Journey through America

Transatlantic Perspectives

Series Editors: Christoph Irmscher, Indiana University Bloomington, and Christof Mauch, Ludwig-Maximilians-Universität, München

This series explores European and North American cultural exchanges and interactions across the Atlantic and over time. While standard historical accounts are still structured around nation states, *Transatlantic Perspectives* provides a framework for the discussion of topics and issues such as knowledge transfer, migration, and mutual influence in politics, society, education, film, and literature. Committed to the presentation of European views on America as well as American views on Europe, *Transatlantic Perspectives* offers room for the publication of both primary texts and critical analyses. While the series puts the Atlantic World at center stage, it also aims to take global developments into account.

Volume 1
Journey through America
Wolfgang Koeppen

Journey through America

by
Wolfgang Koeppen

translated by
Michael Kimmage

Berghahn Books
NEW YORK • OXFORD

First published in 2012 by
Berghahn Books
www.berghahnbooks.com

© 2012 Berghahn Books

First published by Henry Goverts Verlag 1959 as *Amerikafahrt*

© Suhrkamp Verlag Frakfurt am Main 1982

All rights reserved by Suhrkamp Verlag Berlin

Library of Congress Cataloging-in-Publication Data

Koeppen, Wolfgang, 1906–1996.
   [Amerikafahrt. English]
Journey through America / Wolfgang Koeppen ; translated by Michael Kimmage.
   p. cm.
   "First published by Henry Goverts Verlag [in] 1959 as Amerikafahrt"—T.p. verso.
   Includes bibliographical references and index.
   ISBN 978-0-85745-231-3 (hbk. : acid-free paper) —
   ISBN 978-0-85745-437-9 (ebook)
   1. United States—Civilization—1945– 2. United States—Social conditions—1945–
3. United States—Description and travel. 4. Koeppen, Wolfgang, 1906–1996—Travel—
United States. 5. Authors, German—Travel—United States. 6. United States—Foreign
public opinion, German. I. Title.
   E169.12.K57513 2012
   973.91—dc23

                                                                2012001647

British Library Cataloguing in Publication Data

A catalogue record for this book is available from the British Library.

Printed in the United States on acid-free paper.

*This book was made possible by the financial support of the Catholic University of America and of
the Center for Advanced Studies, of the Ludwig Maximilian University in Munich.*

ISBN 978-0-85745-231-3 (hardback)
ISBN 978-0-85745-437-9 (ebook)

for my daughter Ema,

in anticipation of her journeys

Contents

Acknowledgments

I could never have translated Wolfgang Koeppen's *Amerikafahrt* in isolation. My work has continuously depended on the teaching, expertise, and help of others, both in Europe and the United States.

My long debt of gratitude begins with my German-language teachers. Anne Bailey furnished a splendid introduction to the German language. She also had the patience to shepherd a group of teenagers through Germany some two months before *die Wende.* This three-week trip, my initial *Deutschlandfahrt,* left me with a lasting interest in Germany. At Oberlin College, I studied the German language with Heidi Tewerson.

At University College, Oxford, where a British Marshall Scholarship provided immersion in modern European history, I was lucky to read German history with Hartmut Pogge von Strandmann. As a doctoral student in Harvard's History of American Civilization program, I studied American literature with Werner Sollors. Werner is a man of many languages and literatures, German not least among them, and I cannot exaggerate the power of his example or influence. He was a natural mentor for this project. It was self-evident to him why an American student of American studies would want to go and study in Hamburg, Berlin, and Munich.

In the academic year 2004–2005, I was a German Chancellor Scholar and worked in Munich courtesy of the Alexander von Humboldt Foundation. It is an honor to be and remain a Humboldtianer. It has also been of immense practical value to me. This fellowship enabled a year of teaching and research at the Amerika Institut of the Ludwig Maximilian University (LMU). There I was able to work closely—and become friends—with Berndt Ostendorf and Michael Hochgeschwender, eminent experts on the Euro-American terrain who have watched benevolently over this project. Later, the Humboldt Foundation sponsored several returns to Germany after 2005, during which I began my translation of *Amerikafahrt.* The Humboldt Foundation is astute in its emphasis on networks, and the network it constructed, by virtue of awarding me a Chancellor Scholarship, is the network I have relied upon in researching, conceptualizing, and executing this project. Within the Humboldt Foundation and the American Friends of the Alexander von Humboldt Foundation,

I would like to thank in particular: Bob Grathwol and Donita Moorhus, Britta Gross, Katrin Amian, Virginia Barth, and Steffen Mehlich.

For four years in Washington, DC, I lived across the street from the German Historical Institute, a fellow without portfolio. There I got to know Christof Mauch, Anke Ortlepp, and Uta Balbier, three German Americanists and three friends who are colleagues in America as well as Europe. Anke gave a thorough reading of the introduction to this book. Between Washington and Munich, Christof has made countless contributions to this work of translation. He knows the inner dimensions of Koeppen's ouevre and is, as with so many subjects, the ideal interlocutor on the intricacies of this German text. Christof has also helped my translation efforts in many material ways. He has several times invited me to the Amerika Institut, and it was his invitation that brought me to the LMU's Center for Advanced Studies in the spring of 2010 and the summer of 2011. Christof was instrumental in transforming this translation from manuscript to book, a tireless advocate on its behalf who, together with his co-editor, Christoph Irmscher, welcomed *Journey through America* into their series, "Transatlantic Perspectives," with Berghahn Books.

At Berghahn Books, both Marion Berghahn and Ann Przyzycki have been exceptionally helpful, responsive, and interested in this project, from proposal to manuscript to book. They have had the courage to publish a historical document that remains, after some five decades, an avant-garde experiment in language and vision.

It was with Christof Mauch that I organized a Koeppen conference at the Center for Advanced Studies in Munich, in January 2010, titled "Amerikafahrten," or "American Journeys." It was a chance to reflect seriously on the image of America in Koeppen's writing, and amid CAS's characteristic scholarly calm and Schwabing elegance I had the good fortune to meet several distinguished Koeppen scholars: Walter Erhart, Jörg Döring, Hans-Ulrich Treichel, and the director of the Koeppen archive, Eckhard Schumacher. I am grateful to Walter Erhart for inviting me to contribute an article on Koeppen to the *Internationales Archiv für Sozialgeschichte der Deutschen Literatur,* to Sonja Asal for inviting me to release an essay on Koeppen as a CAS E Publication, and to Eckhard Schumacher for his invitation to a spirited roundtable on *Amerikafahrt,* with Walter Erhart, in Greifswald. There I could see Koeppen's point of departure, his hometown, with my own eyes and get a sense of the rich archival materials gathered in his *Geburtshaus.*

The LMU's Center for Advanced Studies (CAS) was no passive vehicle for research. On my first day there I learned that almost its entire staff had read *Amerikafahrt* prior to my arrival in Munich. This is only one way to describe the atmosphere of collegiality and curiosity that reigns at CAS. It was not only a privilege to be a *Dachfellow;* it was a delight as well, and for everything—the privilege of ideal working conditions and the delight of intellectual fraternity—I have Annette Meyer and Sonja Asal to thank. Lena Bouman and Susanne Schaffrath were kind and keen consultants. I would also like to thank Christof Rapp, CAS's genial director, for his support, and to thank the CAS staff for their hospitality, their professionalism, and their redoubtable humor. So many pages of this translation were happily written and revised on Seestr. 13.

The Catholic University of America, my home institution, has shown a steadfast commitment to this unusual project. It never demanded that I be anything other than the scholar I wish to be, whether this means writing a monograph on twentieth-century U.S. history, authoring a book of literary criticism or translating the unknown travelogue of an unknown writer (in his American context). Such is the freedom Catholic University's history department has guaranteed, and I would like to thank my colleagues in two separate columns. First the Americanists: Tim Meagher, Leslie Tentler, and Steve West; and then the Europeanists: Jennifer Davis, Laura Mayhall, and Caroline Sherman. Jerry Muller deserves a column of his own. We share many of the same interests, and when it comes to scholarship I do my best to meet Jerry's exacting standards. His generosity and encouragement make it easier to do so. Tom and Lisa Cohen are not only dear Washington friends but fellow addicts of literature and of the finely turned sentence.

Beyond my department, I would like to express my gratitude to Dean Larry Poos and Dean James Greene at Catholic University. In the shortest imaginable time, they arranged for a generous and urgently needed grant-in-aid. Ernie Suarez, a colleague in the English department, a friend and a neighbor, is a stalwart comrade in the realm of literature and music.

My peripatetic family is to be thanked in a different register. There is nothing mono-lingual about this family, on the American or the Lithuanian side, and with our family more is gained than lost in translation, as has been the case for me since childhood. My parents criss-cross the Euro-American world, from the East Coast to Russia. My brother Daniel and sister-in-law Melinda have added Central Asia, the Caucasus, the Middle East, and Alaska to the list. Speaking of lists, the countries-visited competition is still ongoing with my brother-in-law Redas, sister-in-law Indre and with the next generation, Lukas and Guoda. My parents-in-law are the most generous of hosts in Tolkunai, where I have puzzled over Koeppen's words on the veranda in summer and by the wood stove in winter. An ocean away, my parents have created their idyll in Brunswick, Maine—one part library, one part yoga studio, and one part refuge for gourmets and cinephiles. I have had access to the Center for Advanced Studies in Munich, while working on this translation, and to more intimate centers of advanced study in Dzukija and New England.

My wife Alma is my traveling companion, literally and figuratively. We have had American journeys, Lithuanian journeys, Latvian journeys, Estonian journeys, Italian journeys, German/Bavarian journeys, and Indian journeys, and we are still at the beginning of our journey. My daughter Ema, to whom this book is dedicated, came into the world as I was writing the introduction to this book. May she one day read *Journey through America* as a meditation on the two continents that are by birthright hers.

Introduction

America came to Wolfgang Koeppen before he could go to America. Koeppen traveled to the United States in 1958, and when he published *Amerikafahrt—Journey through America*—a year later, he was at the height of his literary powers. His impressions were the insights of a major German novelist, a postwar writer engaged in continuous reckoning with modern Germany. In addition, Koeppen was an esteemed travel writer who had already voyaged to the Soviet Union in 1957 and whose 1961 travelogue about France was among his last book-length publications. Koeppen's golden age of literary creation coincided with the birth of the Federal Republic of Germany, more commonly known in the United States as West Germany. Haunted by National Socialist devastation, Koeppen had little interest in celebrating the Federal Republic as the democratic, virtuous, and America-inspired antithesis to Germanic authoritarianism. His most acclaimed novels all appeared in the 1950s—*Pigeons on the Grass* (1951), *The Hothouse* (1953), and *Death in Rome* (1954)—reflecting Koeppen's refusal to be an apologist for the (German) past or the (Americanizing) present.[1] *Death in Rome* puts the detritus of National Socialism on display, not in a German setting, but in the central city of European culture. Koeppen set *The Hothouse* in Bonn, the new West German capital and home to a democracy that was inadequate and corrupt, at least in the verdict of this uncompromising novel. *Pigeons on the Grass* captures a day in the life of postwar Munich, teeming with American soldiers and mired still in an unmastered past.

For a European writer of his generation, Koeppen was unusually well versed in American letters. Gertrude Stein's phrase, "pigeons on the grass alas," gave Koeppen the epigraph and title to his most celebrated novel. The technical innovations of Stein, Dos Passos, and Faulkner helped Koeppen to fashion his modernist German prose. These writers taught Koeppen to associate America with fragmented traditions and jumbled experience, less America triumphant than a country in which history could amount to unfinished tragedy.[2] Faulkner's sinful South, burnt into the memory of its children, is a direct analogue to Koeppen's burdensome Germany. From Dos Passos—the Dos Passos of the 1930s—Koeppen understood the parallels between literature and protest, the way in which a cumulative message of dissent could emerge from waves of novelistic description. Stein injected a radical freedom into her sentences and paragraphs, invoking new patterns of literary association. The odd dream-like music of her wording is audible in Koeppen's German-language sensibility: pigeons on the grass alas. European and American writers supplied the cosmopolitan Koeppen with options for telling stories that were unmistakably German. In the 1950s, when Koeppen produced his magisterial trilogy, the United States was an occupying superpower, recently arrived and struggling to remake Germany in its own image.

Thus, for literary as well as historical reasons, Koeppen's journey through America was anything but simple tourism. It was innately and urgently meaningful. It was alive with German meaning, and it was alive with American meaning too, since Koeppen's trip was sponsored in part by the U.S. Department of State. In the eyes of American foreign policy makers, such authors, such trips, and such books contributed to Germany's postwar reeducation.

Koeppen spent three months, from April through June, in Eisenhower's America. He sailed from Le Havre to New York, going down to Washington, DC, to New Orleans, over to California, to Salt Lake City (the nadir of his journey), then back east to Chicago and Boston. From there he returned to New York before heading home, having experienced a European's typical grand tour *à la americaine*. Nothing much happened to Koeppen in America as far as one can tell from his book and the accounts of his biographers. He was content to watch and observe, to be "a passive connoisseur," as he once described Flaubert, whose travel writing Koeppen revered. One could say that America cooperated with Koeppen's intention not to make himself the subject of his journey. Koeppen's trip to America was the inverse of Charles Dickens's valedictory tour, during which Dickens was everywhere preceded by his sterling American reputation, a celebrity bestowing the gift of his presence on an adoring and knowledgeable public. American intellectuals guided Alexis de Tocqueville through American life and history. Simone de Beauvoir was a recognized Parisian intellectual when she came to America not long before Koeppen did. More recently, an American magazine asked Bernard-Henri Lévy to retrace Tocqueville's nineteenth-century journey.[3] Koeppen, by contrast, was entirely unknown in America. The authorial persona in *Journey through America* is a man without a firm profile, it seems from the book, something like a Kafka protagonist with a name designated only by a single initial. The "I" of *Journey through America* is another twentieth-century K., or he resembles Karl Rossmann, the youthful hero of Kafka's novel *Amerika*—expelled from Europe, impressionable if often uncomprehending and mostly alone in the American expanse.[4] In Koeppen's *Journey through America*, solitude serves its own narrative purposes, magnifying America's visibility. America is large enough and its place in the world central enough for it to consume an author's complete attention. And so, Koeppen passes incognito through his own travelogue.

Soft and lyrical, *Journey through America* is also dauntingly ambitious. It presumes that all of America can be contained in a book, and in it Koeppen was presenting a crucial subject to an avid audience. Because America epitomized some element of the German and European future, it was an inevitable point of orientation circa 1959.[5] Koeppen did not belong to the Left or the Right, and for this reason his America is neither an example of capitalist horror nor an agent of low-culture materialism, poised to undo Europe's inherited majesty. *Journey through America* has no sustained argument. Nor does it offer a discreet series of statements or claims about America. At the same time, *Journey through America* evinces a pattern of ideas beneath its stylized surface. For one, America holds the keys to political power. *Journey through America* begins with a reference to American soldiers on European soil—crusaders Koeppen calls them, without rancor—and concludes with an image of the United Nations building in Manhattan. Washington, DC is the center of this global system and the Pentagon a further center within Washington, while New York generates the money upon which the powerful depend. Then as now, this much was obvious. More mysterious is the joining of peoples and nations within the mighty United States. Los Angeles and New York strike Koeppen as model cities in at least one respect. They are places that have brought different groups into harmony and onto a higher plane of civic pleasure, the opposite of Hitler's racial fanaticism, which brought only suffering. Koeppen cannot reconcile this mingled, racially indifferent America with his experience of the segregated South or the less visibly segregated North. He poses a tacit question in *Journey through America*: whether American power will be used to enable a joyous multiculturalism, synthesizing the Pentagon's will with the United Nations' promise, or whether it will extend the chauvinism encoded in the country's white supremacist traditions. The answer to this question, Koeppen believed, was of the essence for postwar Germany.

Wolfgang Koeppen was born in 1906 in the Prussian town of Greifswald. If his life had a single theme, a *leitmotif*, it was alienation, which asserted itself early on. He was an illegitimate child, and when he was nineteen years old his mother died, confirming an adulthood of imposed and chosen isolation. By 1927, Koeppen had settled in Berlin, where he would remain until Hitler took power in 1933, living out the final years of the mythic "Weimar Berlin." In Berlin, Koeppen worked as a journalist paid to write about the city in all its guises, its circuses and cabarets, its countless theaters (in their Brechtian heyday), and its literary scene, everywhere intertwined with the culture of West-

ern and Central Europe. Koeppen, who never finished high school or attended
a university, distinguished himself by the excellence of his prose. He was a vir-
tuoso of the *Feuilleton,* the cultural pages of a German newspaper, somewhat
similar in tone and style to the *New Yorker.* In these years, Koeppen also began
to write fiction, pouring his biography into his first novel, *Eine unglückliche
Liebe (An Unhappy Love)*, in which international travel figures prominently.[6]
The novel was published in 1934. A tangled love story, *An Unhappy Love* is
in no way a political novel. Though Koeppen lived in one of the most ideo-
logically combustible places in Europe—the city of communism and fascism
that Christopher Isherwood chronicled in his *Berlin Stories*—this was not the
environment that captivated Koeppen. He was shocked by the advent of Nazi
Germany, as if it had interrupted the great expectations held in store for him
and his literary art. After 1933, Koeppen lingered on in Berlin, where he was
steadily deprived of newspaper work. He sought out a theater job in Munich,
which the authorities prevented him from getting. Unresolved paternity questions, stemming from his father's refusal to acknowledge Wolfgang as his son,
complicated Koeppen's Aryan credentials. He had difficulty demonstrating his
Germanness. All the while, many of his friends and colleagues were abandon-
ing Germany. Koeppen never decisively rejected the Third Reich for the rigors
of exile. He did not like the new regime, and the new regime made it hard for
him to subsist. By November 1934 he was living in Holland.

Koeppen's exile lasted for four years, giving him time to finish his second novel, *Die Mauer schwankt (The Wall Sways)*, which he published in 1935.
In it, Koeppen traveled back to "the peaceful, bourgeois era" of his Prussian
childhood.[7] The travails of the twentieth century serve as a dividing line in
The Wall Sways. By the novel's end, the civilized long *durée* of the nineteenth
century has yielded to a nervous time of troubles. To get this novel released in
Germany, Koeppen chose to sever long-standing ties with the Cassirer Press,
publisher of his first novel, the Nazis having branded it a Jewish business. He
returned to Berlin from Holland on November 14, 1938, some five days after *Kristallnacht.* Koeppen would later describe the period between 1933 and
1945 as the epoch of his silence: his Dutch exile lent credibility to the claim.
Another, much more famous German writer, living in American exile in this
period, was Thomas Mann, and Mann, who became an American citizen in
1944, was anything but silent in the 1930s. In Koeppen's case, the biographical
record is more checkered and his anti-fascism more ambiguous. Though there
is no evidence that Koeppen believed in Nazi ideologies of politics or race,
he was willing to live and work in Germany, to be a citizen in Hitler's empire
and even to lend it his creative energies. Koeppen was employed in the German film industry, writing vapid screenplays, earning good money, and living
a life of (relatively) glamorous hedonism, first in Berlin and then in Munich.

He was silent insofar as he did not publish fiction in these years, a meaningful sacrifice for a writer of Koeppen's ability.

Between 1945 and 1961, Koeppen wrote six books—three major novels and three volumes of travel writing. Unable to finish large-scale projects in the last thirty years of his life, he died in 1996. Like Ralph Ellison, who lived for decades after publishing *Invisible Man* in 1952, Koeppen's literary greatness accrues to the middle period of his life. This was a greatness tethered to the collapse of Nazi Germany. Having made his accommodations with the Nazi regime, Koeppen had to clear his record with the American authorities after 1945, which he did. He then assisted in the writing of an early Holocaust memoir, *Aufzeichnungen aus einem Erdloch* (*Notes from a Hole in the Ground*), published in 1948 under the name of Jakob Littner. From the murk of anonymity Koeppen rose to fame with his trilogy, which left a distinctive mark on postwar German culture and was translated into many languages. Koeppen's was an impressively disaffected West German voice, his prose style unconventional, realistic and symbolist, documentary and poetic, as musical and bizarre as the language of James Joyce. The tones of pain and complication that color much of Koeppen's writing, from his fiction to his travelogues, were well suited to the spare postwar years, a time of recurring pain and complication. Koeppen's gift for stream-of-consciousness writing, which exposed the tortured psyche of his characters, evoked the mood of German guilt. Yet his was not an innocent imagination putting a guilty country on trial. Perhaps Koeppen's tenure in Nazi Germany helped him, after the war, to write from the inside, not as a Nazi or as a former Nazi and not as an immaculate exile, but as a German among Germans. His novels were historical and contemporary, Faulknerian in their insistence that the traumas of the past and the traumas of the present cannot be disentangled.

Of the three big novels, *Pigeons on the Grass* is the one most relevant to *Journey through America*. One of its major characters is Odysseus Cotton, a black American G.I., his surname indicating his connection to the American South and to the institution of slavery. He shares his first name with the hero of the *Odyssey*. Odysseus Cotton has come to Germany, the modern Troy, on a military and existential quest. America is now inescapably a part of Europe, and once his Iliad of waging war is over, Odysseus will bring Europe back with him to America.[8] Washington Price is another black G.I. in *Pigeons on the Grass,* and his pregnant German girlfriend is carrying their inter-racial child, a portent of the German-American future. The novel's ominous unnamed city is Munich, a self-conscious literary creation like the Dublin of Joyce's *Ulysses*, and much of the city lies in ruins, a realist detail and an effortless metaphor. The black market is thriving, culture is slowly reviving, and the city's energy is frenetic, with the intersecting confusions of soldiers and citizens. The German characters may all be moving forward in some way, making ends meet, making a living, but this is merely the surface of things. Below this surface is an ominous unnamed tragedy. It is not that there was once a Nazi Germany or that there was once a world war. The tragedy is that no line can be drawn across the year 1945 or *Stunde Null,* zero hour, as it is sometimes called in Germany. This might work in a textbook, with its guarantee of new chapters, and it might flatter the best intentions of the occupiers and the occupied, but nothing really new can be built from the crooked German timber. If this is the mission of the American G.I.s, they can only fail. Koeppen's contrasting mission was to portray Germany's willed entrapment in its own terrible history, a history America had absorbed by winning the war.

The afterlife of Nazi Germany suffuses the trilogy's other two novels. Gradually, Koeppen had changed from a writer of the private self, of romantic and erotic tribulations, able to tune out the din of National Socialism in the early 1930s, into a political writer. *The Hothouse* is tartly anti-celebratory, implying that Germany did not elevate itself to virtue and democracy by losing the war. Keetenheuve, the novel's protagonist, had lived in exile during the war. He becomes a political figure in the Federal Republic, and his search for political and intellectual integrity leads to deepening frustration. A visceral corruption runs through German history, a corruption that has not been excised by the Germans or the Americans. Those without the gift for forgetting, and those intelligent enough to know the nature of things, must contend with the grimmest despair. The novel ends with Keetenheuve's suicide. In *Death in Rome,* Koeppen's Rome is not a simile for decadence, as Venice is in Mann's *Death in Venice.* In Mann's novella, an aging writer from Munich meets his death in a dying city, while in Koeppen's *Death in Rome,* an aging German, formerly a Nazi overlord, seems to be living out a death sentence in Rome, banished from his native country and still actively promoting its fascist hatreds.[9] The artist in *Death in Rome,* however, is young, a composer aware of the German horrors yet apprenticed to all the deathless art to be seen and felt in Rome. Bleak as Koeppen's postwar trilogy is, its last installment hints at a European renaissance still entombed in Rome's streets, galleries and buildings. What the Germans have devastated Rome may still be able to replenish.

Each of these three novels displayed Koeppen's literary devotion to place or, rather, to cities. In *Pigeons in the Grass* it is Munich. In this novel, even the American characters all have well-conceived places of origin, from Baton Rouge to Los Angeles. Provincial Bonn is the incomplete modern city in *The Hothouse,* quickly and unimaginatively rebuilt from the wartime rubble, and in *Death in Rome,* the Italian capital is the very soul of Europe.

Koeppen's sensitivity to place, the marvelous instrument of his prose, his erudition, even his penchant for alienation, made him an exceptionally fine travel writer. In 1955, Koeppen went to Spain at the request of the *Süddeut-sche Rundfunk,* the South-German Radio Station, producing well-regarded radio programs and articles from his trip. Then, in 1957, the Soviet Writers' Union invited him to the Soviet Union, an irresistible offer, and a year later Koeppen published *Nach Russland und anderswohin* (*To Russia and Elsewhere*). The book consists of a long essay on Soviet Russia as well as essays on Spain, Holland, and Britain. The dominant political reality at the time of the book's publication was the Cold War, with a consequent pressure on writers to take a position and to situate themselves amid the reigning polarities. Books about the Soviet Union, derived from trips to this post-revolutionary country, were a well-established genre. Enthusiasms and disappointments had a political edge, and documenting one's political reckoning with the Soviet Union—in the hands of a John Reed, an e.e. cummings, a Walter Benjamin, an André Gide, a John Steinbeck, an Edmund Wilson—could make for first-rate in-tellectual drama.[10] Without knowing it, Koeppen was rehearsing for *Journey through America* when writing about the Soviet Union. In both books, the political label—Soviet Union, United States—is discarded for more sugges-tive and emotional words, Russia and America. In both books, the journey is physical and metaphysical, a journey to a place and a journey to a literary geography. Russian literature sustains Koeppen in the Soviet Union, as if he had gone to visit the nineteenth-century writers he first encountered on the printed page. The same held for American literature when Koeppen was in America. Koeppen consciously avoids a political summation in both books, the fanfare of ideological argument at a time when such fanfare was de rigueur. In his terms, Koeppen succeeds if he can hear Russia's distinctive poetry and if he can convey this poetry to his readers. The Cold War is subordinate to this poetry, much as the Trojan War cannot compete with Homer's poetic art in the *Odyssey* and the *Iliad.* Although Odysseus Koeppen did not write verse, his prose often has the hypnotic, musical effect of poetry.

Koeppen's *Reisen nach Frankreich* (*Travels to France*) is a slight book, a tired effort after five extraordinary creations, anticipating the writer's block that would dominate Koeppen's later years. It recapitulates many clichés about France, listing facts and details from guide books, and it casts a flattering light on the two travel books that preceded it, the extended prose poem about Rus-sia and the extended prose poem about America.

Like *To Russia and Elsewhere, Journey through America* began as a radio broadcast. Once again the South-German Radio Station had sent Koeppen out into the world, and the published book, which Koeppen meticulously re-worked from the radio broadcasts, has a tone and tenor that originates in the spoken word. It was the latest addition to a vast genre, the German "America book," and *Journey through America* attracted rapt critical attention as soon as it appeared in print. The literary scholar Walter Erhart writes of Koeppen's book being "celebrated immediately after its appearance as one of the most significant [German] publications of 1959." It was "immensely successful" from the beginning, and since 1959 *Journey through America* has gone through multiple reprintings.[11] In 2008, Walter Erhart published it in a critical edition with notes and commentary.

Koeppen has two modes of writing in *Journey through America*, one fast and one slow. In travel mode, the sentences are crammed with imagery, run-on attempts to capture the traveler's unfiltered impressions. These excited descriptions, culled mostly from train trips, inspire some of Koeppen's longest, most extravagant sentences. *Journey through America*'s epic first sentence, broken into a modest five sentences in this translation, concludes with an admonition to the European reader—*not* to go to America by plane. Too much will be left unseen or seen too quickly, from too great a height. Slower forms of transportation open up the mind, not just to new places and new vistas but to the mind's rapid powers of association. The longer sentences in *Journey through America* prove the point: in them Koeppen ravishes his reader, or reader-listener, with the grandeur of his imagination, the words taking flight as the traveler recalls and embellishes the record of his travels. At times, Koeppen sounds like his contemporary, Jack Kerouac, whose *On the Road* (published in 1957) is mentioned in *Journey through America*. Koeppen's second mode of writing is simpler, closer to factual statement. It is the writing Koeppen does when standing still, his vision and intellect calmly assimilating the world around him. With the exception of a small town in the Southwest, where Koeppen stayed for a day or two, rural America is seen from the train and is portrayed as lonely and brooding (the Northeast), as lonely and mythic (the West), or as lonely and tragic (the South). Otherwise, America exists for Koeppen as a slow-moving urban phenomenon: New York, Washington, New Orleans, Los Angeles, San Francisco, Salt Lake City, Chicago, and Boston. Koeppen walks the streets of these cities, even Los Angeles, gradually assimilating them into the American scene. Cities are the vertebrae of *Journey through America*, the movements of Koeppen's American symphony. A 1927 film titled *Berlin: Symphonie einer Grossstadt* (*Berlin, Symphony of a Metropolis*) had Berlin as its protagonist. In *Journey through America*, America's various great cities are the protagonists as well, with New York in the starring role.

A book of cities, *Journey through America* is also a book of themes. Koeppen's biggest themes are Europe and America, themes that blend into one another. He has a habit of envisioning German or European streets behind the American ones, moveable pieces of the world puzzle. On 47th Street in New York,

Koeppen comes across second-hand jewelry from Europe and his mind's eye pictures European cities that once had significant Jewish communities: "this street was Vienna, it was Berlin, it was Warsaw or Czernowitz." Observing a crowd outside a New York theater, Koeppen is transported back to the theater districts of Weimar Berlin: "I saw myself on Schumannstrasse, on Schiffbau-erdamm, on Kurfürstendamm." Koeppen anticipates a late twentieth-century cliché—that New York and Berlin are cosmopolitan cousins—when he notes that New Yorkers are "related to Berliners." In Washington, DC, Koeppen senses the Bendlerstrasse, a Berlin thoroughfare of the Nazi war machine, running through the Pentagon. This Euro-American map, somewhat like the Russo-American cartography in Vladimir Nabokov's novel *Ada*, is surreal, and it goes in both continental directions. The American soldiers in Germany have "brought Main Street with them…. [T]he loneliness of the prairie has come along on the trip, the hot and cold air of the Nevada desert has come along. …" Because of these American soldiers, American culture is inundating Germany, so that "on evening screens every village boy comes to know Broadway's canyon of lights." When Koeppen himself steps onto New York's Broadway, he is responding to long familiar stimuli, as if he had come home by arriving in New York for the first time: "I recognized New York as the settlement of my time," he writes. Between the European and the American themes lies a sequence of other themes. There is the theme of Europe in America, then of Kafka and America, taking Koeppen to the theme of American loneliness. The theme of loneliness combines with the themes of leisure and the counter-culture, both associated with the state of California. California's inter-racial mixing is paired with the theme of racism and segregation. A final theme is that of the Enlightenment, of literacy and liberty and progress. Europe's recent abnegation of the Enlightenment will be corrected by America's geopolitical pedagogy, or so Koeppen allows himself to hope; but given what America is, given its many internal feuds with the Enlightenment and its own mess of unenlightened problems, his can only be a sober, limited hope. On this note, hope and sobriety co-mingled, Koeppen returns to Germany.

Koeppen titled his radio broadcasts, his first draft of *Journey through America*, "Die Früchte Europas" ("Europe's Fruits"). Europe and America are kin, a single organism, branches of the same tree.[12] America grants Koeppen no respite from Europe, the continent with a "broken heart," as he puts it in *Journey through America*'s first sentence. Getting ready to leave for America by ship, Koeppen is reminded of the never-ending European turmoil: "First I saw the emigrants. There were still emigrants." The displacement of people and the political oppression have not ceased. From a train window in America, Koeppen notices "a city of ruins," a pre-Columbian Berlin: "it was once of awe-inspiring size, perhaps with political power, destined to rule the globe and then destroyed because of the wrong decisions or because of word from an angry god." If Hitler's hubris destroyed Germany, the angry Teutonic god gave something to America. At Berkeley, Koeppen "once again saw what a fine refuge the United States had provided in the years of the latest European blackout," the gentle sarcasm of the word "latest" implying blackouts still to come. America has space for the people Europe might persecute or silence, and Koeppen speculates that in Berkeley "they would have hired and published Nietzsche, had he lived in the madness of our time and had he been homeless." A screenwriter who had worked in the German film industry, Koeppen was familiar with the Nazi-era exodus of German talent, but here he did not arrange the calculus of gain and loss in America's favor. Hollywood is not Berkeley. It is an industry for mass commercialism resistant to European artistry. Late at night Koeppen comes across a bookstore in Hollywood, still open and a focal point for "the film city's inner emigration meeting up near Genet and Beckett, making plans that Hollywood's bankers would never finance." For Koeppen the wartime enmities have all faded into ancient history. The German or German-Jewish Nietzsches who found a way to the New World, where they could persevere and publish, are valuable to the United States and to Europe alike.

Koeppen is appalled by the one unreconstructed piece of Europe he finds in America. This is the German neighborhood around Manhattan's 82nd Street. Here *Journey through America* changes tone, its usual generosity vanishes, and the author goes on the attack. There is Koeppen's Germany, and there is the other Germany. The other Germany may be receding on German soil, but here it is in America, "a German nightmare" still intact. In *Journey through America*'s sharpest paragraphs, Koeppen laments the self-reinforcing principles of kitsch and authoritarianism. The first image is of "Emperor Barbarossa, his beard growing through the table." The last image places Sepp Herberger, the authoritarian trainer of Germany's national soccer team, next to a "picture of Hindenburg on the wall," Hindenburg the World War I hero who had placed the crown of political power on Hitler's head. The culture of 82nd Street horrifies Koeppen even more than its retrograde politics, the "Tyrolean roses in small cinemas patronized by regulars, the song of nostalgia and the ever-blooming lilac of truly false feelings." This German enclave is willfully un-American. Its houses stand "among enemies, stuck between Italian, Spanish, Czechoslovak and Puerto Rican settlements," "embittered, ill-tempered and not finished with America, it seemed"—all this for no reason "in the happy free world city of New York." The U.S. Navy completes the repulsive picture. The sailors come to consort with German girls, "the honest German girls [who] kept up their reputation of being cheap." These images carry an argument. Xenophobic German-Americans betray America with their self-love and their love of strong men, and they betray Germany as well, for Germany is a country they hardly know. With earnestness and emotion, Koeppen invokes the good Germany, which happens to be his Germany. "A sports club had flown in and was being celebrated. The faces of fools," Koeppen complains. Then he shifts gears: "German literature, German art, our present, our life, German spiritual labors ... did not exist for the inhabitants of this German street in New York." National sentiment is not alien to Koeppen. He aligns himself with German literature, German art, and German spiritual labor, but the national must lead out from itself into other worlds. In a world city such growth should come naturally.

Koeppen's (European) guide to America is Franz Kafka, and his Baedeker is Kafka's novel *Amerika*, which was written before World War I and published in 1927. Koeppen's arrival in America moves him to quote from Melville and Twain and Whitman. Yet the definitive voice is Kafka's: "Franz Kafka who never reached America but who nevertheless had the truest dream of America looked upon 'the statue of liberty, already long observed, as in a sunlight grown suddenly stronger, her arm, with the sword, raised as if recently outraged, and breezes gusted around it.'" This sword is a famous "mistake" on Kafka's part, indicating, for Koeppen, the mystical truth of Kafka's *Amerika,* America awash in unusually strong sunlight, touched with anger, the beacon's ostensible lantern exchanged for a sword. Kafka's novel is a major work of German literature and, as such, an obligatory referent for Koeppen, as Tocqueville's *Democracy in America* would be for a French political scientist thinking about America. Koeppen's deference to Kafka and to Kafka's "realism" is more than obligatory, though: it shapes *Journey through America,* the title of which may contain an echo from Kafka's novel.[13] The title could even be a pun, suggesting a trip to America and a trip within Kafka's novel *Amerika,* the trips one and the same. Psychologically, Koeppen may have identified with the hero of Kafka's *Amerika,* Karl Rossmann, who is parentless in America, as Koeppen himself had been while still a teenager in Europe. Koeppen also worked on ships as a young man and could feel literary kinship with Karl Rossmann or, if he chose, with Melville's Ishmael. Kafka was Jewish, lived mostly in multilingual Prague and wrote in a German that was never fully his mother tongue. Posthumously, he stood at the commanding heights of modern European literature, but when he was alive and writing in German he did not entirely command the language or the culture behind it. Often the language and culture were commanding *him,* a recognizably Kafkaesque dilemma. Koeppen—despite being German-born, living mostly in Germany, and standing sovereign within Germany's linguistic and literary tradition—saw himself as an heir to Kafka's bottomless alienation.

Kafka's *Amerika* is everywhere a frame for Koeppen's *Journey through America.* Karl Rossmann discovers an America that is materially impressive, without having the comfort or ease of settled wealth. Indeed, Rossmann's America is forbidding, malevolent, and strange. The classic (American) transformation whereby a foreign-born subject becomes a citizen eludes Karl. America does not grant him self-dignity and agency. He is adrift in America, constantly at the mercy of others, and no less trapped than his cousin protagonists in the castles, ministries and courtrooms of Central Europe. The Hotel Occidental, in Kafka's *Amerika,* embodies the American strangeness, with its endless corridors, its empty spaces, its swarming guests and despairing employees. Koeppen finds such a hotel in Washington, DC and, recounting problems with his stay there, he, "an old reader of Kafka," writes of being especially unsettled. Massive buildings, not intuitively human in their proportions, are a hallmark of Kafka's America. Koeppen's first sight of an American building makes him think that "the hall was America and it was as if Franz Kafka from Prague had imagined it." When Koeppen walks into a broken-down rooming house in Chicago, the sad, unwell occupants filling a building that makes little sense, "it all resembled a chapter from Kafka's 'Amerika.'" Koeppen sees no material incongruity between the American reality and Kafka's disturbing fictions.

Kafka gives Koeppen more than a vocabulary for writing about American despair. Kafka's *Amerika* is an unfinished novel, and especially so in its ending. It depicts gloom and exploitation, without the alleged American liberties, and it arrives at an astonishing destination. The novel "ends" in Oklahama, a second departure from verisimilitude, finishing in bright light and open spaces, with a theater that resembles a circus. Perhaps it was Kafka's dream vision of Hollywood. Perhaps it was his sense that freedom and happiness, in short supply elsewhere, are not to be had in American cities, under the thumb of American capitalism, but in the American West, in the fresh air of entertainment and play. This Kafkaesque America also appears in *Journey through America.* Koeppen is stranded in Hollywood, outside the public transportation net, and is finally able to get back downtown by taxi. From the highway he is captivated by the American motels and their odd unpretentious beauty: "the motels gleamed in the light, the guests sat on terraces and verandas as if on little stages, in courtyards open to the street, beneath garlands of light bulbs, palm fronds and ripe oranges, and I believe I observed happy nomads, wandering actors acting themselves, and again it was Kafka's America that I saw, it was the big world theater of Oklahoma."[14] Such light-filled joy, among the palm fronds and the ripe oranges, is absent from Hollywood, which Koeppen finds depressing. It is found *near* Hollywood, to the side of it, among those who have come from around the country to see the stars and the film studios. Again, these are not Americans in stable communities or in inviting cities or homes. They are nomads and travelers, like the author who describes them, and as such they are happy. Their stage is their domestic world, as they sit together on the motel terraces and verandas. Koeppen, looking in from the street, is their audience. The paradox of their happiness is that they are wandering actors, liberated from home and job and from the conformities that Americans so eagerly sell to one another. For this reason, they are "actors acting themselves," an invigorating oxymoron. Though Koeppen has no contempt for middle-class American life, he does not see much liberty or happiness in it. The liberty and happiness are there on the margins, to the west of center.

The big world theater of Oklahoma is the exception and the loneliness behind it the rule. Americans struggle with a loneliness that they cannot keep at bay. As the New York office buildings empty and darkness falls, "the city did its despairing battle against loneliness." Koeppen emphasizes that this is an *American* loneliness, as opposed to an urban loneliness or a modern loneliness. What strikes Koeppen is "the special American loneliness, which Americans feared and which they hated." Koeppen finds a predictable culprit in the automobile. Where loneliness is, the automobile is as well, and by writing about the conviviality of American cars Koeppen evades a hackneyed critique of car culture. In America, the cars are not lonely; they travel and meet with each other; they have their respected position in this endless country; they seem content.[15] It is only the people they carry who suffer from loneliness. Americans have yet to master their machine civilization. They do not understand its powers for good and must therefore breathe "the acrid train-air of technology." Among the harshest images in *Journey through America* is one of American houses situated on the land like "leprosy sprinkled in great nature's painting." David Riesman's 1950 book *The Lonely Crowd,* which Koeppen owned, conveyed a worry about modern men and women dehumanized by technology and perhaps by modernity itself. The masses had been integrated into fascist and communist regimes, and people melted into masses could be the stunted progeny of capitalism as well, lulled into soulless conformity by mass manipulation and entertainments.[16] For intellectuals on both sides of the Atlantic, in the 1950s, capitalist mass man was typically the American. Koeppen did not endorse this idea at all. "America was no land of the masses," he writes, possibly to his own surprise. "It was a land of loneliness...." Loneliness marks the American poor, whom Koeppen encountered in most American cities, sometimes with a hint of poetry about them—like the "one-armed vagabond with Verlaine's touching physiognomy." Mostly, though, America's un-poetic poor elicit Koeppen's pity. Like Karl Rossmann, they have been set adrift. They are "poor in a peculiarly American way.... [T]he grotesque element [in their clothing] was there to clarify the isolation, their status as outcasts, as step children ... as I had already observed among Negroes." The middle-class loneliness is less obvious, less explicable, and no less profound. It is only that its origins are more spiritual than material.

American loneliness is multi-faceted, and California gives Koeppen the chance to study American loneliness in its full variety. Three Los Angeles neighborhoods serve as variations upon the theme.

The first is Santa Monica, idyllic California, which at first does not seem lonely at all. Koeppen is fascinated by the beach culture, the roller skaters and body builders, the portable radios playing jazz, followed by drummers in the evening. Listening to the music and watching the dancers, Koeppen muses that "nowhere in the New World was Europe further away." The California beach instructs Koeppen in the joining of leisure and industry into a business enterprise. The urgency behind the enterprise is a question of loneliness: "what diligence had been conceived to entertain these people, to amuse them, to stimulate their desire, to take from them the pressing burden of time and loneliness!" Koeppen moves further down the coast and comes to the alternate world of Venice Beach, the anti-idyllic home of the Beats. If Koeppen admired Kerouac's *On the Road*, he was less than enamored of the Beat prototypes.[17] He uses two Protestant comparisons to describe them, one modern and the other early modern. "Every trombonist in Venice was Kierkegaard, who had been thrown existentially … into this hell and was crying out from it," Koeppen writes, as if to fold gorgeous sensual Venice into Kierkegaard's clenched Northern angst. The Beats are congregants in a grim church, sitting "gloomy, disheveled and dirty with their slender beer bottles and recorded jazz that sounded like strict church music[;] perhaps it would have delighted their ancestors, the Puritans." This is a Protestantism without joy and without God. Its power, Koeppen contends, will be its influence on others' style. The Beats' cultivated loneliness will lend its élan to a new kind of conformity, and their rejections will be accepted by others, less pure and less radical. To Koeppen, the connection is clear: "they had renounced the State Department, the Pentagon, the refrigerator, the television and Hollywood once and for all, and so the movie business was just about to discover them." The culture industry will feed on their loneliness—this is the relationship between American loneliness and mass culture. The Beats are ready "for spiritual rebellion and for the negation of conformist thinking, or not-thinking, not dissolute, not satisfied but ascetic and hungry for life. Venice was soil, nourishment for trees, from which the institutions and, as it goes, the new conformity will eventually pick their fruit." The Beats' rebellion is futile. At the same time, it has an established pedigree in American culture, going all the way back to the Puritans.[18]

The final panel in this California triptych is a non-descript Los Angeles neighborhood. It has a "square that was really almost Italian, not the splendor of Venice, but with a Southern poverty and Wailing Wall grief." It is a Jewish area with "sickly looking Hebrew letters" on many of its shop windows. The residents here are no less lonely than the Beats and possibly than the fun-seekers in Santa Monica, though their situation is hardly comparable. Refugees from the Holocaust, they could be characters in Koeppen's postwar fiction, these "Jews from Europe," as Koeppen explains, "who had saved themselves from the raving monster by going as far west as they could." Koeppen shares in their talent for being in America and seeing Europe before their eyes, "old people, teary women, beaten-down men, dreaming of Breslau, of the Hausvogteiplatz, of the Prague old town, of their old Vienna neighborhood." These Angelenos have saved themselves from Hitler by coming to America, their place of refuge, and America has let them be. Yet their loneliness is almost perfect as they sit "timidly, shriveled by fate, reflecting each other's sorrow on little marble tables and on marble benches." Saved by America, they live outside and apart from America, and there is no way to reconcile their European past with their American present. The emigrants Koeppen saw as he boarded the ship to America could in fact be exchanging European trauma for American emptiness. To make this point Koeppen modifies the myth of Southern Californian sun: "the country's friendly sun was shining on them, but I feared that it did not warm these refugees, who also didn't see its light." Had Koeppen not been Kafka's student, he might not have been so alert to the American qualities of this tableau. As it was, America and even California, with its great distance from Europe, was a movie made from a Kafka screenplay. Kafka, born in 1883, could have been among these displaced Jewish men in 1950s California.[19]

Yet another European "America book" solidifies the concordance between Kafka and Koeppen. This is Robert Frank's *The Americans,* a book of photographs published first in France in 1958 and then in the United States in 1959. Frank was born in 1924 to a Swiss-Jewish family. He traveled through America between 1955 and 1956, his bi-coastal itinerary very similar to Koeppen's, though it is doubtful that the photographer and the writer knew each other or of each other's work. Biographical connections notwithstanding, Koeppen's *Journey through America* and Frank's *The Americans* are companion volumes, arrestingly similar meditations on American space, on a distance that cannot be overcome and on people alone and lonely among their resonant national symbols. The mood and the myth-making in these books by Frank and Koeppen can be traced back to Kafka's *Amerika* and its belligerent Statue of Liberty, presiding over America with sword rather than lantern.[20] Tocqueville takes his readers in one direction, to democracy in America, and Kafka takes his readers to an altogether different country, an America paradigmatically modern in its lyrical dissonances. This is exactly the country that Frank and Koeppen happened to discover in the 1950s.

As Koeppen hinted in his portrayal of the Beats, loneliness engenders conformity. Other Europeans, starting with Tocqueville, had noted a tendency toward conformity in America. Tocqueville saw conformity in American culture, in its weakness for general ideas and its fear of aristocratic distinction. A democratic culture should be a culture of individuals and of individualism, Tocqueville postulated, yet the American passion for general ideas often suppresses freedom of opinion. American culture can level individualism. Koeppen elaborates no theory of American conformity: he elaborates upon *an image* of American conformity. This is the flowerbed hat that women—rich and poor, white and black—wear out of fidelity to national style. Sometimes Koeppen uses the flowerbed hat as a metonym for American women. American cities are ordered around the satisfaction of female consumers, and the results are more efficient, more conformist than lovely. American men have their own patterns of conformity, into which they are inducted as boys. Koeppen sees how boys, "out of fear, out of their strangely American man's complex, to be perceived as soft, as feminine … overemphasized their rough-and-tumble behavior and their neglect of a decorative beautiful appearance." One effect of such conformity is a curtailing of eros. As soon as women put on the flowerbed hat, they have tied themselves to the norm of middle-class respectability. Men in America protect their fragile masculinity by exaggerating it, and Koeppen is startled by the shortage of women and the profusion of men in American bars. Even strip clubs in America corral eros, betraying a counter-intuitive fear of female sensuality. Though Koeppen did not write about suburbia and was uninterested in the metaphor of Eisenhower's America, his observations correspond to later American stereotypes of the 1950s, a period when conformist decency was the rage and the rebellious energies, erotic and otherwise, were being kept in check.

The worst American conformity is conformity to racism. At the outset of his journey, Koeppen mentions "the heroic saga of Little Rock" as common knowledge in Germany, but in the America he visits he sees little trace of a civil rights movement. No reference to Martin Luther King, Jr. is made in *Journey through America*. Instead, Koeppen is shocked by the scope and cruelty of segregation, a subject he had already addressed in his novel *Pigeons on the Grass*. To control the present, segregationists apportion one place for blacks and one for whites, and by inhibiting intermarriage they attempt to control the future. Koeppen handles miscegenation both as a hard fact and a malleable symbol. The fact is white Americans' terror of miscegenation. In Washington, DC, Koeppen sees black and white children at a bus stop, standing "among each other in groups divided by race, though a blond boy took a lively interest in a dark beauty." When Koeppen asks "Americans what the prospect was for such a love, love on the way to school … the Americans did not know what to say, I feared they found my question indiscreet, they suppressed a thought that was obviously unpleasant for them." In the play of his prose Koeppen permits the miscegenation America forbids in practice. In the White House he notices "a white and a black piano, touching one another tenderly in wood, as if the country's dangerous colors wanted to make a case for friendship." When Koeppen leaves Washington for the Deep South, where Southern history has brought a nightmare "into being," his train reflects the Southern sun in a curious way: "in the morning the sun was already burning, its rays marrying in the white-black on the train." Nature and language are free where humans are unfree. Coming out exhilarated from a performance of *West Side Story*, Koeppen is aware of blacks and Puerto Ricans on New York's actual city streets "murderously caught up in the danger and stupidity of racial hatred, even when they called themselves with great pride Americans and New Yorkers."

Segregation's foe is not so much the white liberal, about whom Koeppen writes nothing, as the incipient black middle class. Chicago—destination city for the black migration—impresses Koeppen with its African-American bourgeoisie. Looking far into the future, Koeppen writes that one day "this [black] migration will be comprehended as the South's loss; once again the South will lose the Civil War." Koeppen is surprised by an affluent black neighborhood adjacent to an "old black slum." An elite black school "could be Harrow. These Negroes were a new, different generation, no longer stuck in fate's dead-end but extremely active and trusting in the future." Koeppen's curiosity about the black middle class takes him to *Ebony* magazine. The magazine's offices are opulent and its editor charismatic. The magazine itself, however, celebrates the same middle-class conformity that soothes whites in their esteem for the status quo. If segregation is to be abolished, it will have to be challenged, "but it seemed to me that the Negro illustrated magazine had fashioned too comfortable a peace with the world and the condition it was in." Koeppen asks whether *Ebony* is "a mouthpiece for black apartheid." He spells out its accommodationist thinking: "Little Rock is a disgrace but in New York and Chicago please retain your independence and your racial pride while living in a black ghetto." The black middle class is constrained by being a minority within a minority, and the more similar it becomes to the white middle class, the more insuperable segregation will be. Decades from now, the next generation may face a more forgiving racial logic. As for 1958, only in Los Angeles does Koeppen thrill to the Whitmanian energies of a racially mixed American democracy. On a Los Angeles street, "I lingered in order to be amazed. I was aroused, I got excited. I had never before seen such people, whites of all shadings, Negroes light and dark, Asians yellow and brown … a new people, which looked beautiful, proud, uninhibited, free, stepping straight … a new race … no longer distinguished from one another in their life's joy." As long as America lives on a black-white axis, it will be stuck in its segregationist mindset. When other colors, other axes are introduced, the us-them hatred will diminish, and the racial utopia of this Los Angeles street will find its reflection in the nation at large.

An eighteenth-century ideal of fraternity, so brutally minimized by American racism and segregation, leads Koeppen from the theme of race to the theme of education. America is the land of the Enlightenment. Its revolution was a revolution for the Enlightenment, waged by "courageous rebels against the English crown." In their Enlightenment idealism, in their will to realize the betterment of all, Americans remind Koeppen of Soviet citizens. "Only in Russia have I met as many idealists as I did in America," Koeppen writes. "I say this without mockery, and it seems to me the biggest, perhaps the only hope for our world's state of confusion." Even without ostensible mockery, this is a coyly mischievous point, made a year after Sputnik, and it explains the American Enlightenment as perceived by Koeppen: a compelling object of contradiction. Koeppen marvels at America's universities and libraries, not only at their high quality but at the people using them, the flocks of multiracial youth striving for *Bildung*. Koeppen repeatedly associates America with literacy: "the United States was and remained in all its parts the homeland of the literate." The Library of Congress is a "high temple of literacy." Koeppen declares that "the encyclopedists' dreams were being fulfilled overseas," the French Enlightenment realized in America's schools, libraries and universities, though with universities an irony suddenly surfaces. At Harvard Koeppen nears the summit of American education, and here he finds a uniquely American confusion of spirit and money. The German word *Geist* (spirit) conveys more than the English one does, a quasi-religious ideal of self-cultivation. Harvard's Widener library, "with its Athenian-academic porticos of columns, and its collection of Renaissance manuscripts and Shakespeare first editions, was an appealing symbol of the transformation, always possible in America, of money into spirit." Widener's splendor came from the Widener family's money—money made into spirit. Appealing as this alchemy may be, it is only one side of the equation. At a Boston hotel Koeppen sees a gathering of rich alumni. From these alumni it becomes "apparent that with a successful Harvard diploma and brilliant career, spirit had been transformed back into money. Perhaps the cycle was healthy," a conclusion that reads like a punch line.

On the West Coast, Koeppen chances upon another Enlightenment irony. Having found Venice in Southern California, Koeppen finds Athens in the North. In Berkeley Koeppen casts aside Kafka and takes up Goethe, exchanging the back alleys of Central Europe for the open Mediterranean. Modern alienation shades into an ancient oneness with nature: "the university in San Francisco was Greece, it was Hellas beneath the Californian sun." Goethe had left Germany for Italy, from 1786 to 1788, and the result was the most famous travel book in German letters, *Italienische Reise* (*Italian Journey*), pub-

lished in 1816. Italy awoke Goethe to a new sensuality and to a new kind of
European joy; it was travel as revelation and rebirth. Standing in Berkeley,
Koeppen "felt as if Sicily's gift to Goethe was being given to me: the clarity
of the sky, the breath of the sea, the aromas into which land and sky and sea
resolved themselves into a *single* element." Then Koeppen comes to the Greek
Theater: "in its proportions the theater was more real and more perfect than
the old buildings in Greece, in Sicily and in the South of France." This is
Thomas Jefferson's dream, of education clarified in architecture, until a wonderful American circumstance intrudes. The vista of the Greek Theater forms
an "image that would have pleased Apollo. But it was Billy Graham who appeared, the successful itinerant preacher." It is not Billy Graham's religious
fervor that terrifies Koeppen so much as his demagogic fury. Koeppen listens
to Graham with German ears, which receive "the hysterical, cracking voice of
the political agitator, the evil drummer, and for a while I shocked myself by
asking whether I was listening to America's future Hitler." Nowhere else in
his book *Journey through America* is Koeppen as alert to inchoate fascism as he
is in Berkeley, with its Apollonian grace. The students pay little attention to
Graham, to Koeppen's relief, and later Graham comes to Koeppen on a hotel
television screen. The demagogue has vanished, his place taken by a salesman
who synthesizes religion, psychology, and the American knack for market-
ing. This Billy Graham also disgusts Koeppen, though not as acutely as the
Berkeley demagogue. The American Enlightenment is mysterious. It contains
its own antithesis, and only for an outsider, a non-American, is it strange to
hear Graham's hysterical, cracking voice where one might expect a Socrates, a
Nietzsche, or a Goethe.

A final Enlightenment conundrum is New York, "the new Rome of the
much invoked Western hemisphere," frantically consumed with making and
enjoying its power.[21] It is a city of man and of man's dominion over nature:
"its towers did not praise God, they did not inquire into the existence of an
Almighty, they had arrived at their own omnipotence." The city is "laid out
in an easily comprehended order, as if by a playful but not very imaginative
child." This familiar New York, the New York of the grid and the skyscraper, is
only artifice. The charm and the soul of New York reside elsewhere. Koeppen
had wanted to taste the Enlightenment in New York, but the city has other
allegiances: "there was no shiver, which I was ready to feel, before the majesty
of human freedom or before the proclamation of faith in human happiness
compelled by technical, material progress and prosperity." To Koeppen, New
York "suggested a house of cards and inspired thoughts of storms that might
be brewing far away." In New York, Koeppen experienced a version of the
anxiety E. B. White described with such extraordinary precision in his 1948
essay, "Here is New York." A sentence from White's essay, often quoted after

September 11, reads: "The city, for the first time in its long history, is destructible. A single flight of planes no bigger than a wedge of geese can quickly end this island fantasy, burn the towers, crumble the bridges, turn the underground passages into lethal chambers, cremate the millions. The intimation of mortality is part of New York now: in the sound of jets overhead, in the black headlines of the latest edition."[22] Koeppen's anxiousness is similarly amorphous and intuitive: "flame-red, its sirens shrieking, a fire truck roared past us. I had expected it! I already saw a skyscraper burning. Broadway blazing, already I could read the headlines in all the world's newspapers. Violent catastrophes seemed to lie in the air here." If Koeppen's imagination of disaster was colored by wartime memories, he was convinced that the precarious feel of American cities is an American phenomenon, an effect of the urban American psyche, "this strange fear, which one felt … in American cities: something was about to happen, someone was about to start shooting, shouting, screaming, running amok." These words were written after an entirely peaceful trip, decades before the age of global terrorism. Koeppen believed in a counter-Enlightenment of violence and chaos at the heart of America's conventional Enlightenment.

Enlightenment hope and counter-Enlightenment fear converge in the final pages of *Journey through America*. Koeppen is bidding farewell to New York, and already the motion back to Europe has begun. He goes to the East Side of Manhattan, where "the glittering hope of the world raised itself up." Koeppen's concluding sentences flow with sadness and without irony, the absence of irony an incitement to sadness. The United Nations building is "like a tall, shiny mirror before uncalm water," reflecting the world's turbulence. Inside, "the bird of freedom or of peace was being held or let free by an angel. One couldn't say exactly; perhaps the angel thought that the time had not yet come." This new start includes Germany's new start, such that from the U.N. building's windows "the East River looked like the Rhine at Bonn, and beneath its shining surface one could make out dangerous reefs." The building is lovely and unreal, less real possibly than the reefs in the river. Some human dimension is missing "in the perfect architecture, which gave the gift of good thoughts, a creation of our times, the faith of our times and without stain like an artful fugue." This is the Enlightenment promise on international soil, isolated from American and other complexities. The U.N. building is *Journey through America*'s penultimate image. Then, "I went under the river," he writes, "went under the hope of the nations reflected in the water, went under its reefs, which could wreck every hope, to the borough of Queens, to the airfield back to Europe." Throughout the book—in New Orleans, New York, Los Angeles—Koeppen has made a point of visiting cemeteries. "One should never forget to visit the cemeteries of foreign countries when traveling," he instructs his readers. "Graves tell a great deal about a city," and Queens is full of cemeteries. "From the field of the dead I looked over to Manhattan once again; by chance it was a Jewish cemetery in which I was lingering," an ethnic detail casually introduced. "Its gravestones stood so tightly that they seemed, in my eyes, to be a beautiful mirror image of the beautiful and beloved … the people-mixing and most sublime city of skyscrapers." (In the center of contemporary Berlin, close to the Manhattan-like skyscrapers of Potsdamer Platz, is a monument to Holocaust victims meant to evoke a Jewish cemetery.)[23] The distant memory of German crime, strangely palpable in America, completes the picture, just as it completes the book. America, with all its promise, is not like an artful fugue. It is not without intractable difficulties, inherited and self-made, and the American century, already begun, will be a century of difficulties. This insight of Koeppen's is neither tragic nor definitive, and it is not original. Koeppen had encountered it long before setting foot in America, a lesson taught him by Franz Kafka from Prague.

Koeppen received many literary prizes in the 1960s and 1970s. He continued to work—extensively in newspapers and magazines, his original vocation, though only sporadically as a writer of fiction. A disparity widened between his status as a critically acclaimed author and his fraying connection to an international or a European or even a German readership. His moment had been the 1950s, after the war and before West Germany closed its grip on stability and prosperity. In his trilogy of novels he had captured the postwar uncertainties, and the energy of creation carried over to the travel writing, in which he continued to operate as a novelist, inventing from the script of his lived experience.[24] In its narrative structure, *Journey through America* could be compared to a picaresque novel. In one passage, in Chicago, it literally becomes a novel or a short story, Koeppen the observer giving way to a fictitious Minnesotan on a business trip. Then the narrative returns seamlessly to its status quo, as if to say that all writing is novelistic or that life itself is novelistic, and a writer's commitment to realism is, at its root, a commitment to fantasy. The small-town German boy watching fantasy images of America on the provincial movie screen, in *Journey through America*'s first sentence, prefigures the adult Koeppen contemplating the fantasy of international peace, along with other less promising American fantasies, on the book's last page. Building upon Kafka, Koeppen exploits collective fantasies or collective dreams, and this lends his book a political character that has nothing to do with political argument. The German polity circa 1959 is bound up with the American military, the Pentagon, and the White House, and it is equally bound up with fantasy, the fantasies that America sends out into the world and the fantasies about America that the non-American world picks up and spins for itself.

Two publications, both released after *Journey through America*, shed a ret-
rospective light on Koeppen's idiosyncratic method of travel writing. In 1976,
he published *Jugend* (*Youth*), which fostered confusion as to whether he had
written a novel or an autobiography. It could easily be read as both. Having
"fictionalized" his travel writing, giving it the structure and symbolism of the
novel form, he could render his fiction biographical, imbuing it with precisely
described episodes from his own life. The other later-in-life publication, il-
lustrative of Koeppen's creative style, generated a literary scandal. As already
noted, Koeppen participated in the publication of the Jakob Littner's memoir, *Notes from a Hole in the Ground*. Littner, a German Jew and a Holocaust
survivor, had authored a nonfiction manuscript and titled it *Mein Weg in die
Nacht* (*My Path into the Night*). It was given to Koeppen, who reconfigured and
fictionalized Littner's text, imposing an aura of redemptive forgiveness upon
it. As if this were not enough, Koeppen had the 1948 book republished in
1992 as a novel by Wolfgang Koeppen.[25] Littner's journey through the Holocaust had been transformed into Koeppen's journey, and those who learned the
convoluted history of these texts were rightly horrified by what Koeppen had
done. Koeppen's own past made his identification with Littner all the more
deplorable. Here it matters that Koeppen was Aryan enough to survive and
even to prosper in the Third Reich. "A poet cannot be a fascist," he had once
observed in a critical essay.[26] The poetic imagination can never be implicated
in political excess, racism, and cruelty: either the poem is untainted or it is not
poetry, a dubious but telling notion. This was someone who granted literature
enormous liberties, granting himself boundless narrative license on the as-
sumption that art and virtue are cognates.

Journey through America is thus the work of a novelist's novelist, and so it
must be read. It is not a sociological document and has little of empirical value
to offer. Its considerable value begins and ends in Koeppen's fertile imagination. After 1958 Koeppen returned a few times to New York, his favorite
American place, and wrote some short pieces on the city. "I had wanted to live
there [New York]," Koeppen recalled in a 1987 magazine article, "to work, to
write books. It didn't pan out."[27] Perhaps Europe's hold on him was impossible to break, or perhaps he had already said everything in his initial radio
broadcasts, the record of his three months in the United States, from which
he conjured this fantastic and beautiful book.

A Note on Style

Koeppen uses many English words in *Journey through America*. They help to
show what he has taken, linguistically, from the Anglo-American world and

what, for a German-speaking audience, was communicable English in 1959. All English words in the German text are left intact in this English translation and they are also italicized to give the English-language reader a better sense of the German book. They are the only italicized words in the body of this book.

The word Negro, rather than African-American, is used, since it matches Koeppen's use of the German word *Neger*. An American author, writing in 1959, would likely have used the word Negro rather than African-American or black. The same obtains for the adjective "colored," though in its American context this is a more complicated word.

The notes are intended for a twenty-first-century English-language reader, with supplementary information on all but the most famous names, details, and references.

Notes

1. These dates are for the publication of Koeppen's novels in Germany. The English-language translations came much later: *Pigeons in the Grass,* translated by David Ward (New York: Holmes & Meier, 1988); *The Hothouse,* translated by Michael Hofmann (New York: Norton, 2001); and *Death in Rome,* translated by Michael Hofmann (London: Hamish Hamilton, 1992). An earlier novel of Koeppen's, *Eine Unglückliche Liebe,* has also been translated into English: Michael Hoffmann, translator, *A Sad Affair* (New York: Knopf, 2003).

2. On the motif of fragments and fragmentation in Koeppen's writing, in a German rather than American literary context, see Hans-Ulrich Treichel's seminal study, *Fragment ohne Ende: Eine Studie über Wolfgang Koeppen* (*Fragment without End: A Study of Wolfgang Koeppen*) (Heidelberg: Winter, 1984).

3. "Ein passive Geniesser," in Wolfgang Koeppen, and "Flaubert," in *Gesammelte Werke 6,* ed. Marcel Reich-Ranicki, Dagmar von Briel and Hans-Ulrich Treichel (Frankfurt am Main: Suhrkamp, 1990), 126. Dickens came to America in 1842. His travelogue, *American Notes for General Circulation,* published in 1842, led to his American-themed novel, *The Life and Adventures of Martin Chuzzlewit,* which was published in 1844. Alexis de Tocqueville came to America between 1831 and 1832, and he published his two volumes of *Democracy in America* in 1835 and 1840. First published in France in 1948, *America Day by Day,* by Simone de Beauvoir, was published in the United States in 1953. The *Atlantic Monthly* commissioned "In the Footsteps of Tocqueville," a series of articles from Bernard Henri-Lévy in 2005. Henri-Lévy put his impressions into book form in *American Vertigo: Traveling America in the Footsteps of de Tocqueville* (New York: Random House, 2006).

4. Koeppen made the connection between himself and various Kafka protagonists in *Journey through America*: "I had a presentiment that I was K. from Kafka's 'The Trial,' I was the surveyor from 'The Castle,' I was the country doctor following the wrong people, and there was no way to set things right." (121)

5. America as a land of the future is an established European trope. To take only one German example: Wilhelm von Polenz's book about America, *Das Land der Zukunft* (*Land of the Future*) (Berlin: Fontane, 1904).

6. In *A Sad Affair* though the characters are perpetually traveling, they remain stuck in their respective erotic prisons. Its very first sentence is this: "The first time Friedrich crossed the border into a foreign country, the borders were not foreign to him" (Als Friedrich zum erstenmal über eine Grenze in ein fremdes Land reiste, warn ihm Grenzen nicht fremd). Wolfgang Koeppen, *Eine unglückliche Liebe,* in *Gesammelte Werke vol. 2* ed. Marcel Reich-Ranicki, Dagmar von Briel, and Hans-Ulrich Treichel (Frankfurt am Main: Suhrkamp, 1990), 9. Its final sentence reads: "It was a border that they now respected; and Sybille was certainly there for him; and Friedrich was the one who belonged to her. Nothing had changed (Es war eine Grenze, die sie nun respektierten; und Sybille blieb für ihn bestimmt; und Friedrich war der Mensch, der ihr gehörte. Es hatte sich nichts geändert). Wolfgang Koeppen, *Eine unglückliche Liebe,* 158.

7. "Die ruhige, buergerliche Zeit," in Wolfgang Koeppen, *Die Mauer schwankt;* in *Gesammelte Werke vol. 2,* 212.

8. In *Journey through America,* Koeppen again likens black Americans to Odysseus: "young gangs from Harlem were moved forward, their scouts could meet with their Puerto Rican brothers in the many-storied train station [Grand Central Station], they fought, they were voyaging with the Argonauts, with Odysseus, they made their feints in the front lines." (55). On the motif of Odysseus in Koeppen's literature, see Jürgen Egyptien, "Ausfahrt statt Heimfart: Existentielle Inversionen der Odysee in 'Tauben im Gras,'" in *Wolfgang Koeppen "Mein Ziel war die Ziellosigkeit* (Wolfgang Koeppen—"My Aim was Aimlessness"), ed. Gunnar Müller-Waldeck and Michael Gratz (Hamburg: Europäische Verlaganstalt, 1998), 155–68.

9. On the connection between Koeppen and Mann here, see Oliver Herwis, "Wolfgang Koeppens Absage an der Ästhetizismus: die Strategie der literarischen Auseinandersetzung mit Thomas Mann in Roman 'Der Tod in Rom,'" ("Wolfgang Koeppen's Rejection of Aestheticism: The Strategy of Literary Reckoning with Thomas Mann in the Novel *Death in Rome*"), *Zeitschrift für Germanistik* 5 (1995): 544–53.

10. The American journalist John Reed wrote an excited eyewitness chronicle of the Russian Revolution, *Ten Days that Shook the World* (1919); Koeppen's contemporary, Walter Benjamin, wrote up his 1926 sojourn in the Soviet Union, posthumously published as *Moscow Diary* (Cambridge: Harvard University Press, 1986); e. e. cummings' book on Russia is *Eimi* (New York: William Sloane, 1933), recently published in a new edition, *Eimi: A Journey through Soviet Russia,* ed. George Firmage (New York: Liveright, 2007); André Gide conveyed his disillusionment with the Soviet experiment in *Retour de l'U.R.S.S.* (Paris: Galilmard, 1936); Edmund Wilson's *Travels in Two Democracies* (New York: Harcourt, Brace, 1936) was a travelogue divided into American and Soviet halves; and John Steinbeck contributed *A Russian Journal* (New York: Viking, 1948) to the genre.

11. "Amerikafahrt ... unmittelbar nach Erscheinen als eines der bedeutsamsten Buchereignisse des Jahres 1959 gefeiert ... immens erfolgreich." Walter Erhart, "Kommentar," in *Wolfgang Koeppen: Amerikafahrt und andere Reisen,* ed. Walter Erhart, Anja Ebner, and Arne Grafe (Frankfurt am Main: Suhrkamp Verlag, 2008), 289, 293. A partial list of German "America books" preceding Koeppen's would include: Karl Lamprecht, *Americana: Reiseeindrücke, Betrachtungen, Geschichtliche Gesamtansicht* (*Americana: Travel Impressions, Observations, Historical Overview*) (Freiburg im Breisgau: Heyfelder, 1906); Arthur Holitscher, *Amerika heute und morgen: Reiseerlebnise* (*America Today and Tomorrow: Travel Experiences)* (Berlin: S. Fischer, 1912); Ernst von Wolzogen, *Der Dichter in Dollarica: Blumen-, Frucht- und Dornenstücke aus dem Märchenlande der unbedingten Gegenwart* (*The Poet in the Land of the Dollar: Flower, Fruit and Thorn Snippets*

from the Fairy-tale Land of the Unconditional Present) (Berlin: Fontane, 1912); Alfred Kerr, *Yankeeland—Eine Reise* (*Yankeeland: A Journey*) (Berlin: Rudolf Mosse Verlag, 1925); Egon Erwin Kisch, *Paradies Amerika* (*Paradise America*) (Berlin: Erich Reiss Verlag, 1930); Manfred Hausmann, *Kleine Liebe zu Amerika: Ein junger Mann schlendert durch Amerika* (*Little Love for America: A Young Man Ambles through America*) (Berlin: S. Fischer, 1931); Bruno Erich Werner, *Kannst du Europa vergessen? Notizen von einer Amerikareise* (*Can You Forget Europe? Notes from an American Trip*) (Stuttgart: Anstalt, 1952); Gerda Scott, *Und auf tat sich Amerika … Ein Erlebnisbericht* (*And America Beckoned … An Adventure Story*) (Hamburg: Wegner, 1953); Lorenz Stucki, *Im Greyhound durch Amerika* (*Through America on Greyhound*) (Bern: Alfred Scherz, 1955); Rudolf Hagelstange, *How Do You Like America? Impressionen eines Zaungastes* (*An Onlooker's Impressions*) (Munich: Piper, 1957). "America books" could also be books of photography, such as Emil Shulthess, *Photos einer Reise durch die Vereinigten Staaten von Nordamerika* (*Photos of a Trip through the U.S.A.*) (Zurich: Manesse Verlag, 1955).

12. In his commentary on *Journey through America,* Walter Erhart observes that "Koeppen describes North America as a part of Europe—as Europe's continuation and anticipated future" (Koeppen beschreibt Nordamerika als einen Teil Europas—als dessen Fortsetzung und vorweggenommene Zukunft). Walter Erhart, "Kommentar," 267.

13. In an introduction to *The Wall Sways,* Koeppen notes "the realism of Franz Kafka" (der Realismus des Franz Kafka). See Wolfgang Koeppen, "Forward 1983," (Vorspruch 1983) in Koeppen, *Gesammelte Werke 1,* ed. Marcel Reich-Ranicki, Dagmar von Briel, and Hans-Ulrich Treichel (Frankfurt am Main: Suhrkamp, 1990), 162. In *Journey through America,* Koeppen refers to Kafka's American novel as *Amerika*, the title given it by Max Brod; it also has another title in German, *Der Verschollene;* and it bears emphasis, in context, that Kafka's posthumously published novels do not appear in the form and with the titles Kafka might have given them for publication, had he ever consented to their publication. The first chapter of Kafka's *Amerika*, "The Stoker," was the first work of Kafka's Koeppen ever owned. He "bought his first Kafka, 'The Stoker' in paperback" (kaufte ich meinen ersten Kafka, den 'Heizer' broschiert). Koeppen, "Franz Kafka or a Thought, a Fear, a Heartbeat" (Franz Kafka oder Ein Denken, eine Angst, ein Herzschlag) in *Gesammelte Werke 6,* ed. Marcel Reich-Ranicki, Dagmar von Briel, and Hans-Ulrich Treichel (Frankfurt am Main: Suhrkamp, 1990), 240.

14. The imagined "Oklahama" of Kafka's novel is rendered as the existing American state, Oklahoma, in the German text of *Journey through America.*

15. With the American countryside in mind, Koeppen writes that "this garden wrested from the wilderness seemed to be inhabited less by people than by cars. The cars ruled the landscape, they stood in packs before each house, camped in the forest clearings, indulged themselves in the rivers, they had their drive-in restaurants, their drive-in cinemas in the open air, their own hotels and their giant, extremely melancholy cemeteries. At times two cars stood as if lost in conversation, in the most lonely nature, not humans but cars appeared to be the rulers of this land, and they had their appointment to rendezvous." (58)

16. *The Lonely Crowd* was published in Germany in 1958 as *Die Einsame Masse.* On its presence in Koeppen's library, see Walter Erhart, "Kommentar," 273.

17. This is even more apparent when Koeppen goes to Beat hang-outs in San Francisco, finding there the "uniformed nonconformists." The young Beat poets "had the faces of Caligula with the head of Heliogabalis or the young Nero," three of the less appealing Roman emperors. (109).

18. Here Koeppen's rejection of American conformity and Puritanism resembles his critique of Soviet Russia: "it frustrated me that this great, likeable country was so brave, so puritanical and so conformist" (ich ärgerte mich, dass dieses grosse, liebenswerte Land so brav, so puri-

tanisch, so konformistisch war). Wolfgang Koeppen, "Herr Polevoi und Sein Gast" ("Mr. Polevoi and His Guest"), in *Wolfgang Koppen Gesammelte Werkevol. 4,* ed. Marcel Reich-Ranicki, Dagmar von Briel, and Hans-Ulrich Treichel (Frankfurt am Main, Suhrkamp, 1990), 187.

19. Philip Roth would imagine exactly this scenario, of Kafka in America, in his story-essay "'I Always Wanted You to Admire My Fasting'; or Looking at Kafka," in *The Philip Roth Reader* (New York: Vintage, 1985), 281–302. Roth's Kafka comes to Newark, New Jersey.

20. See Robert Frank, *The Americans: Photographs* (New York: Grove, 1959); and Robert Frank, *Les Américains* (Paris: R. Delpine, 1958). Jack Kerouac wrote the introduction to this book. See also Sarah Greenough, ed., *Looking In: Robert Frank's The Americans* (Washington, DC: National Gallery of Art, 2009); and Tod Papageorge, *Walker Evans and Robert Frank: An Essay on Influence* (New Haven: Yale University Art Gallery, 1981).

21. Koeppen often compared New York with Rome and Rome with New York. Goethe's Rome, he wrote, was "New York with ruins" (New York mit Ruinen) and New York was "the new Rome, the old Babel" (das neue Rom, das alte Babel). Wolfgang Koeppen, "A Brother of the Masses He Was Not: On Uwe Johnson" (Ein Bruder der Massen war er nicht. Über Uwe Johnson), in *Wolfgang Koeppen Gesammelte Werke vol. 6,* ed. Reich-Ranicki, von Briel, and Treichel (Frankfurt am Main: Suhrkamp, 1990), 440, 428.

22. E. B. White, *Here Is New York by E. B. White* (New York: The Little Bookroom, 1999), 54.

23. This is Peter Eisenman's Memorial to the Murdered Jews of Europe, opened in 2005. See http://www.holocaust-mahnmal.de/en.

24. Günther Häntzschel uses the term "magic realism" in relation to Koeppen's *Journey through America*. See "Russland, Amerika und Deutschland im 'magischen Realismus.' Neue Lesarten der Reisebücher von Wolfgang Koeppen," *Jahrbuch der Internationalen Wolfgang Koeppen Gesellschaft* 2 (2003): 191–208. Koeppen himself used the phrase "magical realism" in his travel essay on Russia: "I tried to elucidate a magical realism" (ich versuchte, eine magischen Realismus zu erläutern). Wolfgang Koeppen, "Herr Polevoi und Sein Gast," 138.

25. For an extraordinarily insightful and detailed study of Koeppen in relation to mid-century German history, including the Jakob Littner scandal, see Jörg Döring, *"Ich stellte mich unter, ich machte mich klein": Wolfgang Koeppen, 1933–1946 ["I Took Shelter, I Made Myself Small"]* (Frankfurt am Main: Suhrkamp, 2003). See also Alfred Estermann's "Nachwort" [Afterword] in Wolfgang Koeppen, *Jakob Littners Aufzeichnungen aus einem Erdloch* (Frankfurt am Main: Jüdischer Verlag im Suhrkamp Verlag, 2002).

26. Wolfgang Koeppen, "Alfred Andersch," in *Wolfgang Koeppen Gesammelte Werke vol. 6,* ed. Ranicki, von Briel, and Treichel (Frankfurt am Main: Suhrkamp, 1990), 386.

27. Wolfgang Koeppen, "Ein Wiedersehen mit New York" ("A Return to New York"), in *Wolfgang Koeppen: Amerikafahrt und andere Reisen in die Neue Welt,* 234 [Ich wollte dort leben, arbeiten, Bücher schreiben. Das hat es nicht ergeben]. This essay was first published in the travel magazine *Merian* in 1987.

Journey through America

The barracks of the inoculated crusaders on Europe's soil, a renewal of the Roman wall on the Rhine, rocket ramps in a black zone, supply bases on the high school of Salamanca, bulldozers, planing machines, hole-drilling tools, hiding places for fear, shelters for stupidity.[1] The old vineyards consecrated to the gods, to the saints and to commerce; the German planes, the Germanic middle, the continent's broken heart, Maginot's illusions restored, colonies of officers and sergeants with Indian faces, neighborliness and isolation. They've brought Main Street with them, unpacked churches from their suitcases and space for fighter planes to launch their attacks; sand and forgetfulness built up on the outskirts of the free imperial city, the school buses of children confident with promises of security laid down in the crib. Aspirants to world domination, shy and loud in the Old Heidelberg show. Gentlemen in a whiskey ad next to German beer bottles. The loneliness of the prairie has come along on the trip, the hot and cold air of the Nevada desert has come along, unforgotten, the good and evil wind from Chicago the hometown ghetto, vending machines for love and singing machines for the dream of not-being-alone.[2] Four-star generals on the Champs Élysées, radio reports from the Pentagon, the banner of the Atlantic alliance in the friendly forest of Marly-le-Roi, dead the Christian Kings, magisterial the speeches from the president in the White House; urbi et orbi; speeches broadcasting from towers, fear and hope disseminated in the radio news hours, the Marshall Plan's good money, the solid dollar for undeveloped regions, the check written for freedom, the check written against hunger, the check for oil, billions for the research done at Peen-

1. The original Roman wall on the Rhine was built between second and third centuries and was seen, by the Romans, as a border between civilization and barbarism; Salamanca is a Spanish city built into a mountain; it has an ancient university, and the "school of Salamanca" was a sixteenth-century intellectual movement.

2. *Alt-Heidelberg* [Old Heidelberg] was a play by Wilhelm Meyer-Förster (1862–1934), a German writer. It was the basis for the operetta, *The Student Prince,* by Sigmund Romberg (1887–1951), an American composer of Hungarian background, which premiered in New York in 1924 and was made into a 1927 silent film by Ernst Lubitsch (1892–1947), a German-American film director. The city of Heidelberg was also in the American zone of occupation.

emünde, extending to the moon.[3] The *stars and stripes* above the consulates and the libraries of *the American way of life;* on evening screens every village boy comes to know Broadway's canyon of lights, California's sun-bright streets, the family prayer before the shrine of the open refrigerator, the manliness of chrome and horsepower, the breasts and legs of commercially sponsored beauty queens, delighted eyes, drawn weapons, the big war for the Wild West and the battle royal in the urban jungles, figures made from petit-bourgeois desires and immaturity and triumphs in life's struggle, victories in science and O'Neill's crazy lights as well as Tennessee Williams' illuminations, Faulkner's genius, the heroic saga of Little Rock, the terrible discontents of the advertising agents and then the posters from the airline companies, asleep in a hammock over the Atlantic, you've already arrived before you've departed, so much seduction is not to be resisted, even today one should still head by ship for the first pilgrimage to "America-you-have-it-better," to the New World, carried by waves like the truly remarkable Columbus, and not thrown through the air like your contemporaries packed off by their travel agencies, you understand once again that the two continents really are separated by an ocean, while the traveler flying in pink chewing-gum seats is all too likely to see New York as a suburb of Berlin or Paris, and to see London, Frankfurt, the airport madness and what's lying around it as the satellites of Manhattan.[4]

In Paris, by the St. Lazare station, right near Balzac's old rue d'Amsterdam, France was blooming, the net of fantasy stretched from pillar to pillar and history indulged in laziness. The long passage, glassed-in with milky absinthe, it seemed, was the nineteenth century, embodying a great French epoch, it was comic and amazing, it was indecent and seductive. The small bright jack o' lantern of the Enlightenment and literature's touching colorful magic lamp had shone then. They are shining still. I asked myself, for how long? The blood of glory and freedom had irrigated the ground, seeping from layer to layer. The aroma of chicken-in-a-pot was in the air, like the wolf's hungry breath, like the breath of uprising, the stink of malaise, the perfume of scandal grown stale and the sour smell of power, which had blown for centuries around the Bastille. I felt at home here. I had read that only someone who had lived in

---

3. Marly-le-Roi was the French town that served as NATO headquarters until 1967, and *urbi et orbi,* "to the city and to the world," is the phrase used at the beginning of a Papal address. Peenemünde was a German village isolated for military research in Nazi Germany; its mention here suggests too smooth of a transition from World War II to the Cold War.

4. America-you-have-it-better," "Amerika, du hast es besser," is a famous line from a poem by Goethe (1749-1832), "To the United States," composed in 1827 and published in 1833. The stanza reads: "America, you have it better/ than our continent, the old one / you have no ruined castles/ and no basal. / You don't have within / the lively times / useless remembrance / and pointless conflict."

France in the eighteenth century knew the pleasure of existence; still, one loved the revolution in Paris, the never-ending assault on all castles of coercion, the spirits of rebellion from time immemorial were invited to a banquet, here where upheaval was wanted, here I was a European, which is what I wanted to remain. A dish of milk was set out for a mouse, a cat observed the mouse covetously and languidly. Algeria and torture were far away and near. On newspaper stands the word of conscience was postered, Sartre and Mauriac called out Zola's "J'accuse," and the general sang the Marseillaise before a hundred camera eyes.[5] In front of a bistro shaky chairs invited charming dalliance. There they served dry white wine, which, according to Georges Simenon, is beloved by French police commissioners, a human quality, though on the Quai des Orfèvres the wine disappoints.[6] Women, born to be embraced, hurried to work with serious business faces. On a billboard a luxurious blonde, Renoir's offspring and dressed as a sailor, advertised a foaming beer.

But on the platform of the Compagnie Générale Transatlantique the sinking of the Titanic was being played out. First I saw the emigrants. There were still emigrants. There were still the dark places, the hells, the hiding places for people, the pens, the camps, the barbed wire, the huts, there was still the drawing of borders, expulsions, repressions, denunciations, the old continent's revolutions. They were fleeing, the shadows of persecution accompanied them, the clouds of violence seemed to be hovering over them still, and displayed the pallor of cramped quarters. They looked to the West, they saw holiness in the course of the sun. They called for freedom of conscience, freedom of thought, freedom of religion, had freedom been lost along the way, were they only craving bread or already the dream cars of the glossy magazines? Head scarves from the countryside or of days past? Shy children in black wool stockings, the curly beard and godly hat of a pious Israelite. The emigrants took down heavy trunks; property, plunder packed in blankets, they kept memories of the impoverished room on home soil, which had been no paradise for them, and mothers of families, matrons, who were staying behind in order to die, lamenting the departure of those from whom they were separating, as if they were not stepping into a train but right into the grave. With all the sadness a glow transfigured the scene, it was the hope of the poor, the legend of becoming a millionaire, and in the station's smoky fog the light suddenly gleamed, it was the sun over the gold digger's dead body in the desert, it was the lonely

---

5. François Mauriac (1885–1970) was a French writer and public intellectual; Émile Zola (1840–1902), whose famous polemical tract, "*J'accuse*" (1898), was an attack on French anti-Semitism; the general in question is Charles de Gaulle (1890–1970), who founded the Fifth Republic in 1958; by 1958 the war between France and an independence movement in Algeria was into its fourth year.

6. Georges Simenon (1903–1989) was a Belgian writer of detective novels.

ray on the fallen gangster's cement epitaph, deep below ground in a garage. Those traveling the sure way, having been born millionaires, stood before the first-class luxury section holding court. This was the world of *Harper's Bazaar,* Barbara Hutton and the Duchess of Windsor met up, and the photographers bought the faces cheaper by the dozen.[7] The masters were once again in Paris, they were once again traveling through Europe, they were looking around for new ways to polish their status, for the bizarre decoration of their oh-so-boring legends in the society pages of the papers. They had succeeded once again, the gossip columns were filled, a month of empty life buried, and someone from the embassy and the regulars at the Ritz brought them to the boat train, though even here there were tears, last kisses, and farewells as if forever, even here time came to an end and eternity was terrifying, since it means death.

I saw the proud ship, which I had not yet entered, smashing into an iceberg, an employee of the company rang a little death bell, Le Havre–New York departure, we got into our cars, and the poor and the millionaires all sang: closer, my God, to thee.

From the train window, the impressionists' landscape glided by, Maupassant's row boats were still rocking on the Seine, the little bateaux mouches were still enticing, and again young men in row boats were proudly displaying their muscles to their beauties, while polite, very professional French bureaucrats gave travelers the old country's departure stamp.

Over the customs booths of Le Havre towered the red smoke stacks of the "Liberté," which had steamed its way across the seas as the "Europe," bursting with Bremen's Hanseatic pride, and now it stood for French freedom; and it was the ocean that came next, the ocean observed from a luxury hotel, but still the same untamed, heavenly ocean—for six days endlessly far, endlessly empty and harshly misanthropic. The inexperienced travelers believed that they would encounter other ships here, that they would see sails and plumes of smoke in the firmament, symbols of man's land-based power over earth, but the passengers beheld only stormy or smooth waves, the sea remained unnavigable, and so might the passengers, exposed to the utter indifference to their fate all around them, understand the despair of the caravels' crew who believed they were traveling ever further into nothingness, or the passenger could marvel at the courage of the old immigrants, who with certain wind were willing to drift toward the absolutely uncertain for the sake of belief, for the sake of human rights and for the sake of hope.[8] This courage had created America. This courage was creating America still today.

---

7. Barbara Hutton (1912–1979) was an American socialite.

8. Caravels were boats used by the Spanish and Portuguese for the early exploration of the Atlantic.

In the on-board cinema flickering shadows traveled along with us, our ob-trusive mirror images. The minister made his greeting, waved and smiled. The general made his greeting, waved and curried favor. We got the latest from Washington and from Hollywood. Egg dances on the edge of the abyss, so-ciety cha-chas over the ocean's depths, above the sleep of hidden monsters, above the grave of those who had gone down, burned, torpedoed, bombed, sacrifices to the murderous orders, to the fetish of the flag.[9] Traveling priests were absorbed in their prayer books or in looking at God's gray creation on the cabin-class deck, black birds near the deck games, a black-tie gala, spruced up penguins beneath the crystal chandeliers trembling gently to the engine's pounding pistons, orchids from south-English greenhouses on powdered skin and the trains of dresses and perfume from Rond Point; closed portholes and light in the cafeteria turning the tourists and immigrants pale, much re-read tourist brochures, disintegrating letters from relatives, believed and already doubted promises and all the burning expectation of the coast![10] "There now is your insular city of the Manhattoes, belted round by wharves as Indian isles by coral reefs—commerce surrounds it with her surf. Right and left, the streets take you waterward. Its extreme downtown is the battery, where that noble mole is washed by waves, and cooled by breezes, which a few hours previous were out of sight of land."[11] With these words Herman Melville described the New York of 1850, where he hunted Moby Dick, the white whale, his chimera. And Franz Kafka, who never reached America but who nevertheless had the truest dream of America, looked upon "the statue of liberty, already long ob-served, as in a sunlight grown suddenly stronger, her arm, with the sword, raised as if recently outraged, and breezes gusted around it."

The New World greeted me with cold wind and gray air. Anticipation had driven the travelers out of their beds a day before, but the closer land came, the less we were warmed by the desire gradually taking shape. A herd of ama-teur photographers swarmed over the decks like startled sheep. The Statue of Liberty rose out of the sea in a dissipating coat of fog and was a dowdy sister of the beloved giants, Bavaria, Germania, or Berolina, into whose hollow head one can climb to see the mutely extending horizon from its blind eyes, a nation's mother complex, a matron in an ill mood, holding out a wet lantern, but illuminating nothing.[12]

---

9. The egg dance is a dance, of some antiquity in Europe but popular in America as well, in which a dancer tries not to destroy eggs laid on the floor.

10. Rond Point is a luxurious neighborhood of Paris.

11. This is a citation from chapter one of Melville's *Moby-Dick* (1852).

12. Bavaria, Germania, and Berolina are all allegorical female figures, representing, respec-tively, Bavaria, Germany, and Berlin.

The famous *skyline* stuck out from behind the home-baked Statue of Liberty, the skyscrapers met at the tip of this most secure and expensive rock. I thought about economic statistics, about success curves graphically represented, I saw the stock prices climbing, rockets rising up, the heavens should be stormed, but here paradise was as hard to see as elsewhere, and in the eyes of the guest nearing land the richest city in the world left the impression of a village grown megalomaniac, instead of being overpowering it seemed a familiar sight, the painting was more clearly arranged than gigantic.

The ship slid slowly pulled by tugboats toward the new Rome of the much invoked Western hemisphere, its towers did not praise God, they did not inquire into the existence of an Almighty, they had arrived at their own omnipotence; but there was no shiver, which I was ready to feel, before the majesty of human freedom or before the proclamation of faith in a human happiness compelled by technical, material progress and prosperity. The city of New York, as it stretched itself out in the morning mist, a theater prop made from steel, cement and glass and old stone walls as well, suggested a house of cards and inspired thoughts of storms which might be brewing far away. Other buildings crouched beneath the highest roofs, looking smaller than they were, like simple booths, almost like ground-floor barracks; they gathered the giants around them, wanting to make them all the same and everything seemed provisional and arbitrary, though laid out in an easily comprehended order, as if by a playful but not very imaginative child.

Luckily I saw compact old-fashioned ferries going over the shallow bay, and they enchanted me as they crossed the Hudson, wheels rolling, beating foam, with their heavy human freight, the America of my expectations, they made me think of Mark Twain and Walt Whitman, even if the Mississippi and the green hunting grounds and the poet's days were gone. The docks already mentioned by Melville still surrounded Manhattan like black honeycombs, the "Liberté" was swallowed as if by a mouth, and the de-boarding of the ship followed a strict old ceremony. First the favored from the first class were let into the country, then the cabin class was emptied with all its black-clad priests, and at the very end came the rows of emigrants, now pressed into the demigods' rooms, onto thick carpets, loaded into the brocade chairs of the big hall, where the customs officials sat at cleaned-off tables used for luxurious dinners, the pride of the shipping line. I was not asked if I wanted to murder the president. That was a tall tale. The officials were friendly and relaxed, they used their stamp generously, leaving it up to the foreigners whether they would murder or not.

Big America trusted me. It trusted me from the beginning. It expected that I, with my own eyes, would recognize the States as God's own land. It was an expectation I was involuntarily afraid of disappointing, and this embarrassed me. Was I traveling with the wrong passport? I was granted permission to enter, went over the boat's plank, over the last material thing connecting me to Europe, and went over the bridge into the giant customs hall.

The hall was America and it was as if Franz Kafka from Prague had imagined it, a room with such a swinging ceiling, with such a wide vastness that it dissolved into itself and seemed entirely unreal. A pallid sun refracted through milk-glass panes into glimmering shafts of dust, the concrete floor was worn down and scratched, and countless numbers of the most primitive wooden barriers and the cheapest desks were everywhere, among them was Europe's flotsam and jetsam, raised from the belly of the "Liberté" and somehow ordered alphabetically according to the names of their owners, little mountains of luggage strewn about like harvested piles on a field, transformed into a true heap of misery.

This is the moment when the immigrant wants to tear the clothes from his body and burn all the things he has brought, to step into the new life naked and weighted down by nothing, with his gaze on other, more brilliant possessions. Since such conduct wouldn't be ideal in America, as elsewhere, and might have destroyed all the efforts to travel so far, I waited for the customs official. His arrival was leisurely. From the star on his chest I recognized in him the good-humored policeman from the movies, but he had an old-Prussian commitment to duty. Every bag had to be opened and thoroughly searched. What contraband did he fear in the land of abundance? He didn't find it. My baggage got the entry stamp, which one had to show at the hall's last barrier.

I went through the door. I had arrived in America. I stood in New York. I had often dreamt of this, and now it was like a dream. The dream of being here had been fulfilled, and, as in a dream, there were no foreigners. I was also at home here, and America lay before me as if it were solid property. I sensed freedom. I felt freedom. The freedom was the wind. Nobody asked me where I was going, what I was doing, what I wanted to begin from the Atlantic to the Pacific coast, from the Gulf of Mexico to the icebergs of Alaska.

The taxi was as big as a locomotive, and it was painted gray-yellow like a German postbox. On its roof a blue-red light signal shone, it resembled the blinking vigilant eye of the police, and for a moment I felt that I was a dignitary, being escorted and brought to his destination away from the country and the people. The car's upholstery was hard, and its naked steel floor was dirty; the passenger was offered transportation, nothing more. Continuously transmitted messages came through to the driver; the invisible spoke to him, cursed him, tormented him, hounded him. Every now and then the man answered the spectral voices commanding him from the air; he spoke, sullenly and irritably, talking against the windshield, he swallowed his syllables in a convincing economical way, though I did not understand a word of his self-defense.

Perhaps he was only telling his big brother that he was driving a *greenhorn* to his hotel.

Flame-red, its sirens shrieking, a fire truck roared past us. I had expected it! I already saw a skyscraper burning, Broadway blazing, already I could read the headlines in all the world's newspapers. Violent catastrophes seemed to lie in the air here. How did New York smell? Here it still smelled of the sea, of ships, I felt a breath of Holland, I sensed the colony of New Amsterdam. But how did the continent smell? Only when a country wind came did the continent offer up its smell, the smell of grass, of the blooming or withering prairie, of cleanly cut grass around the homes of Americans, but the city itself smelled of overheated damp, of the white fluffy vapor that continuously pressed up through the street surface, suspended beneath the automobile tires, enveloping pedestrians' feet in fog and allowing them to walk on clouds like allegorical figures. Later I was told that a great heating system emitted this vapor, but at first sight New York rose out of volcanic soil, and curb and asphalt and masonry were holding off a dangerous eruption.

At the same time the street we were traversing repudiated the world city. The street mimicked; it played. Old Amsterdam, it was very cozy, all kinds of cats and caged birds and mixed-race dogs looked out from dusty friendly windows, little shops had green vegetables and cheap provisions for sale. On the sidewalks people were moving, people at home with themselves, people in slippers, there was provincialism in New York too and neighborhood pride, neighborhood chats as in Paris, London, as in old Berlin, no hurry, nothing of the American tempo, which is a fully false European notion of America anyway; what was American, new to me, foreign, was people perching before the doors of their homes, women, children and evidently unemployed men sitting for hours on wooden or steel steps, which led up to small verandas or wrapped around the house as fire escapes.

Soon, however, the buildings were growing, as one had expected, as films, picture books and dreams had shown, and the street became a canyon, we were driving deep down on the floor of a gray cañon, and the sky above was an endlessly distant, very narrow but friendly blue stripe.

The hotel was a skyscraper naturally, but it was not a big building. It resembled a highly set narrow iron that wanted to touch the sky with its top, and it was a hostel strangely painted candy pink for travelers who on Greyhound buses, the gas-guzzling greyhounds of a transportation company that stretches cross-country, come to New York from all the states, to do business or to marvel at the city. These buses were stocky and massive, equipped with a viewing area, proudly covered in foreign dust, they were fast rhinoceroses, overcoming endlessly long streets mile by mile, mountains, wild waters, prairies, deserts, having seen the horizons of the Indians. Youth streamed out of their Trojan horse bellies and filled the hotel's narrow lobby, youth in colorful shirts, bright hats covered with advertising slogans on heads that were either curly or shorn. Those who were already old had a youthful demeanor at least, they had chosen shirts that were grayer and hats that were more daring, and it seemed that they all wanted to climb onto unsaddled mustangs and not the public transportation of a world city.

Then everybody had to stand in line; it was disappointing and like being in the middle of a war. In long lines we waited before a table where the rooms were divvied out, before the counter where we could pay, before the self-service elevators, and everyone showed themselves to be patient and found it self-evident that they had to wait. At first this seemed, surprisingly, to indicate a certain shortage of accommodation and comfort, but it was only a passing difficulty, as it luckily proved to be, an almost charming lack of organization in apportioning abundance.

Once again America trusted even the most foreign. The guest was not asked for any verification of identity, there were no papers to fill out for the police, it was enough to put down some kind of name, one's real name or whatever one felt like writing at the moment, to be entrusted with a customer card and to get the room key. In the elevator all the men took off their colorful hats and caps when a young girl got on with us, taking a small mirror from her bag and decorating her lips with devotion—a queen, honored in this city like thousands of others. The jumping light of the display showed that we were climbing with furious speed, to the tenth, to the twelfth, to the sixteenth floor. There the red fire code was horrifying, warnings, fire hoses, steel doors in narrow corridors, arrows pointing to the black fire escapes outside on this giant building. Once again I sensed that in America a catastrophe was expected at every moment.

Excited voices burst from the room I was supposed to occupy. A shot rang out. A woman screamed. With the caution of the great detectives I opened the door. A television blared, telling the guest that he was not alone even in this unfamiliar place, and shadows, the shadows of criminals in this case, had spoken to the four walls of the room until I entered. My bed, white as washing powder propaganda and therefore looking innocent, had witnessed a murder. An ugly young man in a cowboy outfit, shaved bald, was asking me in his whiny voice to buy a particular kind of drop, the most delicious, the most wholesome in the world. Already in Europe I had been especially struck by the distorted way Americans dressed their boys and the provocative way they dressed their girls, and in the preferential treatment of the girls I recognized a clever preparation for new-world life, for the position of women and men in American society. The whining cowboy threatened me with a pistol, and right after a man aimed his *Old Shatterhand* rifle out of a log cabin.[13] But the window offered an overwhelming view. The skyscraper city was shining before me in the mid-day sun, its highest buildings surpassed my high hotel, I recognized New York as the settlement of my time, and I liked it very much, it enchanted, fulfilling all expectations. Like towers and castles of steel, aluminum, concrete and sparkling glass, the skyscrapers rose up everywhere out of a maze of other roofs, relatively and astonishingly low, cut by streets into right angles, and they, the great buildings, seeming to be greeting each other above the ridge of the small buildings. There was a continuously pleasurable blinking and winking in the air. The wind blew freshly and had much room. The sky was high and blue, and I felt myself being drawn into a great general happiness. "I was Manhattanese, free, friendly and proud!"[14] Walt Whitman's voice was over the buildings. Far below on the street cars drove in comic loudly colored rows like a rolling toy through a children's paradise.

According to the street map I had to be near Broadway, right by Times Square. The memory of many film images, of the glittering Armistice Day, a new year's eve swarming with ants, the confetti for Lindbergh's triumph, the intoxication of Prohibition's end, drove me there inexorably, and as so often happens reality disappointed the dream. At mid-day the famous corner between Broadway and 42nd Street looked shabby. In daylight Broadway looked like Hamburg's Reeperbahn, before the pleasure lights of evening have gone on and before the girls have made themselves up.[15] Women wandered by in clothes cut to the newest Paris styles, by a homegrown tailor gone crazy and given to grotesque exaggeration, and to their theatrical robes the women matched big hats with blooming flowerbeds or overripe fruit, on colored or powdered hair. They were met by wide, sturdy, upright, well-proportioned Negroes, who as a provocation wore casually elegant suits with round comic waterproof hats, a consciously silly touch, which lent their faces a strangely arrogant aura. In a display window the film star Jayne Mansfield hung life-size for the onlooker to buy, a hot-water-bottle of glaring red rubber and with pressed-rubber breasts, embarrassingly voluptuous and sticking out. Everywhere there were shops with magic objects, joke products and trick machines, with objects that crudely disfigure and mock the organs of sex and excretion, and there seemed to be customers who found this taste funny and brought

---

13. Old Shatterhand is the protagonist in a novel cycle, set in the American West, by the German writer Karl May (1842–1912) and the German-American friend of the Indian Winnetou; May, whose fiction is mostly unknown in America, though beloved in Germany, visited the United States in 1908.

14. This is a citation from Whitman's 1856 poem "Crossing Brooklyn Ferry."

15. The Reeperbahn is the main thoroughfare of Hamburg's substantial red-light district.

these things home to their family or friends. Another equally successful business sold the most grievous insults, expressed in sayings and pictures, as greeting cards. In a laundromat naked puppets, sickly red or poison green, were on display, putative Parisian coquetry, and the passer-by could believe that on this afternoon he had come across the sad hell for the sensuous. Open purgatory flickered beneath pieces of meat, advertised as Texas steaks. In long rows those who were greedy, not those who were hungry, victims of the fire and the seduction, lined up for a meal that turned out to be as tender as tire trucks, as if it had been roasted on the plate, burnt and glowing. Behind the curtainless mirror of a bakery, as big as a sports field, women with the flowerbed hats on their well-groomed, purple-powdered, silver-dusted hair sat beneath artificial palms, near glittering fountains of light, eating enormous portions of a strangely aroma-less, glaringly colored strawberry cake. The women seemed to have an endless amount of time. They seemed to have endless hours at their disposal, their day wanted to stretch itself out endlessly; hung with jewelry, believing they would be taken care of, the women were sure of their time and of their place in society. And soon I came to the streets of legendary affluence, the world's luxury lay behind glittering panes of glass, at my feet the earth was wooing me; in secure many-storied castles one wrote, counted, did business, one was striving, producing, extracting, inventing, decorating, concealing, deceiving, stowing money away, chalking up interest, and all this industry and all this work, all the country's capacities and products seemed to belong, in the end, to women and to serve them alone, the women with the flowerbed hats who sat by the fountains of light and ate aroma-less strawberries.

At the corner of 47th Street and Fifth Avenue the jewelry treasure of an unfortunate generation of European women was for sale in many jewelry stores, grandmother rings, yellowed pearls, unfashionably cut diamonds, given up for bread or cigarettes because of war, expulsion, putsch, imprisonment and smuggled over the ocean by clever businesspeople. This street in the middle of New York's elegant shopping district was a black, or at least a gray, market, over which an east wind blew. This street was Vienna, it was Berlin, the corner was Warsaw or Czernowitz.[16] One did business behind barred windows or, from hand to hand, in the open air. The restaurants here cultivated the style of old-fashioned bars, set up like soup kitchens, the guests stood around, hats on their heads, and consumed fat sausages, and steaming coffee was poured from giant enamel machines instead of the blinking espresso machines otherwise common in America. This area was very much like Berlin's destroyed Scheunenvi-

---

16. Czernowitz is the German name for a city, Chernivtsi, currently in Ukraine; it belonged to Romania in the interwar years and was occupied by both Soviet and Nazi troops during the war; like Vienna, Berlin and Warsaw it was a center of Jewish life and culture before the war.

ertel, except that everything was played out here under the weight of at least twenty stories, which restored the street to its American perspective.[17]

The open portals of Rockefeller Center resembled the mouth of a giant vacuum cleaner; they sucked up the passers-by like quicksand. This was a city in the city; these walls were striving to reach the heavens. The address book for Rockefeller Center named thirty-five thousand inhabitants; there were visitors in the hundreds of thousands. Caught up in an inescapable stream of people, I remembered that I had grown up in a community of ten thousand souls. It had streets, a marketplace, two churches, two cemeteries, one courthouse, one prison, three schools, hunters' barracks and paths leading out to the sea and forest. Here all of this and much more was packed into a single house. I stepped over the mirrored polish as if over a frozen sea, went through forests of marble and wandered beneath a sun, moon, and stars inebriated with neon lights.

Reason, man, or electrodes controlled the climate, the elevators were floating avenues, the labyrinth was moving, with jumps, crashes and thrusts, it was skipping rope, and the straight-backed conductors drove toward success and to the willing garbage chutes. Before I knew it, I was in the cellar in underground galleries getting seduced by smiling puppets and enchanting offerings, getting Americanized. I had last summer's straw hat on my head and a tie with a wild horse and lasso looped around my neck; unexpectedly I stood in a post office, behind the counter sat a Negro with horn-rimmed glasses like the strict judges of Hades, I fled to a snack bar where milk and coffee flowed from the walls, an open bible pointed to Moses, tablecloth-thin garishly colored meals were conjured by women wearing flowerbed hats who cheerfully spooned them up, while the awful, horribly familiar signs terrified me, the admonishing arrows: to the air raid shelter.

Again the Rockefeller tower trembled in the wind, and the explosions resounding in the hallways were the short energetic thuds of high heels, belonging to proud groups of girls. Song rang out, music, they acted, they danced, they broadcast, they performed a play about being happy. In a courtyard flowers blossomed from heated beds, water games splashed a small Versailles, the flags of nations strong in purchasing power flew above expensive shops, as if the residents of all countries, or at least the well-to-do ones, were invited to a party.

All around competitors were growing and threatening even the size and glitter of Rockefeller Center. Smaller and older buildings were getting torn down, building pits were being dug out, so deep, so wide that a village could be sunk into them; men with white, yellow, and red helmets on their heads oper-

---

17. Scheunenviertel, a poorer neighborhood of Berlin, was heavily damaged in World War II.

ated heavy machinery, continuously transforming the city's face, and I could observe all this through round glass windows, inserted in the construction area specially for onlookers and admirers like myself. A crane made iron beams flutter like feathers, a steel skeleton stretched and expanded, forging a new path in the sky, going even higher and storming the heavens beyond where all the others could go, but at the feet of giants trees bloomed green and there was a lovely little park behind the New York Public Library.

All the races of the world were striving for the book, for knowledge, for discovery, the encyclopedists' most beautiful dreams were being fulfilled overseas, all the wonderful mixed races of the city were hungry for learning, there to be seen in the fullest youth, strolling amid the fresh foliage as if they were in the school of Athens, and America was indeed free and beautiful. The evening came in golden light. Manhattan revealed its island self and seemed to be suspended. Every street led to water. In its breezes New York married maritime Venetian with prairie American. After the workday people flooded out from offices like dancers, rushed like butterflies over to the busses, sank down like black ants into the pits and shadows of the subway. Babel, too, had its dusk. No chair, no table on the street, but warmth and humanity in artificially dark and mysteriously kept caves. Everywhere Aladin's magic lamp was burning. Not the reed-green of Pernod in a glass, but the gold of whiskey, the clear sea of a dry martini spread its spirit in fancy glasses, and men and women sat at high bars, exhausted from the day, though not yet tired for the night, cosmopolitans, who, as Gottfried Benn would put it, were waiting for movement in the evening scenery.[18]

And already neon letters were writing pleasures on the sky! A mounted policeman swam against the stream of cars. They had torn down apartments to make room for parking lots, and, freed from houses, the land was much more valuable. In front of the theater the world's most charmed audience caucused in a flood of white light. This was the audience for Reinhardt and Jessner, for Charell and Brecht, which I was encountering here once again, I saw myself on Schumannstrasse, on Schiffbauerdamm, on Kurfürstendamm, I heard the old talk of anticipation, the conversation of habitués, the dialogue of expertise.[19] Unceasing demands, never-ending thanks to the artists!

---

18. Gottfried Benn (1886–1956) was a German poet and essayist who took his own journey to America in 1914.

19. Max Reinhardt (1873–1943), Austrian-Jewish actor as well as a theater and film director, emigrated to the United States after the *Anschluss* of Germany and Austria in 1938; Leopold Jessner (1878–1945), was a German actor who moved to the United States in 1937; Erik Charell (1894–1974), a German actor and director; the celebrated Deutsches Theater was on Schumannstrasse in Berlin; Schiffbauerdamm, a street of several major theaters in Berlin; Kurfürstendamm, an elegant Berlin street also with many theaters.

New York was not foreign, it was familiar; even in all its foreignness it was familiar. Undraped the windows of the nightclubs. The public. Democracy. A young Negro woman stepped through a bar, she approached in skin-tight red tights and it was her black skin that appeared to burn. A Chinese man who was otherwise normal suffered a nervous breakdown, shrieked, howled, beat his own glass with small fists, because the bar's television was broken and he couldn't see his show, his shadow girl. The monster of the day was a doctor from Puerto Rico. He had shot a nurse in Brooklyn. The choir of newspaper sellers shouted about the tragedy and raised up pictures of the protagonists. It was unenlightening to see the victim, more beautiful girls crossed the street without getting shot, the murderer's eyes blinked near-sighted and vacant behind rimless glasses.

A battlefield din resounded on upper Broadway, before Broadway led into the leaves and the dark of Central Park, the scanty lawns, the stone gardens, the shimmering lanterns, the romance of horse-drawn carriages, into the fairy tale of theft and the murder saga, mythologized daily. On 52nd Street, in the middle of the theater district, were the Catalaunian Plains of the adolescents.[20] Battle raged in the shooting galleries of skillful entrepreneurs. The technological toys for advanced youth lit up and emitted rings, bangs and rattles. In airplane cockpits they knelt down behind canons and finished off their enemies. One finds such emporia in every city of the Western world, but here on Broadway I seemed to have found the primal cave of noise and of pointlessly wasted time.

An enormous store, brightly lit, attracting people like a magnet, open all night, it was a sublime temple of noise. Cacophonies thundered like Niagara Falls, here canned music was for sale, stars of song and instrument looked out coolly from the walls like freshly minted millionaires. The primeval forest of the Voodoo Suite, the melancholy of the *Modern Jazz* Quartet, girls and boys, figures almost indistinguishable by gender, short-haired, slender, pale, the disappointments of the young years in their bleary eyes, they stood, each one for himself, each in his own dream world, as in a trance there, and listened to music, which turned the store into a forest with many babbling brooks.[21]

Further East was a street devoted to the burlesque. There were murals illuminated by spotlights, life-sized color photographs of female flesh, chilled pink, microscopically stretched by magnifying glass, strangely naked skin, the circle dance of the half-naked, the fashion of *striptease,* a despairing clinging to corporeality. Doormen praised the performers' charms, their brutal mouths

---

20. The Catalaunian Plains (in modern-day France) was the site of a battle, in 451 B.C., between the Romans and Attila the Hun.

21. *Voodoo Suite* was a 1958 album by Perez Prado (1916–1989), a Cuban bandleader and composer; the Modern Jazz Quartet, which would record and perform for decades, was founded in 1952.

spoke in praise of women, and among the strip clubs stood, in macabre irony, the carved bloody bodies of animals in the dazzlingly bright window of a large slaughterhouse. The mighty head of a *Black Angle* bull, separated from its body, looked at me full of seriousness and worth and dignity like the powerful old god of the night.[22]

A search light roamed over the city like the outstretched hand of death. Music, laughter, voices from a thousand bars and restaurants. Music, laughter, voices from the procession of cars. Meetings, matings in the broad parking lots, cars the still voiceless witnesses. Many of the skyscrapers looked like trees of light, others like lifeless rocks in a diffuse moonlight. In the display case of a seafood restaurant two big lobsters fought a duel to the death. In their dark armor they resembled knights drawn by Albrecht Dürer. Turkeys, big as a roc, stood ready for carving.[23] Ham like wagon wheels, roasts as if from elephants. The black cook sharpened his knife, hacked off slice after slice from a steaming piece of meat and lay the slices between pieces of bread white as chalk. Yellow, white and black seas, milk, juice and coffee, mouths that were always greedy, always thirsty.

The cheap bars on Sixth Avenue were endlessly long, very narrow corridors, where black and white men sat at the counter peacefully like disheveled birds in a cage; the shining wet street of booze. I thought about Eugene O'Neill's iceman, death for drinkers; but they looked upwards spellbound, not at the heavens, but at the television screen, chases, shooting, suffering and dying flashed across it, interrupted occasionally by the extolling of pleasures manufactured for our short lives.[24]

A stream of bus travelers flooded through the hotel in their colorful traveling outfits, never diminishing, even after midnight, stretched out in chairs, telling each other jokes, making calls to Nebraska, letting themselves be carried up and down by patient elevators. On the sixteenth floor, behind all the fire doors, cries of excitement and laughter. The television shadows were tireless company. Lights glittered expansively in front of the window, as if the Milky Way had sunk down to the earth. The city did its despairing battle against loneliness. A Bible lay on the night table. I opened it and marveled at the bell tower that is the English language: "*And there appeared another wonder in heaven; and behold a great red dragon, having seven hands and ten horns, and seven crowns upon his heads.*"

The morning came sweetly. Fog blurred the bold contours, and the roofs of the skyscrapers now seemed to have reached the sky. So many companies were

---

22. Koeppen is likely referring to Black Angus cattle here.
23. The roc was a giant mythical bird that figures in *A Thousand and One Nights.*
24. The 1939 play "The Iceman Cometh," by Eugene O'Neill (1888–1953) features many alcoholic characters.

suspended in the clouds. A polite man appeared on the television screen and taught me about the weather. The man announced that there would be sun. The doctor from Puerto Rico was shown in handcuffs, his victim lay beneath a white sheet. The doctor's facial expression had changed, he no longer looked at a loss. Now he was playing a role, he had become a star.

In the corner drugstore an athletic Negro beat an egg on hot tin. The egg was sweating like a company of soldiers on the parade ground. The Negro was a god. He moved with elasticity like a shadow boxer.

I sat on a high rotating stool among American citizens. Maple syrup, smelling of the forest, flowed yellow onto buckwheat pancakes. Ice-cold juices, glowing hot drinks, burned toast. The citizens were on their way to work or they were coming from night jobs, intelligent faces read the *Times,* young people called out the results of games, friendliness predominated, breakfast equality, world-city tolerance. The girls were beautifully decorated; they were not arrogant, as was their reputation, they smiled like comrades. The white owner of the drugstore stroked the bristly barbered hair of a Negro boy.

Buses rolled by cheerfully, taxis swarmed happily. The army of clerks, secretaries and sales girls fanned out. Behind the windowpanes of Fifth Avenue lay the wealth of the world, not yet looked at. Pigeons had conversations on the ledges.

The Empire State Building, one knows, is the tallest building in this giant city, and it held its own, having surpassed the seven wonders of the world, having surpassed the pyramids, the temple of Diana in Ephesus, the powerful Zeus of Olympus. Who was adored here?

They pressed into elevators and took a trip to the heavens. The hair salon in the basement was set up like one of the better surgical clinics. For a shave one was put to bed, as if for an operation. The body was covered with sterile towels. The hairdressers wore professors' glasses and came with unclothed arms. Manicure girls, red-headed nurses, ready to anesthetize, took hold of the patient's hands. Black hair waved over the shoes. Steaming compresses burnt youth into the cheeks. The *mister* could show himself. He could travel up to the bosses. He could hunt the dollar.

Directory tables glittered. Confusing text. Who counts the branches, knows the tricks? In-house police controlled the traffic in front of the elevators. It was like a big train station. School classes, visitors from the country awaited the start of the viewing season. The express elevator shot upwards, shocking the stomach. Exit onto the ninetieth floor. Twelve more floors to the viewing platform. The Cologne cathedral was happily overflown, the cathedrals sank in prestige. One was suspended in the clouds. One thought that they could be grabbed hold of.

Manhattan lay beneath a white haze like a ship that isn't very big, one stood atop its highest mast. Was this Babylon? Then the sight of Babylon is too powerful for men. Enormity shrank. This ship here could go down. The eye sought out spots of green. They were here and there like small prayer blankets. Parks, so observed, are strangely light and gentle. The ocean liners are toys. The four-engine airplanes are toys. From this altitude street traffic was an interconnected stream and resembled a man's pulsing bloodstream in a display about hygiene.

But the real living man did not miss the chance to send greetings to the world, by postcard, from such an elevated standpoint. A post office with its own stamps documented this life from above. This was the way to suppress, while thinking of aunt, uncle, wife, lover, colleagues at the office, what each had felt, the deep eeriness of this high place, the idea of having witnessed transience in enormity.

Madison Square, Washington Park, the green meadows.

Madison Square was an artificially planted desert, poverty on the benches, exhausted sleepers, sad unemployed and those who had said no to work, joyously free, and all around streets of cheap shops. The market was gaudy, colorful, attention grabbing, clearance sales every day, liquidations in the evening, new beginnings in the morning, junk for the immigrants, a web cut into thousands of pieces, sewn with a hot needle for those from all over the world who needed something to wear.

Whichever language you speak, and even if you speak no language, the dollar finds a place for you, makes you equal. I heard the word dollar everywhere, in rich and poor areas, it was always talked of with devotion. You're a consumer and will be courted. You're a consumer with your first cry or with the first time you set your foot on the new earth. Whatever the color of your skin, whatever your religious denomination. You forget your fatherland, you soon learn your mother tongue. You want to be an American. Your children are American, proud children, who hold you in contempt, since you come from Rostock, from Lodz, from Messina, Nagasaki, from far away. You will never have the naturalness of those born here, of the customer king. The equal race of buyers wandered around and strayed, it was demanding and controlling, ready to be treated with courtesy, ready to be betrayed. Who knelt down before whom? In a shoe store the white American does before all the feet that come in here.

America rejuvenates, America gives you a new face every day. The paradise of uniform prices, the great *Woolworth's*, with a beauty bar for every woman.[25] The white misses, the black *lady*, the yellow sister, they sat with each other

---

25. Woolworth's, a retail chain founded in 1878, was broken into smaller parts in 1997.

peacefully in front of flattering mirrors, obediently trying the powders, the pencils, the ink of this flowering industry, and a lotion either darkened or lightened the hair, and a paste made curly hair straight, made it into a Jolly Josephine, uniting the Creole Antilles, the Bonaparte Palace and the new Capitoline equalities.[26]

Washington Square, Greenwich Village, the Washington arch, like the Arc de Triomphe in Paris, but bourgeois, humble, on the edge of the square, not in its middle, old beautiful trees, shadows, a fountain, a bohemian neighborhood, a sight to see, the guide book assures us. Here too there are sleepers on the benches in the morning, men in sweaters, men with melancholy moustaches, men of all skin colors, zealous readers, somber students, America is a nation of literate people. There is a playground with Wonderland equipment, not yet in use, tables for chess under a canopy of trees, not being used at this hour, girls in tight pants walk extremely distinguished dogs, old manor houses all around, facades like good grandmother's faces, perfect washing machines for bachelors nearby, run-down rooming houses, dream palaces of the golden youth; no longer the straight streets with consecutive numbers, crooked little streets, a perfume of Paris, an imitation of Rome, a breath of poetry.

A schoolyard enclosed by a high steel fence; dusty floors, white and black children, starched slips, ballet outfits from colorful wool, ball games against the red fire-wall.

Toward the Washington Market the neighborhood was Naples. A market for flowers, for vegetables, for fruit, for imports, symphonies of colors, smells, sounds, all before a curtain of decay, before houses from the nineteenth century, disintegrating in their unique and dirty way into wetness and dust.

I hailed a taxi, I wanted to go to the fish market on the East Side, I crossed the old tip of Manhattan, turned towards the sea and to the island's origin. European street names burdened with tradition. Nassau Street, Frankfort Street, St. James Street. The taxi driver was a white-haired man from Miropole in Galicia.[27] He looked like a wonder-working rabbi, as a child he had studied the Talmud in synagogue, he had traveled overseas, and now he was driving me to the fish market. He felt my clothing, testing the material, inquiring about the production and the price.

---

26. Jolly Josephine was a popular hairstyle in Germany in 1959, meant to be reminiscent of hairstyles in the Napoleonic era; Napoleon's wife, Josephine de Beauharnais (1763–1814), was from Martinique, in the Antilles; the Bonaparte Palace is a villa built in Rome, in 1660, which served as a residence for Napoleon's mother. The Capitoline equalities could be a reference to the mixing of classes and races described in this sentence.

27. Galicia is a region of Eastern Europe, between Poland and Ukraine; it was home to a large Jewish community before World War II; Mirapole is now a city in Ukraine.

We drove down the Bowery, two grey house fronts looked like they had been painted by Buffet.[28] The Bowery was once New York's street for wealth, it was the first millionaires' place for parties and for depravity, now, whoever was dying from America staggered down an avenue of miserable bars.

Then there was the Jewish area; they had brought their cross with them, the Hasidim's sick dreams, the dybuk was there, visible to all, the golem had immigrated.

Containers, warehouses on the river, the big loading docks, the companies of the old Puritans. Brooklyn Bridge hung over the busily active water like a God-given memorial to efficiency. Men carrying sacks, carts with sacks, *trucks* with many axels, the white cold-storage units from Alaska to the Sargasso Sea, from the Caribbean to the *Waldorf Astoria Hotel,* to the housewife's table, the *Fulton Fish* Market, internment camps in black sheds, cemeteries of the sea world, dredges poured them into giant containers, millions of shining, tightly-packed eyes, looking for the moment here at their hell, captive immigrants.

Before Battery Park, bright with green, paths for recreation in the cloudy air, a patch of grass with canons English kings had left behind, the Hudson and East Rivers embraced one another, the bay was there sparkling, the ocean broadened out, puffs of smoke from ships appeared and disappeared, one's mind wandered back to the old countries, the view to Europe.

They had landed here, they had arrived here, all peoples, the Protestants of all denominations, the honest democrats, the anarchists, the assassins of kings and the princes fleeing capture, the rebels, the adventurers, the lost sons, the souls without a fatherland.[29] Hats off to them! They built the city, they were the New World.

Seen up close, at the feet of the first skyscrapers, the skyline rises up before the onlooker like a defensive wall. The view is very unfriendly; the city seems impossible to conquer. The tall buildings are built more out of granite than steel. That's how the solidity of speculation and of the founding period had been proven.

This was the district of the Astors, the Vanderbilts, the Rockefellers, and look, here one stands before John Pierpont Morgan's bank. In such moments, the world reveals itself to be an eternal fairy tale, and letters for Rübezahl are addressed to the *City Bank Trust.*[30] Everywhere on lower Broadway one encounters figures familiar from childhood, the devil, of course the devil too,

28. Bernard Buffet (1929–1999) was a French expressionist painter.
29. The "lost sons" here could well be a reference to Kafka's *Amerika* and to Karl Rossman, whose family sends him to America after he impregnates a servant; the novel has another title in German, *Der Verschollene,* the Lost One.
30. Rübezahl, fairy-tale spirit of the Sudeten mountains, controls secret treasures.

but next to the devil, comfortingly, lucky Hans, the Seven Dwarves, those who went out to learn about fear, and I saw Catherine, who wanted to invest her savings.[31]

The streets were deep valleys in the shadows of power. The noise sounded like it came from a pure-gold bell. The solid, magnificent, massively built headquarters of the great shipping lines recalled the old noblemen's palaces; their time had past. Here time was racing. What would otherwise take thousands of years had been packed into a hundred years. The airline companies had their wind-blown aerodynamic neon stars streaming in the middle of Fifth Avenue, while Cunard put steamships on display in lower Manhattan, in an honorable but somewhat gloomy hall. The show had a deathly effect, life had passed it by, it looked like a cemetery of ships, though no one spoke of capsized ships or praised the "Titanic." Above the old queens of the sea hung photographs of their captains, the great *commander*, golden bars on his sleeve, weather-beaten rocks accustomed to storms but hollowed out, washed up.

A lift lowered me down to the cellar and to a bar for men who make their living at sea. Near secure walls of a vault, the tools of the trade over one's head, one drank as cozily as if one were in a sunken cabin. There was every kind of rum, every brand of whisky for the pirates who had kept the judges busy, the red wine noses of stockbrokers and the super cargos twinkled, the sailors' agents were at rest, no writer had been shanghaied here, but I still saw Melville at the bar signing his contract with the whale hunters. Cod liver oil was on offer in the trade journals: guaranteed to be without taste.

Wall Street begins with a church and a cemetery, with a prayer and with graves.

In the cemetery I stood among skyscrapers as if at the bottom of a deep box.

The gravestones commemorated the men who had created the American nation. Did they have any idea that the stones around here would grow to the heavens? They were printers, typesetters, editors, school teachers, literate people chased here from somewhere, kicked out, they became unauthorized generals, and they were all rebels, obsessed with ideas, utopian founders of states. "*Born in Old England, he came over to America 1692 ...*" in weathered script. How far the ocean was at that time! Two months driven before the wind, and there was only the future!

In the Trinity Church there was an epitaph for Robert Fulton, who invented the submarine and was the first to steer a steamship across the Hudson. Did he know where the trip was going?

---

31. Hans im Glück, lucky Hans, and Katerlieschen, Catherine, are characters from fairy tales gathered by the brothers Jacob Grimm (1785–1863) and Wilhelm Grimm (1786–1859).

Old men sat on the benches by the church wall, they looked like they had lost their money on the stock market at some gray time and were still waiting for their long-devalued stocks to rise; they blinked like blind men in the thin sunlight mistakenly shining into the cemetery's dark interstices.

I looked past the stock market to the river below it. Voices murmured: the throne of money. Voices whispered: here the wheel is turned, here the world is ruled, here the decision is made about war and peace, life and death, here the road begins, the path to wealth or to misery. I thought about the armaments boom. I thought about the lessons of the crisis. I thought about the leap from the twentieth story. But external appearances were hardly demonic. If the walls did not loom so high, Wall Street could also be in the Hamburg downtown. I saw a building in neoclassical style, with columns, in which America's history glorified itself, the entirely alive time when America became a state, honored everywhere. It was the old treasury, and before it stood a monument to Washington, by his feet lay fresh flowers. A man spoke to me. He looked like the often described Midwesterner, a Yankee, half farmer, half priest, and he was from the Midwest, even though I took him for a con man, while he enthused with such naïve and stirring admiration about Washington, this great man. And he, who came from the Midwest, had no farm, no church but some kind of a business in some *Main Street,* and now he had traveled to New York to see the castles of money. Pointing to the man of stone, he said that Washington was a contemporary of Frederick the Great: Washington is the man of freedom, if we are free, we have him to thank.

A policeman stopped traffic and let a Negro school class cross the street. The young Negroes were making the pilgrimage to the *New York Stock Exchange,* the biggest in the world, which determined all other prices, and I followed them.

In the dollar's dance house we were welcomed by blonde, narrow-hipped girls in red suits. The fabric color recalled Hussar regiments from the color-happy past, while the young women's hair coloring, their lacquered mouths and their eyes shadowed with blue or green allowed one to hope they were like contemporary call girls.[32] The girls, however, were the chaste Vestal Virgins of high finance, pretty sirens, singing money's song of songs, and adroit seductresses of youth. It was swarming with children, not only the little Negroes, all of them brought here for instruction, and among them one could observe older people from the provinces, who probably wanted to see what they, in their hard-working lives, had missed.

---

32. Hussars were light-cavalry.

In the great room, beneath the proud stars and stripes, the brokers cried out and taunted each other. White numbers jumped on blackboards, hopped, fluttered, transformed themselves, and the teleprinter ticked, moved by a ghostly hand, like the seismograph of a weather station. The red Vestals led us assuredly across the gallery, led us to a theater, where we were shown marionettes, shown how smart and how fun it is to save money, to carry it in a sack to good uncle stock market, and how, through shouting, boards of numbers and teleprinter ticks, one can become a little Vanderbilt.

The red sirens were tempting even in the movie room. This time a class of schoolgirls accompanied them and me into the darkened room. Giggling, a flurry of frills, sweet chewing-gum aroma, the first scents of *make up*, floated around me, while, on the flickering screen, I looked at the chance to be a millionaire or a president, which had sadly by-passed me, my father, my grandfather and forefathers. The little girls were shown the last remaining paradise. This paradise was called the *Stock Exchange*. Of course no Black Friday came into the picture. No one fell from the high window faster than the index itself fell. The little girls had become very still, sitting reverently as if they were in church. A clever little girl, twelve perhaps, looked at me, as if brooding on whether I was already a millionaire. After a quick inspection she seemed to give up on me; perhaps she also remembered having read that millionaires don't go to the movies. I took my revenge by bestowing upon her a rich dumb husband in my thoughts.

At the end, the red guides led us to telephones, which, when the one put the receivers to one's ear, painted a rosy future and promised a shining world of perpetual prosperity.

Outside, before the stock exchange, disappointed-looking pamphlet sellers, screaming with all their strength: *another depression.*

It had reached midday. I moved with the clerks and the stenographers to a big feeding station, where one sat at crowded round counters, like little arenas, at the middle of which was a Negro woman, adorned with a pointed cap, giving out thousands of pale sandwiches, pouring milk and juices and hot coffee from test tube flasks, which revealed the meal to be something like a chemical necessity, limited to the metabolism and the preservation of strength, unrelated to the pleasures of the palate and the joys of the gourmand. There were not enough chairs for the hungry. The clerks and stenographers stood around, in order to tank up. Those who finished their pale sandwiches and drank their juice, their milk, their coffee courteously abandoned their place. The gears of the mass society functioned smoothly.

Then they promenaded for a while beneath the facades of money, sat at Washington's feet or in the little cemetery of St. Paul's Chapel, the district's other historic church, perhaps on the grave of Sieur de Rochefontaine, born in 1755 in Champagne, died 1814 in New York, officer of the French Army, of the Dominican army and of the U.S. armed forces after the King's death. Hawthorne bloomed on the gravestone of this artful, this transformed knight. The sun did not come over the roofs, but the air was humid. The clerks and stenographers hurried back to the artificial climate of their offices and unsettled the world.

I went up Broadway. Long rows of banks, global firms head to head. Poor people, who wanted to become Americans, pressed themselves through City Hall's columned portal. Their English contained many different accents, and a policeman, who had already become an American, patiently showed them up the steps to their happiness.

I wanted to see Harlem, the Negro city, the festering wound of New York, as many call it in anger, the dark ghetto, populated by the descendants of slaves, the children of the commodity that was valued as highly as black ivory, flooding New York African every morning, offspring of those forced to come, driven early to the coasts, aristocrats of the New World, American as the Mayflower pilgrims.

I went to Central Park South. The park is not Harlem. It lies some seventy streets away from Harlem and is, with some exceptions, an excellent area, an expensive address for corporate lawyers and medical experts, and U.N. delegates looked out of the windows of the distinguished residential hotels, decorated with shiny Swedish furniture and worm-eaten Madonnas, apartments that cost fifty dollars a day, horrified at the terrible American storm over the dust-covered trees, and here the Negroes are only doormen and shoe shiners and dish washers, bringing ice for the bars' zinc tubs, though legend makes them out to be the terror of the night and demons of the primeval forest even in the day's shadows, and I went to the park, a grove amid skyscrapers, leprous, cultivated green on evil rocks sparingly covered with earth. Agate pond basins, concrete playgrounds, and I sat myself down on a bench, and others sat on other benches, couples, children and teachers, the tired elderly, and two powerful drunks stumbled by, staggering with their seven-mile steps, violent, deeply black figures, porters, cotton pickers, men who boxed in booths, killers in the movies, brandishing empty bottles, the others slipped away from the benches as if a storm were coming, the skyscrapers stood like distant ghostly palaces, like castles with elevated drawbridges, and the park was a wild free state, a jungle, a mango grove, and the black drunks sat down by me, to my left and right, and they mumbled something about a quarter of a dollar for a drink, and I felt as they did, felt that those who cleaned other people's shoes, carried things, washed dishes, took out trash were allowed to, that they should get drunk, and I gave them a dollar, and we laughed and shook hands, and their faces were like two black suns, and afterwards I was told that it was very foolish of me to have stayed seated on the bench and to have given them a dollar.

At Columbus Circle, where one split the city open, as if obligated to excavate Troy in front of New York's Coliseum, the proud exhibition hall that looked like an ordinary badly built garage, I got into a bus and went along the park to Duke Ellington's *Negro Heaven*.[33] We passed streets of bygone, evaporated wealth, getting a feel for the homes of a strange class, rooms that were too big and too festive, with cracks already and crumbling plaster. Outsider communities, Mediterranean peoples, mestizo races, the bus was a melting pot. But the white element increasingly melted away, drop by drop at the bus stops, then the Southern, the equatorial and the Latin American colors melted away, and I sat among Negroes.

It was like an about-turn, a desertion to the enemy, a jump into another continent. Black passengers, black children, black poor, black rich, black cart pushers, black owners of luxury cars, out of all windows black faces, colleagues, brothers, people like you and me, shops, businesses and display windows as there are everywhere, a black community, not an unusual area and yet a foreign place, Africa above the subway and yet not Africa, America, New York of course, Africa was gray pre-history, Africa was the long-forgotten ancestors, Harlem belonged to Manhattan, belonged to the United States, belonged to today, and perhaps the future belonged to it. Black skin of all shades, mixtures in the millions, consequence and conclusion of the slaves' bondage. And then the unbridled black pride!

The last station was far away at the end of *Lenox Avenue*. The area had a strangely bare aura. Perhaps the open spaces were construction sites. Perhaps they were a damned, eternal wasteland. Another wind blew here. Sand blew as if from the desert. Suburban houses, slum barracks, almost villas, intimidating columns, a civic sense keen on cleanliness, naked depravity and borderless indifference touched each other, rubbed up against each other. The modesty of those badly born, the efforts of the odd-job men and the submission to fate of the aged lived next to the rage, co-habited patiently with a fury gathering to the bursting point. The youth strolled in bands. A young tiger trot. Beauty, strength, gracefulness, rags, fools' hats, the loudest colors. *Blue jeans* girls stood before a bar, narrow-hipped, curly-headed, deer-eyed, bold like the ephebes

---

33. Koeppen may have the 1926 novel *Nigger Heaven* by Carl Van Vechten (1880–1964) in mind here.

of classical antiquity.[34] A black policeman, built like a bull, surveyed the landscape. He had the impenetrable face of the Sphinx. Whom did he serve, whom was he protecting?

In front of a church were long rows of automobiles, shining in the sun, big chrome-plated family ships. The church's brick and gothic exterior resembled Kaiser Wilhelm II's Garnisonkirche.[35] Well-dressed Negroes streamed into it.

I paused at the entrance, I didn't want to stand out, but the black church leaders came up to me, dignified, friendly men, black bankers, black doctors from all branches of medicine, they greeted me as if I were the prodigal son who had come home, they shook my hand with friendliness, I the foreigner who had shown up by accident, and they invited me in warmly, invited me to take a seat in the front pew. A woman, who smelled of very expensive perfume, extended a hymnal to me with a mild smile. An older woman sat at a harmonium. She wore a flowerbed hat, looking strict in her rimless glasses. The woman was a typical older American citizen, very enthusiastic, full of good will, very friendly and very, very moral. America had shaped her, only she was the black side of the coin.

Then we all stood up and praised God, the choir was very melodious, very heartfelt. And angels came into the church, black children, in starched shirts white as snow, their skin and hair like ebony, their painted mouths like blood, and they sang a heartfelt song, and a preacher appeared, white-haired with a medieval face, as if painted by Lucas Cranach, and he spoke and thundered like a real prophet, and an angel came to me and pressed a bag for donations into my hand, which looked exactly like the pay slips of a well-organized business, and I was called upon to give what I wished to spend for the Sunday school, for missionary work, for the weekly prayer devoted to sick neighbors.[36]

Towards the end of the service one of the dignified church leaders came and asked me to join the community, and I was embarrassed by my answer, I'm not from New York, I live in Europe, and I saw that he didn't believe me, that I had disappointed him, and he looked at me sadly, bowing finally, and said that my visit had been a great honor for all of them, which again made me feel very ashamed.

On 125th Street, Harlem's main street, display window after display window enticed, and one shopped here as in Düsseldorf or in Frankfurt or on Fifth Avenue, but on this dark boulevard the goods were somewhat shabbier and the prices somewhat higher than on the lighter colored streets. As always the

---

34. *Epheben,* or ephebes, Greek for young men, are associated with ancient Greek sculpture.

35. Kaiser Wilhelm II's *Garisonkirche,* the *Kirche am Südstern* in Berlin, was completed in 1897 and built by Kaiser Wilhelm II (1859–1941).

36. Here Koeppen is referring either to Lucas Cranach the Elder (1472–1553) or to Lucas Cranach the Younger (1515–1586); both were German painters.

weaker were cheated. Black salespeople, black customers but white shop owners and white mannequins. The white mannequins looked sick and anemic
in this colorful world. Why weren't there black mannequins in the display
windows? Was it easier to sell a black girl a bridal gown displayed on a white
body? I roamed through the shops. When one grew accustomed to the fact
that everything here was happening among blacks, the stores became unin-
teresting. Palmolive is still Palmolive. We live in one world. In the Western
world. In the East there were other brands.

The black faces. Dream faces. Daily life faces. Similarities. Memories. My
grandmother met me as a Negro. A dead friend walked by. My old teacher
waited on the corner. I believe that Egon Erwin Kisch had once observed
something like this.[37] They didn't pay attention to me. They looked past me.

Out of the Teresa Hotel skyscraper, run by Negroes and where only Negroes
stayed, a woman emerged, as if exiting from some grand hotel, and started to
walk her white poodle. The woman's hair was colored bright red, and it sat like
a shock of flaming wig on her dark pretty head.

In a cinema the sinking of the battleship "Graf Spee" was playing.[38] The
German flag of war sank before a thousand black faces.

In another theater life in a white nudist colony was being shown. Pale English bookkeepers cavorted nude with their pale naked secretaries in a sparse
vacation landscape, and the Negroes, dark in a dark room, watched them si-
lently and with wide-open eyes.

In a bookstore, however, a new consciousness, hostile to New York, was being propagated. In the shelves there were works on African folklore, I found
Frobenius' ethnologies, and pictures of Negus and the president of Ghana
found favor with the bookshop and its customers.[39]

Emperor Barbarossa, beard grown through the table, old Teutons on bear
skin, the mead horn swinging, the trumpeters of Säckingen, an undulating
Lorelei and no compliments for Heine, Bismarck in a breastplate and Bismarck with the slouch hat, almost a devotee of the St. Paul's church, though

---

37. Egon Erwin Kisch (1885–1948) was a Czech-German-Jewish writer. He published a
book about his trip to America, *Paradies Amerika, American Paradise*, in 1930.

38. The *Admiral Graf Spee* was a German warship launched in 1934 and sunk, by its captain,
after being damaged in 1939. Its sinking was dramatized in a 1956 film, *Pursuit of the Graf Spee*,
which is likely what the audience described here was watching.

39. Leo Frobenius (1873–1938), was a German ethnographer who wrote extensively about
Africa, influencing later celebrants of African culture and of *négritude;* "negus" is a word for king
in several African languages and was used for the rulers of Ethiopia before 1974 and Eritrea
before 1890, in context referring to Haile Selassie (1892–1975), Ethiopia's emperor from 1930
to 1974; the president of Ghana at the time of Koeppen's visit to America was Kwame Nkrumah
(1909–1972), the first president of Ghana and a leading figure in African politics.

the liberals who had fled across the Atlantic in 1848 did not belong here.[40] Hindenberg in his field uniform, stiff-backed, and Hindenberg in a top hat, bending his neck, the soccer stars from Kaiserslautern, Dortmund and Hamburg, and Tyrolian roses in small cinemas patronized by regulars, the song of nostalgia and the ever-blooming lilac of truly false feelings—all to be had on this street. Sausage from Göttingen, cottage smoke from Holstein, the small packed stores of my youth, still in the imperial style, a royal town, and the restaurants were called "The Heidelberg Keg" and "Grinzing" and "In a Cool Hollow."[41] Beneath commemorative song wreaths, marksmen's targets and gymnasts' flags one could eat an old-German Sauerbraten and Thuringian-style dumplings on Kaiser-Wilhelm-style tables. I was in the German quarter, in New York's 86th Street, a strange world with medium-high houses out of late nineteenth-century Stettin or Chemnitz, there among enemies, stuck between Italian, Spanish, Czechoslovak and Puerto Rican settlements, embittered, ill-tempered and not finished with America, it seemed. Even after years of residence overseas they communicated with each other in a language concocted from never-learned English and already forgotten German. The travel agency advertised package tours for the Neckar and for Rüdesheim. German airlines, German ships made their invitations, one wasn't entirely poor, one wasn't rich in dollars, though measured in Deutschmarks one was making good money, for three weeks one could play the uncle from America in the old homeland.[42] One longed for crown glass window panes. Did one want to stay in the towers of Rothenburg? This was possible. But did one want to go back to Düsseldorf? One was saving for a grave in Queens, but one cherished a dream of Germany, precisely the dream from which one had fled, one retained German closeness, German provincialism, the heavy national surliness. In the "Kühlen Grund" they charged me twenty-five cents to hang my coat on a hook; this was done for free in an American hotel, but German order had its honor and its price; the girl in the coatroom was from Saxony and my amusement at her request for money annoyed her. In this melting pot of peoples, in the happy free world city of New York this was an extreme, not of German peculiarity,

---

40. Barbarossa, Frederick I (1112–1190) was Holy Roman Emperor and darling of twentieth-century German nationalists; "The Trumpeter of Säckingen" was a popular Romantic poem of 1853 by the German writer Joseph Victor von Scheffel (1826–1886); Heinrich Heine (1797–1856) was a German writer and poet, author of the 1838 poem "The Lorelei," and he merits no compliments, in context, because he was Jewish; the St. Paul's Church in Frankfurt was important to the 1848 Revolution in Germany and, in context, a symbol of German liberalism, as opposed to Bismarck's authoritarianism.

41. Paul von Hindenberg (1847–1934), World War I general and president of the Weimar Republic when Hitler first became chancellor in 1933. "In a Cool Hollow," *In einem kühlen Grunde*, is the name of a poem by Joseph von Eichendorff (1788–1857), also sung as a folk song.

42 The "uncle from America" is a figure of proverbial wealth and generosity.

but of German cutting-itself-off from the world and of provincial weirdness. Dusty knights' tankards, hair kept in pigtails. The girls had Dreimäderlhaus haircuts, they were young and they were from yesterday, they were New Yorkers and they were home baked.[43] They were sought after. The U.S. Navy sat in the "German Oak" drinking German beer, a Bavarian folk chorus played the "Fisherwoman from the Lake of Constanz," circle dances, good rhythm, kisses on the cellar steps, the moon over the East River, the marks of small sweaty hands on white sailor suits.[44] With the Navy the honest German girls kept up their reputation of being cheap. In the "Heidelberg Keg" club members strutted to a long table. A sports club had flown in and was being celebrated. The faces of fools. German literature, German art, our present, our life, German spiritual labors, even the German cultural attaché in Washington did not exist for the inhabitants of this German street in New York. Germany was a German Heimatfilm, it was a German kitsch museum, a German book of drinking songs and a German soccer ball.[45] I already believed in Mr. Herberger as Germany's president, near the picture of Hindenberg on the wall, looking down on the Thuringian dumplings, on the orderly row of coats and on the kind cheap girls.[46] Eighty-sixth Street was a German nightmare.

I praised Manhattan's beautiful variety. I stepped out of Teutonia and down to the subway. I lost my free will after passing through the turnstiles. I had become part of a dough that flowed sluggishly but inexorably through the shaft. The dough pressed into an express train. We stood and sweated beneath whirring ventilators and, like rockets, we were pushed through dark canals. In a jolting, jerking, screeching second we reached Grand Central Station, the center of the city and another world.

It was Saturday evening, an underground witches' Sabbath raged in the belly of the train station. Migrations, as if on the river Styx, transpiring in neon light, streams that crossed and battled one another. Every nation, every language was represented. Tibetan monks, Confucian Chinese, Indian saints, Russian castrati, cell-gray nuns, bishops of self-made churches, fire worshippers, the grandchildren of cannibals and all those crippled by life extended a pleading hand for themselves or for their communities. Game rooms, tin vending machines, greedy evil robots swallowed the weekly salary of healthy limbs.

---

43. *Das Dreimäderlhaus,* The House of the Three Girls, is a musical first performed in Vienna in 1916; in 1958 it was made into a Swiss-Austrian movie.

44. *Die Fischerin von Bodensee,* The Fisherwoman from the Lake of Constanz, was a sentimental German film from 1956.

45. *Heimatfilm* is a sentimental genre glorifying the homeland; the *Heimat,* the home region, could be a particular region within Germany.

46. Sepp Heberger (1897–1977) was the head coach of the German soccer team from 1936 to 1942 and from 1950 to 1964, a figure who was both authoritarian and popular.

Young gangs from Harlem were moved forward, their scouts could meet with their Puerto Rican brothers in the many-storied train station, they fought, they were voyaging with the Argonauts, with Odysseus, they made their feints in the front lines. Together they observed, with big eyes, the mechanized and gargantuan feeding stations, the mass drinking troughs of glittering metal, citrus forests, porridge oceans, liquor ponds, cereal fields, herds of cows were devoured here. Gutenberg's paradise was glowing, the world's printing presses supplying the market, printed products in all idioms, the Sunday edition of the *New York Times,* which weighs several kilos, a wonder work of journalism, lying by the wall and heaped into towers, demolished by the industrious hands of readers and piled high again by sweating sellers, a truly Sisyphean job. I imagined I was seeing a castle of black-white magic with phantasms of colorful freedom and the traps of secret seduction.

Advertisements blossomed on *Times Square,* people formed a crowd, tender was the night, in the words of one of the country's poets, who died from his wealth.[47] Neon letters carried the world's fear, stupidity and misery around the newspaper's headquarters. The good financial news bloomed red. It was the witching hour. All the businesses were making their invitations, their open doors wanted to embrace the crowd. Goods were extolled with angels' tongues, they were sold with the enticing appearance of bargains or sold off in quickly called-out auctions. Salespeople shouted their word in the street like fishermen throwing nets into water rich in booty. In alleyways pictures of half-naked girls waited, and they were sought after, as if there weren't girls enough in the streets. People from the provinces pushed themselves here, people from the suburbs, people from crowded apartments, escaping work's controlling clock for the weekend, and among the people were soldiers, sailors, pilots, soon the masters, soon the destroyers of the world, soon they will be at home on the moon. Light games, alcoholic drinks, choirs. One was compelled toward all sources of pleasure or toward quick anesthetization. A ghost, a woman in a kind of harem dress, was surrounded by yelling boys, she rolled her eyes, showing off her substantial breasts and backside with hysterical degeneracy, and her black hair was set strangely high and it shone like a tower of lice rubbed with fat.

What a picture! What activity! What size, what an aberration, what a novel! I sat down exhausted on a stool that belonged to a Negro, I sat at the edge of the street, sat near the stream of people and waited in the shining, the tender, the roiling night of the New World, and the Negro knelt down and

---

47. Koeppen is referring here to F. Scott Fitzgerald (1896–1940) and his 1934 novel *Tender Is the Night,* the title of which was taken from a poem by Keats; it might be more accurate to say that Fitzgerald died from his eventual poverty.

cleaned my shoes, rubbing with his friendly hands, and he said, Germany, only Germany has the most beautiful women. I was flattered but I advised him to look around, on *Times Square* where he was kneeling down, up and down on Broadway, below ground in Grand Central Station, up in his Harlem, everywhere I had seen beautiful girls, but the Negro got worked up, overcome with memory, his eyes shone, his voice trembled, he said Munich, he said Hofbräuhaus, and with a swing of his brush he made a very clear, very indecent and at the same time very enthusiastic gesture.[48]

On Sunday morning the cozy drugstore on the corner was closed, the city's inhabitants were sleeping in the suburbs or already cutting their grass, and even Midtown Manhattan shared the holiday desolation of shopping streets in all big cities, the streets and squares were bereft of people, only a few dogs were sniffing around and people who weren't doing well in New York, who looked very gray, as if turned to dust, searching in the open wastepaper baskets for food or for fallen money, they were shadowy figures, and one could imagine the gigantic metropole without any people and inhabited only by ghosts.

Pennsylvania Station, the big spacious train station that belonged to one of the country's private train companies, was also sad at this hour. With its mighty empty halls, the station evoked a castle from a vanished kingdom. The shiny metal of a new wonder auto, displayed on a revolving stage, seeming to triumph over all aspects of train travel, caught the few rays of sun coming through the windows. Benches for waiting with high, wall-like backs, solid wooden chairs as in church. Old people sat there, and they too were still and solemn as in a church. Cleanly brushed decency. A Negro family passed by, the woman wearing the flower hat, he wore the churchgoer's Sunday clothes, the children were lit up with white collars and bows; one couldn't tell whether they were here to wait for a train or simply to enjoy the Sabbath.

A group of older women sat on their suitcases before the tightly bolted gates, unfree in the European manner and leading to underground platforms. They were dressed in uniforms of sky blue with military caps on hair powdered purple or silver gray. They resembled a club of former airline stewardesses but they were a very powerful, very influential group, the Daughters of the American Revolution, guardians of morals. Their faces were masterpieces of the cosmetic arts, their mien strict and good-natured at the same time, many had the Puritan mouth of John Foster Dulles, hardened by negotiations, many had probably sent their husbands to an early grave, after joyless lives hunting the dollar, washing dishes, cutting the grass, now they were doing good with pious hearts, occupying themselves with public concerns. They were enthusiasts in

48. Koeppen's novel *Tauben im Gras* was set in Munich; it featured an African-American soldiers' club near the Munich Hofbräuhaus.

their own way, caring for the arts and for public welfare, as they understood these things, administrating and watching over the women's rights that had been earned and fought for, that had come down to them, after menopause they had the status of senators, it struck me as uncanny and admirable, they were a good match for the native, bitter-to-digest whiskey, which I began to look for immediately, but the bars and alcohol stores were closed on Sundays as these women had decreed.[49] The door of the bar was bolted, and the bottle ghosts were asleep.

The train to Washington reminded me of cans in a row, its wagons looked like tin plate scrubbed clean by strenuous housewives' labor, using strong scouring sand, and indeed one was packaged and bottled and stuffed into a kind of vacuum, the doors were sealed with pressurized air, no window could be opened, though over a long distance the artificially created, carefully considered climate kept the passenger fresh.

A black servant in a white waiter's jacket took my luggage. I stepped over carpets. In the parlor car, elegantly made chairs, real soothing dentists' chairs awaited the passenger. The chairs could be pneumatically adjusted, raised, sunk, altered in many ways, the body could relax as it wished, feet could be stretched up, the head lowered down, the chair was a secure castle, but it was also an operating table, the body was straightened out for a serious intervention, and the first time one traveled through America one underwent an operation—the country sucked one dry.

What did this land offer its colonizers? Green pastures, green hills, green, wooded, wild forests, streams, widely welcoming to ship travel and discovery, a friendly picture promising nourishment and homeland, and yet the land possessed a vast terrible eeriness, a continent full of hidden danger. Europe also had its pastures, its streams and forests. But here these had never been mastered, they grew, ran wild, they enclosed themselves, they were voracious without end, they had never fully fallen under the citizen's hand, they still threatened to consume people. Even the highways, the secure fast streets, seemed like mere forest paths, and if those living here didn't watch out, the wilderness would reclaim them.

Outside the great cities human settlements clustered around this route, leprosy sprinkled in great nature's painting. One-story houses, surrounded by verandas, were placed on mowed plots of lawn as on green carpets, right by the wide pastures, by the dark, impenetrable forest, this was the house the American loved, thin-walled, always provisional, beneath a television antenna, where he seemed to believe that he and nature were friends, cradled in his rocking chair on the sunny terrace, but his house is a dismal tableau of loneliness and

---

49. John Foster Dulles (1888–1959) was Eisenhower's secretary of state from 1953 to 1959.

approaching death, doomed, something Thomas Wolfe had so strongly felt, and the friendly nature, with which one imagined oneself in harmony, would soon lift its terrible paw, would come with a shocking storm, with the glowing sun, burning grass and tree, with hurricanes in the summer and blizzards in winter and always gigantic.[50]

As if suddenly overcome with fear, it seemed, the settlements unified themselves into a *Main Street,* into a little Broadway with lit-up advertisements even during the day and under dazzling sun, with garages, with movie palaces, distinguished from the garages only by facades borrowed from one of their films, the supermarket spread out its cans, the housewives wheeled the small shopping carts, as if seeking protection together in the treacherous security of our technological century.

The land I saw, this strip of land in front of the not-yet-humanized forest, this garden wrested from the wilderness seemed to be inhabited less by people than by cars. The cars ruled the landscape, they stood in packs before each house, camped in the forest clearings, indulged themselves in the rivers, they had their drive-in restaurants, their drive-in cinemas in the open air, their own hotels and their giant, extremely melancholic cemeteries.

At times two cars stood as if lost in conversation, in the most lonely nature, not humans but cars appeared to be the masters of this land, and they had their appointment to rendezvous.

The South already begins on the New York-Washington line and so does segregation. Black settlements, white settlements, forming a light and a dark chain, are tumbled together in a "hedgehog," like the moving front of some horrible war.[51] The houses, the fields, the cars of the whites. But one settlement wasn't much more shabby than another. From the train one could hardly notice a difference. The *Main Street* was always the same, the businesses were similar, the churches were interchangeable, though they had either a white or a black clientele. The heavens enclosed them all in the same melancholy.

A storm came up, gathering over forests and rivers, pressing down heavily to earth, the black sky hung deep, it was night at mid-day, shaken by the wind the trees were a green wavy sea. In no time the horizon had grown narrow and apocalyptic, a deluge of rain fell, lightening was a continuous fire. In houses that seemed totally lost, already washed away by the flood, lamps cast a terrible light, the cars had put on their headlights, placing civilization's optimism in front of them, an intimidated, an endangered, a bold life tried to assert itself. The train drove on like a diving boat with observation windows through an eerie underwater landscape. The world seemed to have sunk, to have been

---

50. Thomas Wolfe (1900–1938) was an American writer.
51. The "hedgehog" is a pawn position in chess.

pulled down to the bottom of the sea, but in the parlor car black servants served whiskey on ice. Politicians, deputies, lobbyists took the proffered glass in their hands, feeling saved by the calming cool of American comfort. Again they studied their stocks. They talked. Gossip grew like weeds. Others read the reports in the Sunday papers, researched the rich market, mainly there to entice women, looking for new ways of making profit, and a cadet in the dainty toy-soldier uniform of West Point watched, like a nice rabbit hypnotized by a snake, his blonde-headed girlfriend, who cared for her beauty like a strict idol in the light of the flaming sky.

What did we grasp of the world we traveled, of the atmosphere of darkness, wetness, electricity and anxious life through which our train was roaring. We drank our whiskey, we thought about our business, we looked at the vain beauty, envied and sympathized with the cadet who had fallen for her, we traveled in an artificial climate, in the tension-less domain of a Faraday cage.[52]

Only when the train arrived in Washington, only when the luxurious can, in which we ate, only when the wagon was opened, did the air meet us like a slap, the slap of a heavy steam-drenched towel.

We had caught up with the storm; here it was gathering for a new attack. The sky was steely, the clouds threatening, the wash room atmosphere made suit and shirt stick together. Everything seemed to crackle and to be eerily illuminated in a St. Elmo's fire.[53]

Children played by the ticket counters, black children, their black skin further darkened in the tension-filled air, their skin blended in with the black leather benches, over which they were climbing, as if adapted to protect them from hunters, and their voices were shrill like the cries of frightened birds. Everyone was in a stir. Everyone was striding with luggage carriers. Once again I was surprised by the sudden lack of services to which Europeans were accustomed in wartime. Suddenly there were not enough taxis at the station. We stood and waved in vain, and when a car finally hurried by, its driver used the chance and crammed three, four different groups of passengers into the back of the car. My hotel didn't appeal to the chauffeurs; and they left me standing.

The first flashes of lightening moved over the black sky, thunder came both lazy and dull, the first heavy drops fell. The capital city gave an impression of countryside. In front of the station stretched a big free square, and at the end of a broad avenue, as if on a theater brochure, the dome of the Capitol rose up, veiled in gloomy clouds and revealed for only a moment in a flash of lightening.

---

52. Michael Faraday (1791–1867) was an English chemist whose Faraday cage separated internal from external fields of electricity.
53. St. Elmo's fire is the generation of light during electrical storms.

Finally a car drove me through the streets, which seemed strange to the foreigner, like Faulkner's South. In the oppressive pre-storm atmosphere the black population sat, sunk in their own shadows, like ghosts on the steps of verandas. It was an image almost without movement, in a light which the old masters had painted when they wanted to show Jerusalem on the day of crucifixion, and only the children jumped and whirled over the roadblocks in dark, daredevil groups. There were many trees, their thick foliage sheltering the way in night-like darkness. This city did not feel like a city; in these streets Washington resembled a settlement that embodied no solid homeland, it was accidentally jumbled together and damned by God. A bridge led high up over a river, over sensuous green hanging jungle plants, over the deep gorge of the Potomac, of old, wild Indian water.

It was another world on the other side of the shore; there were villas here and the wide horizons of a golf course, pale-faced provinces, the white-faced conquerors of the red and the black man. The Sheraton Hotel, a tall brick mountain with a columned entrance, as if constructed from children's building blocks, rose out of a park, and there was a little excited train, as if from an exhibition, in which serious men sat, looking like senators and secretaries of state, they probably were senators and secretaries of state, in airy toy wagons under an awning painted blue-white when bad weather threatened; they relaxed from governing the world in the society of serious, worthy spouses, decorated with their flower hats, who made their husbands' lives beautiful.

The whole world was striving for the Capitol; everyone sought representation for themselves or their companies or their states in the most famous and most expensive inn, in this the capital of the Western world. Representatives and ministers thronged in the hall. One stood around, one offered, pleaded for a room, one insisted on advanced orders, on one's personal or borrowed standing. The in-house servants, black-skinned or white-faced, condescendingly inspected the guests. Humidity, like hot cotton wool, pressed through the portico and mixed itself in with the air conditioner's cool. The hall was a hot-and-cold-water bath that assaulted the senses, possibly compelling action.

One of the black servants led me through long halls, luring me upstairs and downstairs, leading me through elevator shafts to a room that had been granted to me. An absinth-green metal Venetian blind was lowered before the door. The thermostat hummed, a breath of polar air was over the Chinese silk carpet, and the large, polished shining television, which could be controlled from bed as with a horse's reigns. Outside the bad weather started to unload itself. In a glaring flash of lightening I read that my room cost thirty dollars a day. I was very shocked, I was ashamed, I struggled with myself, pulled myself together finally, called the management and spoke about a misunderstanding, I'm no minister or bank director.

A new servant came, he came very arrogant and led me down new long passageways to another room, again ghostly pale lightening flashed through absinth-green Venetian blinds, again a television dominated the room, which was supposed to cost twenty-five dollars and whose last guest had not yet moved out; he had washed his shirts in the bath and hung them out on a string to dry. Twenty-five dollars also seemed like a lot of money to me, I wanted to live more cheaply, arousing displeasure and confusion. An elevator carried me under the roof; no more television; no more artificial climate; thunder raged in hammer blows, a big, rusted-iron ventilator hummed, digging into the almost solid air like a plough. God knows who this room was right for. There were open doors everywhere, leading to rooms with white refrigerators, with electric cookers, though the spacious apartments weren't kitchens or pantries, uncovered light bulbs burned everywhere, and there was not a person to see.

All this unsettled me, an old reader of Kafka, quite a bit. I was very much in need of a whiskey, I thought about the advertisements, I went down to the lobby and asked about the hotel bar and was looked at punishingly, as if I had inquired about something indecent. No alcohol was served in Washington hotels on Sundays; and in the capital's bars no thirst could be quenched. That was the law. Those who were clever had prepared beforehand, going around the law, bringing bottles in their luggage, ordering ice and soda water to the room. I had not been clever. Finally they comforted me and said that in the restaurant, with food, I could get a beer.

The restaurant's chef was from Heidelberg. The beer was from Dortmund. The man from Heidelberg told me that he had already served the German chancellor and the minister of finance and Franz Joseph Strauss and that next he would buy Heidelberg.[54] The beer from Dortmund cost a dollar fifty, and I believed the man, striving for success, that he would soon have the first hotel in Heidelberg. In the meantime, a tornado was furiously forming outside behind the red damask curtains. The air was a vortex, fire and flying branches, but inside in the dining room the ladies and gentlemen watched the end of the world with indifference, standing in line with dignity before the cold buffet. I too took a tray and a plate and got in line, and my countryman from Heidelberg blessed me with lobster and turkey and fatty sweet salads. I had no choice but to order myself another Dortmund beer, while musicians dressed in the high society styles of my grandmother's generation sat in an ivory gallery and fiddled the "Waltz King" against the wild-west storm.

The music from Vienna calmed the American elements. The storm had died down, the cloud burst had moved on. The air was purified. Now I saw that the area was a single big park. All the houses stood on fields and beneath

---

54. Franz Joseph Strauss (1915–1988) was a prominent postwar German politician.

beautiful trees. Well-groomed elegant dogs sniffed the damp ground. I went to the shore of the Potomac, looked into the deep gorges, observed the green jungle, while from the radio of a car, grazing close by, evening news of unsettling European conditions touched the air, the ghosts of Indians whispered, derisive and scheming, in the tree tops.

The inhabitants of the thirty-dollar rooms got up early. They didn't rest long, they didn't get rusty. On big signs they had written their name or the name of their company, their corporation, the name of the God they were representing and they put these signs on their collars. They greeted one another with morning freshness. Contacts were cultivated, first probings tried out; every handshake was made with the pathetic gesture of irreversible friendship for life. The lobbyists buzzed by like vultures. *The early bird catches the worm:* I had read this sentence in my English grammar book. Had the president's secretary accepted the fur coat, was he stumbling over the carpet that had been given as a gift? In the newspaper his face expressed tired arrogance, perhaps a justified contempt as well.[55] Excitement over trivialities; the moon rocket had missed its goal. The morning papers were flown through quickly; blunders were being made, one had to be involved with world politics. Chaos came from everywhere, Germany was not the navel of everything that happened.

For all transactions one fortified oneself in the breakfast room and in the coffee shop; those who were already above breakfasted in the ballroom, those who wanted to come up were in the shop. Vitamins, nourishment for the nerves, to strengthen the heart and feed the muscles, renewal of energy, getting pepped up, optimism, *keep smiling,* freshly pressed juices, stewed fruits, iced cream, germless milk, grated cereals, soft grits, hot pancakes, fried bacon, eggs, toast, butter, streams of coffee. Health, strength and wonderfulness were served by black waiters, who in their white suits resembled trained madhouse attendants.

The conference rooms were waiting. The microphones had been set out. Conference offices had been set up before the doors. Six women crouched behind six typewriters at a long table; six flowerbed hats sat like six tightly-fit helmets on the six undulating representative heads.

It was raining. This time it was a normal steady rain. The fields and trees around the hotel were a soaking wet green, and one looked through the panes of the veranda hallway as into a sad aquarium; old men were suffering it out on the golf course, though, experienced old boys, whose secretaries kept umbrellas over their expensive, world-ruling skin with obedient steps.

---

55. This could be an oblique reference to the 1952 "Checkers" speech by Richard Nixon (1913–1994), in which the vice-presidential candidate denied that his wife owned a fur coat, an allegation connected to charges of financial impropriety; in 1958 Nixon was Eisenhower's vice president.

Big automobiles armored like cruisers on the high seas and on a dangerous journey. Without a car one was inclined to despair. Washington was built in wide distances, miles didn't count, and the Sheraton Hotel lay at the outermost circles of power. Again taxis seemed a scarce commodity; only after much futile waving did a car finally stop. A Negro woman was driving it; she looked like a young doctor. She picked me up, and then she charitably took along others, who stood like shipwrecks on the road giving signs of their helplessness.

Where were we going? To the capitol of course, through wide avenues that came together in traffic circles and then ran to the next meeting point in tree-lined streams. Washington rarely resembled New York or Chicago, it was always a park, often a mid-sized English town, at times one drives in the city streets through provincial America, here too there was a *Main Street,* the rows of houses more erratic, unplanned development, architectural anarchy, then Southern Negro districts, shabby row houses; in its wasted space the political center resembled the most expansive lawns, flower gardens, tree-lined roads, vistas and pools of an old German palace, the capital of a not-so-big duchy, a Weimar or a Schwerin.

I was struck by an inclination for monuments, for all that remained of a short history, for historic weapons, for decorative canons, for the columns and obelisks of self-glorification, but I soon recognized that here all these symbols, which Europeans find suspicious, were not dead schoolbook pieces, the fetters of growth and development, but a still-living present, a joy still felt, a state had come into being, grown together from the whole world, and not through conquest, through subjugation, but through rebellion and emancipation. Free will, not compulsion, had given birth to greatness. The beautiful thoughts of human rights, the pride, refuge of the persecuted, the place of religious freedom, of conscience, to be a citizen and not a subject, and a still palpable anti-colonial feeling—indeed, often worried and confused today by the politicians' tricks—pleasantly enlivened the air.

School classes from all over and the inhabitants of this wide country, brought here by a huge fleet of buses, stormed the tourist sites, the temples, the historic places. On the broad steps, in the marble halls and passages of the Capitol were little Negroes, there were little Chinese, Filipinos, all the people of the world were proud to be American. I was calmed and comforted to see the sight of Negro children in crowds with blissful faces before the image of the emancipator, the great Lincoln, and behind and near them, equally devout and rapturous, their white contemporaries from Georgia, from Alabama, from Louisiana, from the places of terrible news, of school strikes, of defamation, of hate, of fear.

I let myself believe in this living veneration of America. Everywhere paintings celebrated the great uprising for the earth's independence and for the human rights of all who had sought the New World, and statues of glittering marble showed the courageous rebels against the English crown: the wind drove the coattails of these men as it did the revolution.

Near these valiant figures I also saw senators from a later age standing carved in stone, then the exuberance sank into demagoguery. Probably it was right to have banished some, so represented for eternity, to the cellar of the Capitol. All the same it struck me that among these banished statues were a few brave boys too, and I wasn't able to figure out why one was angry with them.

In the cellar hallways of the uplifting, world-ruling house it smelled like disinfection and the wash room, of Latin class and of puritan-scented dishes from the different mess halls, all resembling simple cafeterias, which nevertheless were jealously ordered for hierarchy, separation and isolation. Signs stated *"For Members Only," "Press Only," "For Deputies."* Black men and women served the governing and the others, who observed the business of government or were fishing in the networking pond. In the serious underground halls of national greatness, on the edge of world events, the Negroes behaved like happy children. They laughed, they chattered, they stood about, seeming to be hiding from one another and perhaps from destiny.

Congress, possibly the most powerful parliament in the world, met in a high room, and the land's inhabitants and the school classes occupied the gallery, looking on curiously.

Members of Congress, as everywhere in the world, gave themselves time. They arrived in a leisurely manner, as if distracted by civic business or as if they had not been too horrified at the bell, which had called them to session and taken them from their restaurant chats. It was not an important day. It was a routine meeting about small stuff. But it was festively called to order by a prayer, spoken by an earnest priest at the rostrum, which was not surrounded by deputies; the invocation of God was also routine and did not alleviate the boredom. Some of the people from the provinces fell asleep in the gallery, dreaming of their farms' broad horizons or of the city's seductions, of temptations they had not encountered.

Disorder stirred among the school children; perhaps they had expected to see the face of white power, the countenance of the wondrous promised future shining like gold.

The laws were discussed in the Senate rooms where the committees met; one could go in and see how they worked.

Everywhere the people had unrestricted access, a continuous coming and going ruled in all the meeting rooms, one passed the doorknob from hand to hand, glanced in the room, looked around, asked about the next one, behaved with disrespectful bustle; but these people seemed to me the kind of people who belonged to a clan, to the augurs, to the curtain, to machinery, while all others probably relied on their press representatives, on young people who sat relaxed at a long table and looked as if they were telling jokes instead of listening to the discussion.[56]

Nevertheless, in all the American papers the reporting from the Capitol was detailed, informative, conscientious and first-rate.

The committee for workers' rights met in a cozily paneled, noble room, its natural grandeur enhanced by marble busts and peacefully placed columns. The hands of an old English grandfather clock no longer moved; its time was finally up.

The chair of the commission surprised me with his youth. He looked friendly, and his young face appeared sensible not assiduous. Invited union leaders sat before the committee at a big table, which stood in the middle of the room as on some isolated, unconnected surface. They looked clever and often brow-beaten, they looked powerful and at the same time powerless. The bosses answered the Senators' questions with quiet, calm voices and without getting up from their seats.

Secretaries came and went with notes and questions, and with their mincing high-heeled walk, beautiful make-up colors and blowing coiffeur, some of these women resembled cheerful circus horses.

Now and again the photographers' flashbulbs would light up, professionally dependent on the unabashedly bored face.

A matter-of-fact and good working atmosphere predominated, as with all ceremonies of state power, without any evident presumption for the law makers, though even this meeting of free citizens betrayed a gentle eeriness.

In the Library of Congress I stood in the high temple of literacy. As a young man I had dreamt of such a palace for books, gradually I had buried this dream; but here in America, in Washington, I saw it realized: I lingered in the ideal library.

The library's holdings were marvelous and its organization exemplary. The librarians did not conduct themselves like state officials, they were true servants of books and good friends of the reader. One always got friendly service and any desired book in a minute's time. "Awake and read" is an American slogan and no mere phrase.

Decorous or functional, the broad, wide reading rooms were full of people looking up words, studying, pondering, and again it struck me that among those drawing themselves to the sources of knowledge was a big share of colored people, the Negro above all of course, though I also saw Indians, Chinese, representatives of the biggest and smallest peoples sitting at the desks, taking it in, daring to do things and writing.

---

56. Augurs were priests in ancient Rome responsible for interpreting the will of the gods.

In the vestibule of this library, which cannot be praised highly enough, was an exhibit of White House photographs. No divinizing the state, no cult of personality! The photographers had worked to capture the truth. The president of the United States was shown as man and as citizen in these portraits, always in a slightly comic posture, always a bit caricatured, never was he a mere office holder or only a general.

But apart from the first man of the land these White House photographers to be appeared captivated by disaster. Again and again they recorded violent death in their images. Planes and cars appeared not only as the servants of man but more often as his killer, capable of smashing him into pieces, and nature, America's big untamed nature, casting up storms over and over again, fire and water like God's scourge over God's own country.

In the Library of Congress, history was painstakingly preserved and proudly displayed, documenting the short span of American becoming, the world since Gutenberg, who was a cousin of Columbus. Old expensive prints stood there, German, Dutch, English, Italian, Latin texts, on the table Brandt's *Ship of Fools* lay open next to the works of Erasmus, and the great Mainz Bible and *The Bill of Rights* rested, guarded by heavy-set policemen, equal under the law and under glass.[57]

A colored engraving from 1850 was titled: "German Gymnastics in Cincinnati." The German gymnasts sat beneath black floppy hats, emphasizing manliness around a German keg of beer and swinging frothing-over beer mugs with strength and excitement. In this I saw the final destination of the Paul's Church, the emigrated German democracy of 1848, fraternal, Germanness beneath the black floppy hats, which Bismarck then stole from them, and already they were cultivating the wrong German romanticism, the fatal-sentimental homeland feeling of New York's 86th Street, the longing for the oak of a German inn, which today is best satisfied by German football players.[58] Even little Bavarian stories were housed in the library of the American Congress. A picture was called *"Lola comic,"* another *"Lola has come,"* and they showed Lola Montez first with her happy and then with her sad royal protector.[59]

Paintings from early American painters inspired fascination, they derived from a sky that was still foreign, the whole magical allure of forests untouched by immigrants' feet; these colonial painters saw the Indians, those old inhabit-

---

57. Sebastian Brandt (1457–1521) was a European writer whose 1494 satirical book, *Ship of Fools,* was widely read in Germany; the Mainz Bible was printed by Johannes Gutenberg (1400–1468).

58. On the St. Paul's Church, see note 39.

59. Lola Montez (1821–1861) was a European dancer and actress and the mistress of King Ludwig I of Bavaria (1786–1868), "her sad royal protector."

ants of the earth condemned to death, as pure villains and also naively, Jean-Jacques Rousseau style, as the better men.

A young Negro, his taxi, his radio drove me with jazz sounds through the American Valhalla, gasping trombones, screaming trumpets, songs of wildness and holiness. White columns, manicured lawns, temples, the landscape of classicism, the garden of the ideal, the streets of the transfigured revolution and of state making. The Washington Monument was an obelisk enclosing an elevator; one reached the heavenly heights of this stone and this mark of memory, and across lovely green meadows one could see the law makers' dwellings, the houses of those currently governing the political experiment grown into the first superpower. It was not a material but a spiritual landscape. The Lincoln Memorial, a columned temple of marble, observed itself in the canal buried before it like a mirror. In the dark water the will to good swayed reverently. Abraham Lincoln sat sunk in thought in a grandfatherly armchair, and in this form one could also take him home in a little pocket edition. The Jefferson Memorial was a little pantheon, a tribute also to Rome and to Paris, but here in the open landscape it was lonely and solemn. My young Negro driver drove me, and we sought and found the famous words of the third president chiseled in stone: "I have sworn upon the altar of God eternal hostility against every form of tyranny over the mind of man." The words moved me. The sun's reflection shone on the face of the young Negro. Then we looked across to the golf course on the Potomac's other shore. We saw small figures in the gentle terrain. We did not see the ball, which they were driving forward with clubs. Perhaps the president was relaxing there from the world's business. The bridge swung boldly over the river; it cleared a direct path for the generals from the Capitol to the five-storied strange fortress, where they believed that world peace was well protected.

The bridge was new, the servants of peace could use its two wide lanes, and my driver, my black friend, believed that they were built for fast crossings, it was almost an acrobatic act, a leap over the abyss, and we felt like commanders, tearing forward behind blue light and police sirens, hunting the shy angel with the palm. But in the New World the palm branch did not just signify peace, here it was a martial symbol looking good on uniform collars and hats.

The Pentagon made a strange impression; perhaps because it did not seem such a secret. It probably wanted to inspire amazement from the air, astonishing eagles and doves. I first thought the building was a water tower, then a bare hydrocephalus, and when I looked more closely it resembled a modern prison, familiar from shows about gangsters and prison breaks. In the end it was probably the tower of Babel, and thousands upon thousands of cars had gathered themselves around it, praying to it in motionless herds. Airplanes constantly

floated past the five-story castle, past the Bendlerstrasse, past the great general
staff, the army's high command in the land of limitless possibilities like bees
around their hive, and their irritated buzzing led me to think that, loaded with
atomic bombs, they were probably demonstrating the permanent readiness for
revenge and death, which was so often proclaimed.[60]

Buses and taxis were steered into a tunnel, its light bulbs vaulted an underground heaven both splendid and eerie. An army of employees whirred in and
out. Briefcase carriers, salary gatherers, meal consumers, pensioners of discord,
shareholders of fear. The women marched along with equal rights, they too
carried their briefcases, they too went to work. I saw hardly any uniforms. No
watchman was visible, though I had the feeling that an invisible eye, an elec-
tronic Cyclops was watching me, making an x-ray of my heart.

"The pentagram imposes pain upon you," says Faust forebodingly to Me-
phistopheles.[61] America's big military pentagram is supposed to prevent the
devil from entering; within it the witches' multiplication tables of world destruction would already have been talked through in order to save the world;
probably the last, the final game of war would be practiced on desks and
typewriters, no longer in the sandbox, hardly by generals any more, more by
graduates of the Institute for Advanced Studies or by scientific robots behind padded doors. I didn't see them, Einstein's fearless dreadful students, the
young Fausts; they were all too well protected by the secretaries.

I discovered only the mostly clearly observable and most orderly and, indeed, the most bewildering labyrinth in the world. I wandered through a forest
of signposts. For weeks, for months I could have walked by millions of rooms
in these sober halls unnoticed except by the Cyclops' eye, rooms where Pando-
ra's box was kept laboriously closed with the tapping of typewriters, the ring
of the telephone and the ordering of files, and in which peace, recently made
impossible to share, was being dangerously administered. Now and again we
encountered carts that brought milk, tea and sandwiches from office to office,
I did not dare to ask for a bite, but I was relieved to see that they were transporting no rockets, no bombs and no general staff maps marked with targets.

Only a few minutes by car from the fortress, where the time of our death
is decided, lies one of the world's most immense, most noble cemeteries, the
Arlington National Cemetery. If the future had depressed me in the five corners
of the Pentagon, by the graves I was glad to breathe the relatively mild and
shining air, the humane aura of the dead, of heroes who have war behind them.
On green hills, in the free expanse and under very white gravestones rested

---

60. The Bendlerstrasse was a Berlin street central to the Nazi military bureaucracy.

61. This is a line from Goethe's *Faust*, part I, line 1396. The pentagram is, in context, a powerful and mystical sign.

those who had fallen in the Civil War and the American victims of the last two world catastrophes, American friendly, American in their lack of a grave mound.

The young Negro drove me slowly through the long alleys in this empire of the dead. It made a melancholy impression. One of humanity's hopes was buried here. America too had failed to find the peace it sought; it could not hold itself aloof from Europe's self-inflicted carnage, which its immigrants had fled. The white stones lay there like a bountiful terrible crop, and from the cemetery the Pentagon looked just like apocalyptic architecture.

A Negro singer sobbed in the radio waves reaching my driver and my car, making me think of a Great Mother figure, a moving lament for all the earth's dark children.

I was away from the company of the statesmen, the ministers, the ambassadors, managers, representatives great and small, away from the *high-life* and ambitious hotel, having moved to a place that was more middle class and more average and surely more typically American. Only a small class traveled on expense accounts, spending dollars without thinking. Others watched their dollars closely, the almost sacred tone in which the word dollar was spoken, betraying that in the United States it was also hard to earn money, important as money was to have.

In the new hotel I had a little kitchen in my pleasant, affordable room with a refrigerator and a stove, with pots and silverware, and like the other guests, officers and government employees, called to the capital city for instruction or to make a report, I could shop at the nearby drugstore or in the convenience store, carrying home what I needed, very practically packed in big bags.

In the evening there was sizzling in all the pans. The American style was neighborly. Most of the guests kept their door open. One saw them, comfortably dressed in undershirts, busy, dividing their attention among the warming cans, the frying meat and the never-tired television, tuned in this house mostly to baseball, as was the case all over this country and for foreigners, at least on the screen, incomparably boring.

School classes, come from far away to marvel at Washington, the city and the man, also stayed in this decent middle-class hotel instead of in youth hostels. They also loved keeping their doors open, participating in unfamiliar life, offering it their own company. I saw them in their happy, excessive use of bath, bed, stove and elevator. I liked them. They were colorfully dressed, they were clean, they moved through the halls, through the lobby, even through the restaurant, run by a butler-like Filipino, with self-confident assurance, not fearing teachers or adults.

The Filipino had the film villain's perfect skill, appearing soundlessly behind me and terrifying me with a jug of ice water, which he placed on my table.

Officers, ministers of every sect, old women, the self-worshipping youth all drank up whole fountains and, with them, store houses of laid-away juices.

I breakfasted in a drug store outside the hotel, to make friends with daily American life. The drug store was a barrack, a one-story temporary dwelling on a wide street with businesses and banks. A ventilator battled in vain against the heat from the sun and the kitchen.

Already in the morning there was a roasted potato with the fried eggs, the toast tasted mushy, it was coated with melted butter and it stuck to one's hands. But fresh juices, fat milk, excellent coffee. The lowest level of the bureaucracy and business world breakfasted here, messengers, drivers, small-scale employers, students, young lawyers, young politicians, journalists-on-the-make. The secretaries were dressed up by the tailor's art and taken care of by cosmetics; they looked more disciplined, more energetic than the men and were much more womanly than their European colleagues.

We hunched harmoniously on the bar stools and read the *Washington Post* in order to keep up with conversations about the latest in the world and in the nation's capital. I was excited by the newspaper's range; on weekdays it was as thick as a Sunday edition in Germany, its news agency was terrific, its cartoons were stupid and its advertising pages were a gold mine.

The daily seduction was tremendous: sales, sales, sales. Comically, most of the exhortations with the sentence: you can save money. The pockets of poor wage earners were empty from extravagant saving. The young people who breakfasted with me counted their pennies, the girls' fine clothes purchased, at great cost, by the mushy toast, by the simplest meals.

It was the morning hour of the students. They waited at the bus stops, which went to Georgetown, to the old Jesuits' university, to a sister school and to other institutions of learning. White-cheeked and dark-skinned youths, dressed in the same teenager and college style, which had gone out from America to conquer the world, stood among each other in groups divided by race, though a blond boy took a lively interest in a dark beauty; I understood his excitement, I felt for him, and I asked Americans what the prospect was for such love, love on the way to school, and the Americans did not know what to say, I feared that they found my question indiscreet, they suppressed a thought that was obviously unpleasant for them.

Georgetown was pretty, and the morning trip with the country's black and white young blood was beautiful. Strangely enough, a piece of old England had remained intact in the capital of independence. The houses in the style of George II were in the English colonial style, Britannia carried over the sea, placed on a foreign, even tropically overgrown lawn, though it was clipped in the English manner, and English dogs with their proudly raised tails were everywhere on the raked lawns. Everything looked freshly washed; here, as I was told, the whole area had been given up to deterioration, consigned to being a Negro slum, and not long ago, during Franklin Roosevelt's presidency, young New Deal intellectuals had discovered their taste for a feudal bequest, restoring the houses of the king and hanging their Renoirs and Picassos on the wall.

They were still living there, diplomats, secretaries of state, the stars of journalism. Washington was still a swamp in the English era, and the current inhabitants of Georgetown might also consider the seat of government a swamp flower. They rushed to work in European sports cars, diving into the cloud of vanity, maneuvering through the haze of intrigue, parking in the morass of political prophecy.

One avenue led directly to the White House. There the sirens sang. An air raid alarm was sounded, its howling, unforgettable tone hung over the capital of the New World, the castle to which Europeans had fled, the symbol of Western security. The handwriting on the wall was audible in the air, the streets grew empty, I hurried with the others in an office building, where employees and wisecracking seekers of protection gathered like gaily patterned tiles on a chess board, glad for an interruption, for a change, and one laughed heartily at the fun, as one had once happily laughed in Berlin. The exercise was over quickly. No fires blazed, no walls were knocked over. The sky was clear, not darkened by a single cloud.

The White House stood nobly beneath the old trees. It was no king's palace, more the house of a well-off and cultivated man. The house told of inherited wealth and of handed-down culture. The president's residence did not emphasize the elevation of the state, nor did it emphasize world power, it did not symbolize a bloody history, its white was the white of innocence.

I joined the visitors' line. Schools. Schools. Schools. America's schools seemed to be always traveling. The school, which surrounded me before the White House, was from Tampa. The little girls from Tampa were dressed, once again, like young ladies, waving their petticoats, already wearing flower bed hats, and they were talented in the art of jewelry, while the boys were, sadly, no young cavaliers, but out of their fear, their strangely American man's complex, of being perceived as soft, as feminine, they overemphasized their rough-and-tumble behavior and their neglect of a decorative beautiful appearance.

Despite their marble walls and crystal chandeliers, the public rooms of the White House looked more plain than pompous. The rooms conveyed no showy affluence, testifying instead to a natural elegance, the good way with people and the tradition resting on the independence, freedom, civil rights and revolutionary ideals that is the best of Americanness.

On the walls I saw the portraits of dead presidents or of those no longer in office, and here too, as with the senators in the Capitol, the men of the old era had good heads, exuding excitement, intellectual energy, high spirits, strong character and a passionate will to create, not just an American nation, but a better humanity; but those who came after them, who later ruled this house, were lawyers and businesspeople, showing smooth, conventional faces, washed with the water of sobriety.

In the small ballroom a white and a black piano were touching one another tenderly in wood, as if the country's dangerous colors wanted to make a case for friendship.

In the park by the White House an experienced band of grey squirrels lived in old gnarled trees, feeding themselves astutely and honestly on the nation's tribute.

In Washington one could also eat Italian, Japanese, Armenian. The restaurants were a piece of Italy, a speck of China, they were Asia Minor within four walls. Many tables remained empty, their owners showing their concern on their faces. Occasionally a cocktail was served before the meal, a small onion swimming in it; it was like a pearl of bitterness served by a woman's hand. I ate in a drug store by a Marilyn Monroe, who found it unspeakably funny that I used my fork in the European way. Her ringing laughter was not unkind and she promised more than her hamburger did. During the day I ate at a nightclub, and on its ghostly, empty dance floor short-hand typists, pale in the evening's neon light, consumed sweet-and-sour ragouts prepared in a Chinese style. The city's secret boozers paid their visits to a Mexican-themed restaurant; one couldn't find a single drop of whiskey or gin at the bar, though at the tables strong rum cocktails were given out with food, and men with dark faces chewed on huge steaks, as if in good time they would be atoning for the rum. A particular melancholy fell over Washington at night. The time when the offices closed was, as elsewhere, the hour of overfilled buses, stopped up streets; but then—where are these people to be found?

As usual, the sky was heavy with storms, the air was oppressive, and the streets were empty. The clouds had a reddish sheen. Occasionally a big car drove through the empty, still streets, seemingly in search of something that probably wasn't to be found. Young Negroes came out of a church's vicarage, behaving with a very considered craziness, not natural to the social situation in what was still a white neighborhood.

In a long, narrow room three Creoles played a beautiful wild jazz, and extremely furious but silent young men sat on the long-forgotten sides of the bar, as if held up by string. They belonged to the white population, not a single Negro was among them; and there was no girl to be seen. The young men brooded somberly to the music's provocative rhythm, and I feared that they had hidden pistols in their pockets and would suddenly start to shoot blindly, for some trivial reason, merely out of apathy. The Creole musicians outdid one another in the ecstasy of noise, the ear, the walls resounded, but all the shrill, ringing sounds seemed, in this bar, only to intensify the pressure into a cauldron which was about to explode.

I was very surprised by the bitter absence of girls among these young men, who were not at all inclined toward homosexuality; it did not correlate to the uncoerced, free relationship of the sexes at school age, to the children's dates, to the school dances and early marriages. The young men in this bar sat between school and marriage as if in a sexual quarantine, and here the jazz was like a fence around a caged criminal.

The Negro neighborhood began behind the public library, which America's dark citizens also used industriously; everywhere among the open stacks black girls and black boys were running as through a colorful forest, and men, still in overalls from work, crouched on the green lawn and read Robinson or Hemingway, Camus and Oppenheimer in lantern light.[62]

The others, women, men and children, sat on stoops in the long straight streets, sometimes close together, leaning against a wall or standing free, saying nothing; and where there was no light, in the shadow of firewalls, tree leaves, smashed lanterns, one hardly saw them crouching there, motionless, in the cloak of night and as in some great silent expectation.

Lit-up halls stood at the border between the white and black quarter, as in no man's land, with time-killing machines, mechanical games and peep-show boxes with pictures of half undressed girls, and there were also places for strip shows and for showing nudie films. Their customers were always white-faced, they were never black.

The disrobing took place on scaffolding illuminated by spotlights as in a boxing ring. One sat around the ring in the sheltering darkness as in an amphitheater. One could believe that one was alone, with the way she offered her obdurate smile, alone with the girl bought for one's dreams. Once again one got a heavy sense of loneliness here, the special American loneliness, which Americans feared and which they hated.

As I left Washington, I was once again driven to the station by a Negro. He drove me through the Negro streets of my arrival, drove me by those sitting on their stoops motionless day and night, past the children hurrying like dark wind-borne sand, noisily playing ball with rusted cans, and when the driver recognized from stickers on my baggage that I was German, he said to me that he found Hitler the most meaningful phenomenon of the twentieth century. I gathered that experience had taught him to speculate on his tips, and I replied by saying that he had gone to too much trouble. But this Negro tolerated no

---

62. Edwin Arlington Robinson (1869–1935) was an American poet, and J. Robert Oppenheimer (1904–1967), an American physicist.

objection, he got passionately excited, turning back to me, and complained with great theatrical gestures, neglecting our safety so that the car swerved dangerously, while its driver consigned the city of Washington, the president of the United States and the politics of the capital to the devil. This Negro was a nice, a decent, an intelligent man, he was educated and literate; it was only hatred that made him blind and allowed him to see the great translator, an eschatological phenomenon for black people, in Hitler, who preached the superiority of the Germanic race.

America still knows the romance of the railway. The massive distances, the country's monstrous size, the time change from the Eastern to the Western states, the confusion of a passenger's sense of time still makes a trip in the great trains crossing the continent into a genuine adventure.

From Washington to New Orleans I was once again pleasantly and oppressively preserved in an artificial climate. In my car, rubbed bare as if with scouring sand, I once again had canned food, I had rented a roomette, truly a small room with a window that could not be opened, a chair, a toilet and a ventilator, and at night a mechanical invention was supposed to transform it all into a bed.

But I was clumsy, acting like Chaplin, pressing the wrong buttons, setting chair and walls into strange motion, finally I was pressed out of the room by the mechanics, I guessed there was something under the bed and in the end I was banged with it back into the wall.

The conductor, who had been called to help, did not show himself to be very capable. This black conductor was a real American. The American is good-natured, but he believes that the foreigner must learn how to figure things out in this country. In general, the traveler, still wearing clothes of European make, is not taken for a tourist but for someone who has just immigrated, who would do himself good by quickly becoming comfortable with the native customs. The American finds it hard to believe that someone who has had the good fortune to make it to the United States would not want to stay there forever. I always aroused astonishment and true compassion when I mentioned my departure, which was coming ever closer, and people who hardly knew me often offered to vouch for me, so that I didn't have to return to old Europe in my won-over condition, won over by being in America.

When the bed was finally tamed and conquered and lay smooth before me, I found traveling in the roomette wonderful. I put out the light, pulled up the window curtain and from my camp I saw the land at night, saw again the seemingly impenetrable green forests, the endlessly broad fields, almost nowhere did I see agriculture or cultivated fields, and again everywhere the headlights of isolated cars in an overpowering void of people, a light in a barren hut seemed to be alone in the world for a while, the only, the last shimmer of life far and wide, until the loneliness suddenly massed together, cars gathered in the open expanse, and enormously big and already to be glimpsed from a distance, the face of a film star stood over them in the night, his excited, his dumb threatening mouth, his eyes meeting only the darkness, a drive-in cinema, and I did not know from where the cars emerged in the empty night, to worship this star.

Then after new miles of sleep, when the earth was dead, a hotel, terrifyingly close, rose out of the night's dark and green loneliness with a gaudy show of light, this too conceived more for cars than for people, ramps and doors seemed to be made so that one could drive with the beloved car into bed, one should also have driven by a buffet standing beneath the starry sky, which offered sandwiches to people and gas and oil to cars in a corpse-white neon light. And then, once again, a *Main Street* dipped out of the expanse and the desolation, they always seemed to be ordered from the same factory for main streets and, once completed, thrown in the endlessness, a sudden long row, a Broadway amid unused land. As always, lit-up script, hypnotizing offers, calls to buy and save in all colors of the spectrum beckoned—a colorful monochrome. The drug store, the convenience store with its empty wire baskets, the car dealership, the gas station, the scrap yard, in the progressive night they all seemed abandoned in the light of their neon tubes, lost and very much not at home there. There was not a person to be seen; only the cars driving, as observed from the train, in a silent procession through the straight streets, which were immediately and hopelessly swallowed up again by the expanse and the darkness.

My journey was to the South, going from the latitude of Naples to that of the Nile. The train went through Virginia, which the great Elizabeth had named to honor her virginity, the train crossed Carolina, which Charles II had loaned to eight aristocrats, who possessed a touching, if arrogant, faith in the wisdom of the philosopher Locke, a beautifully enlightened constitution for their fiefdom, still in effect for their children and their children's children, and the train pulled us through Georgia, which George II was supposed to have boasted about, the European kings were obsessed with overseas glory and with distant bondage, the journey went through Alabama, Mississippi, Louisiana, through the old French conquest, and they were all feudal, they were white-and blue-blooded and aristocratically inclined, and in the solemn asiento they had won from Spain the right to gather Negroes overseas, five thousand a year, not counting contraband, trading in souls and bodies in order to possess them like a dead thing, to whip them like a hated, captured enemy, to embrace them like an expensive lover in the loneliness of the hot night, so one could remain a master in vast plantations, living off the fruits of slaves' sweat, and so, from all that the forebears did, out of their cleverness, their pride, their lethargy, their hearts of stone and their sleep in black dreams, a nightmare has come into being.[63]

In the morning the sun was already burning, its rays marrying in the white-black of the train, by afternoon the air was like a Turkish bath and the sky a heavily pressing exhausted haze.

The train went right through a small settlement, continuously accompanying a main street for a while, letting one look in at verandas illuminated by the sun, a rocking chair was rocking itself, a ventilator was spinning above a white, then above a black face.

We had come into the dark states of racial segregation. Waiting rooms, cafeterias for this or that skin color, perversions of human worth, a grill for colored by a little train station behind a mesh door, the scene appeared frozen, presenting itself like a panorama built for a stereoscope; the passing-through of the express train was probably the event of the day, though eyes that looked blind peered at us from expressionless faces. Life was evil under this sun. Half-grown Negroes squatted in the dust. They were like a part of the dust. A white woman came over. She wore very short, very tight shorts. She went with long legs and with provocative slowness. The Negroes looked rigidly into the eerie emptiness, their eyes, beneath their comic, intentionally dented felt hats were like white discs in the hot midday. Inert white boys stood, their shirts open at the chest, down to their bellybuttons, against an old, dented wrecked car, they too were not moving, it was taken for granted that they would not let their companions of the other, the despised and disquieting color out of their dark view.

We rode through the night, we rolled through the day, we overcame the monstrous distance, the broad land, each of us sat in his roomette, each locked up to a certain extent in a water closet and in an artificially cooled climate, which kept us alive, we traveled like grotesques drawn by Saul Steinberg, tragi-comic knights of progress, which had already moved on past the railroad, we were serious pilgrims of the earth, business people, officials, engineers, a rabbi from the army was among us, and the black conductor brought iced whiskey with an indifferent face, or he brought none at all when we were in a state where law forbid the sale of alcoholic drinks, we lost our feeling for time, for place and we lost contact with all the world, at the rare train stations there were, surprisingly, no papers, no clocks and no station signs, "find your

---

63. *Asiento* refers to permission granted by Spain to sell slaves, in effect from 1543 to 1834; Charles II (1630–1685) was King of England; John Locke (1632–1704) was an English philosopher whose Fundamental Constitution of the Carolinas was adopted in 1669.

own way, don't ask, figure it out," was what it meant here in the real American argot, and finally we traveled through an hours-long storm over rail-narrow dams, over the bay-wide Mississippi delta and, wrapped in rain and in a veil of thunder, confused, exhausted and each amid his individual loneliness we came in the night hours to New Orleans.[64]

One has probably heard about the New Orleans mardi gras, has seen confetti streams over masked processions in news reels, one thinks of the old courtly France, of Mark Twain and of the broad Mississippi steamboats, of the show boats and the dance ships, of Gerstäcker's river pirates too, and I thought about Faulkner, about the despair, about the crazy absinthe fumes, about the courageous fighting for their life in his novel *Pylon,* and with Faulkner I seemed to be in the right frame of mind, it was raining, the streets through which my taxi was driving had a suburban character, celebrating monotony, the joylessness of the provinces, a bad mood dripped from all the roofs, and even the trees on the avenue, into which we finally turned after a long journey, sadly shook their rain-heavy heads.[65]

The guest house awaiting me was a real plantation, imposingly spacious, pleasantly airy, and built mostly from wood; the columns, which stood before the two stories, painted white and trying to resemble the Pantheon, were also wooden. At any moment, I thought, Uncle Tom must step out the door, though it was only two terracotta Moors holding two milky round alabaster lamps over the wide veranda steps, and in the lobby one man, the owner of the house, in the breeze of a powerful rusted ventilator, relaxing in a rocking chair in front of a television, watching an ice show from New York, an impoverished inheritor of the plantation perhaps, who was effusively warm and who led the guest over wide, much-polished stairs, past blue screened doors, behind which another rusted ventilator was humming, to a big room with worn-down planks smelling of spiced wax.

The night had a tropical glow. It was full of a vanilla scent, of foreign smells, of heavy, warm rainfall, of distant thunder claps, of whispering trees, unfamiliar bird calls and the dark fog horns of the old steam ships, calling out, as if from a powerful breast, to the nearby, fantasy-awakening storm. But insects

---

64. Saul Steinberg (1914–1999), European-born graphic artist, drew cartoons for *The New Yorker.*

65. Friedrich Gerstäcker (1816–1872), a German writer, wrote books on America such as *Die Flusspiraten des Mississippi* (1848) [*The River Pirates of the Mississippi*], based upon his travels; William Faulkner (1897–1962) set his 1935 novel, *Pylon,* in a fictionalized New Orleans. On the role of Gerstäcker and May in *Journey through America,* see Jerry Schuchalter, "'... Und Gerstäcker, Karl May, Cooper und Sealsfield reisen mit uns,'" in *Wolfgang Koeppen - Mein Ziel war die Ziellosigkeit,* ed. Gunnar Müller-Waldeck and Michael Gratz (Hamburg: Europäische Verlaganstalt, 1998).

were soon buzzing around all the lamps, humming through air beaten by the ventilator, descanting, evil-minded stinging animals, and big beetles, brown-black or shimmering in all colors, crawled over the ground, the night table and bed and gawked with basilisk eyes up at the traveler waiting to sleep, so that I got up again from my place and went down to the lobby where I found my host, awake long after midnight, still in his rocking chair, still lonely and sunk into watching television.[66] My complaint did not surprise or upset him; he took a pest spray, followed me calmly, sprayed an odorous stream over the bed and wished me good night.

In the early morning the giggling of unusually big laughing doves who sat plump and heavy on the cornices. The insects had hidden themselves away peacefully. The promise of a hot day lay in the air. The host was sleeping, the house was sleeping, the streets were sleeping. It was sleeping beauty's empire through which I went, long uncut hedges, avenues empty of people, grandeur and decay, quiet, beautiful houses, aristocratic in their own way, on both sides of the street, polished wood columns, tree trunks split by lightening, prehistoric foliage on the terraces, weathered palms and through the enchanted street rattled Tennessee Williams' street car named *Desire,* with only one passenger, an old Negro on the yellow benches, going to its final station, desire.

It took me to the "Vieux Carée," the old French quarter, which was like a closed museum at this hour, through which only cleaning ladies were walking. Such a moment gives even the Mona Lisa its innocence back; the sights to see have been purified from stain, by looking, and are once again themselves.

In New Orleans tourist buses were offered a dream, a place of exile, a place of collapse, here there were houses of the old immigrants, living places of the banned, who had taken their proud France with them, who had remained cultivated, rich in culture, courtly at any price and who had documented their fine manner of living and their horror at the foreign, at the hot air, at the strong sun, at the hurricanes in delicate balconies, which circled the houses in artful metal work, Valenciennes lace made out of iron, the little palaces à la Orleans, once again the houses had walled courtyards, Spanish-Roman patios, where one could be with family or friends, wishing to dream of the Sun King.[67]

The streets were still named after the Bourbons, honoring the Dauphin, playing Chartres and Rue Royal.[68] I went through very quiet courtyards, whose current occupants were still sleeping behind drapes and curtains and in artificial coolness, I was amazed by the splendor of the azaleas, saw agave widened into big fans, in this house Napoleon should have found refuge, and

---

66. Basilisk is a mythic reptile.
67. Valenciennes lace originated in the North of France.
68. The *dauphin* was the heir to the French throne.

before a window a colorful bird was hanging in a golden cage, commemorating the great days of the singer Adelina Patti.[69]

The day changed everything. The streetcar named "desire" was now completely full, and in the front sat the white and in the back the black passengers, as decreed by law.

In the little drug stores depressed pale faces provided grumpy service, which in New York had been provided by cheerful Negroes. In New Orleans a taxi with a black driver would not pick me up. The little white man ruled the city, the little white man decided the elections, the little white man feared for his daily bread and watched jealously, tense and brutal, so that no kind of slave would take it away from him. Complete segregation ruled, white taxi drivers for white people, black for black. Who wanted to speak about suppression? Justice and a decency pleasant to God himself ruled. The setting changed first at the top of the social pyramid, first at the distinguished St. Charles Hotel. At the St. Charles the black chef could be a complete gentleman, in the St. Charles there were excellently schooled black waiters, black elevator girls and black bar men. In the St. Charles the old plantation atmosphere ruled, a benevolent use of black talents, for the guests in this great establishment did not fear their dark brothers as competitors, and perhaps they were tolerant or arrogant enough to accept the Negro as a researcher or as a U.N. ambassador, then he would not push equality so far as to stay or to dine at the St. Charles.

The main stream of New Orleans, Canal Street, named after a filled in and already forgotten canal, led down to the harbor, going the way of the Ramblas in Barcelona, but it was a Ramblas without trees and without charm, a promenade without coffee houses, terraces, awnings and flâneurs, the streets looked as if the noble-born and conquered inhabitants of New Orleans wanted to outdo their conquerors, the Yankees, in their soberly ugly, anarchically bare city building.[70] In a world of stone structures the sun strung heartlessly, the air was full of dampness and electricity; whatever one wore stuck to the skin, whatever one touched would crackle.

I fled to artificially cooled stores, visited the abundance of goods, which was also astonishing in New Orleans and intended for women, in many drugstores I drank quantities of lemonade, I sat at long cool shelves in the acrid train-air of technology, after a short while I was trembling from the cold and returned to the hot street, looked at the storm gathering itself for the attack and believed that I would suffocate in New Orleans. The city was a bath of contrasting temperatures, charming to all the senses, oppressing the heart.

---

69. Adelina Patti (1843–1919) was a European opera star.
70. Las Ramblas is a prominent pedestrian street in Barcelona.

The Negroes were welcome as customers in the stores, in the juice bars the thirsty were not let in. No black child reciprocated a white man's smile. Something had gone bad in New Orleans, in New Orleans the streets made one feel sad.

At the end of Canal Street the Mississippi flowed broad and lethargic beneath a sky still furious around midday, and there were also the wide, heavy five-story steamboats, ready for an evening dancing trip toward the Gulf of Mexico, past the green jungle of the bayous, the crocodile's old homeland, the swamps of the slave hunt, of pirate treasure: the proud masters of the river carried a cargo of passionless love, adventure recreated without danger, of bourgeois, touristy routine pleasure for a night hour beneath the Mexican moon.

The wind came out of a hot land, blowing from the empire of old murdered gods; it smelt of poison, of blood that had run, water that had been fouled and of cheap marijuana smoke.

The seamen's bars around Canal Street and its side alleys were really an Aztec world. The bars revealed a fear of the sun inherited from the Spanish. Their windows were thickly hung. Often there was only a single light bulb, like a candle in a piously dark church, full of sanctity, in the ventilated bar room. Guitars sounded from the jukeboxes, high tenor and warm alto voices sang, moving in hard, choppy rhythms, songs about despairing, deadly love. These sea-going residents of the gulf, with their shabby Southern, mestizo elegance, drank a misted-over beer and looked with eyes, which resembled dogs' eyes in their pleading and simultaneously threatening expression, at barmaids who were always chubby, always blonde, always sallow-complexioned and immobile.

Across from the bar stood the fleet's solid company house, untouched by any drunkenness. In its doorway a poster advertised for the women's marine corps. I saw a skinny, fresh American dream girl, evidently smelling of good soap, proud and looking to distant coasts full of expectation.

In the evening a stream of visitors hurled themselves at the old French Quarter, always ending up on Bourbon Street. What these visitors awaited, what was offered to them, was a Montmartre, a Montmartre of their imagination, it was Parisian dissipation sterilized in the American way, it was French depravity in the parameters of the law, it was an object of calumny for the American women's clubs and proof of their need to exist. The visitors strolled through the striptease street with their strange American superstition about the wickedness of nudity.

Before the door of every bar there hung a big photographic reproduction of the exhibitions on offer. One establishment praised, as a particular attraction, mother and daughter in similarly naked pose, and it had not guessed wrongly; its chairs were all occupied. The clientele was well dressed, bourgeois, out for a night's entertainment; the women had put flowers or Pforzheimer jewelry in their powdered hair; escorted by at least two men, they stepped with long legs and with a sweet shiver through the swamp.[71] There was a monstrous quantity of girlie shows, their quality, however, was pure conformity, a general agreement to find not-very-fresh thighs and breasts, awkward contortions, commercial tricks, a conveyor-belt smile of moderate promise depraved and exciting.

One sat at the usual long bar, drank one's drink and saw, where bottles normally stood on shelves, women stepping with dance steps over a footbridge slowly taking off their clothes, commented on usually by a stupid master of ceremonies with bar-room wit, before they disappeared completely naked behind a plush curtain, with fanfare and lights-out. In its constant one-dimensional repetition the event was as banal as it was ridiculous. Having slipped back into their clothes, the girls tried in the usual international rip-off style to get money from those without female accompaniment through ample consumption of colored water drinks; it astonished me how ineptly, with how much charming shyness they did this in America and how much they still had to learn from the Place Pigalle. But the life confessions which they felt compelled to tell their customers were, as everywhere, recreated as "true stories," dripping with morality, sentimentality and a guilt-less guilt. None of the women acknowledged their already demonstrated nakedness, their night profession or an existence that was not middle class.

I looked for the New Orleans jazz. There was none, it was no more. It had emigrated to the North or the West, to tolerant places, or it was traveling through Europe, playing in Paris, getting raves in Hamburg, selling itself for a lot of money to the record and radio companies. I could easily find the old celebrated places, the *Paddock Lounge,* the "*Famous Door,*" the memory of Papa Celestin, the yellowed photographs, though only the photographs of Basin Street heroes and the torn-down Creole quarter.[72] That must have been a joyful world of gods despite all the poverty and injustice. Today one still honored the memory of the blues masters, the fathers of this great jazz style, but on the stage there was only the most common and commercial entertainment.

The few black musicians who played for tourist groups from Texas, Washington, New York or Chicago worked without wanting to, earning their money, as they had to, and how could they be happy or even sad in a good way when their black people were not around in the clubs, when there should be no intoxicating dancing, when the desire and rebellion of the sounds was not registered and no beloved god of the Negroes was being summoned?

---

71. Pforzheim is a town in Southern Germany known for its – Pforzheimer – jewelry.

72. Papa Celestin (1884–1954) was a bandleader, singer and trumpeter whose band played regularly at the Paddock Lounge.

And so, I soon had enough of the lights, of the thousands of advertisements, the girls undressing for business, the listless musicians, the legends of Bourbon Street, I searched for the old New Orleans in its back alleys, strolling through the night and through strangeness.

Napoleon made out of porcelain, half life-size and colorfully painted, stood in a lit-up entrance hall, looking, as if at a lost battle, at an old, very, very noble lady with a tiny white dog who was shrieking like some madwoman of the South, created by a poet, and an old gray-haired Negro, who was walking a hysterically yapping Chinese Pekinese on a leash, answering the woman in a sing-song out of a King Vidor hallelujah film, at the same time devoted and accusatory.[73]

On the wooden veranda of an old ballroom black nuns were moving, darkly clad, pleated night after night, as if they wanted in this sad way to repeat the celebration once given here to honor the Marquis de Lafayette.[74]

Music sounded behind a balcony, behind slightly open shutters, a violin, a piano, a flute sang out, and the tones came mysteriously from these old houses into the dark, still streets, like a monologue of ancient loneliness.

Through the openings in beautiful artfully made railings I looked into gardens and courtyards, I saw candles burning, and old men, perhaps already dead, seemed to be dining there in the softly flickering light, a fine ceremony of world-hating isolation.

Dazzling arched lights, however, illuminated the old Congo Square soberly and without mystery, it has not been called this for a long time, and the cold utilitarian facades of new office buildings looked without interest out onto the square, robbed of all its magic, where bulls were fought in the Spanish period, where slaves had danced Africa's dances, swinging their chains against the moon, crying out to the great voodoo god to fall on the city and all the damned plantations with lightening and storms.

One street went further. Walls hemmed it in. I listened to the step behind me. It kept its distance; when I stood still, it too was still. Who wanted to stand there like that? Someone afraid of the night or someone else, someone to be feared? The quarter was full of silent people; suddenly they grew out of the night, out of the wall, in the late hour's shadows they were long, still gloomier shadows somehow reproachful like the ghosts of insulted isolates.

At the next corner two bars kept watch on each other like two battalions lying across from one another. One bar served white drinkers, the other black

---

73. King Vidor (1894–1982) was an American film director whose 1929 film *Hallelujah!* was a story about African-Americans, with an all-black cast.

74. Marquis de Lafayette in New Orleans (1757–1834), French aristocrat and hero of the American Revolution, took an extensive trip through the United States between 1824 and 1825.

drunks. They were indistinguishable in their gloominess and rage. I entered the black bar, and they showed me across to the white bar. They were not unfriendly, but they wanted no troubles on my behalf. Poor whites and poor Negroes from the neighborhood drank the same cheap liquor, beer of the same brand, but the distance separating these bars seemed unbridgeable.

Nevertheless the Negroes accepted white shadows greedily and interested themselves in the flickering bland problems of young European citizens; a cinema played "Bonjour Tristesse" for black eyes and it had stayed open the whole night.[75]

Brought out of their sleep by the lit-up ads of the cinema, the heavy plump laughing doves of New Orleans hovered gabbling in the velvet Louisiana air at twilight, on the monument skin of Simon Bolivar.[76]

Behind the curb varnished black posts rose up everywhere from the ground, with horse heads cut from wood and with iron rings, to which gentlemen of the old school and perhaps today's great bandits and celebrated murderers had tied their horses. Every corner told old stories. Against whom had one not conspired here, against whom had one not lost out? One had murdered with a light hand and been sent to hell without remorse. Black early-morning workers, porters, damn builders, machine workers were already going down to the harbor, hearing the echo of their steps in the arcades, in the rusting, delicate balcony rails and bay window supports of the long-ago conquered French gentlemen.

Visitors to New Orleans met one another at the *French Market,* the night owls at the usual last station. Whiskey and smoke steamed from their clothes, their skin, their hair, exhaustion rolled over their faces, a disappointment of which they were hardly aware, and life's emptiness yawned before them. At the market stands they offered coffee, Creole spiced chicken broth and oysters for sale, which, broken open, looked like fat gray toads, mussels from the warm Gulf; first I was disgusted by them, but then they tasted deliciously of tropical depths, and a striptease master of ceremonies with a stupid whinny, for whom I had felt embarrassed in the evening, was suddenly likeable to me, as he sat near me at the marble oyster bar, a serious man, selecting his sea food with connoisseurship.

On the nearby *Jackson Square* a monument to the great General of the South rose up, a monument to the Confederate heroes of the Civil War unforgotten in the South, shining in a sun that was still red and already hot, and

---

75. *Bonjour Tristesse* was an American film made in 1958 by Otto Preminger (1905–1986), an Austrian-Jewish director who had moved from Europe to Hollywood.

76. The New Orleans monument to Simon Bolivar (1783–1830) was erected in 1957, shortly before Koeppen arrived in America.

on this morning and in this sun Jackson rode his horse to victory and not to death.[77]

The little park of dust-dry plants was the old Place d'Armes, the parade grounds, the place of surrender, where the Louisiana colony was sold to Spain by France, then by Spain back to France and finally by France to the United States. In the shadowless garden they were hustling the products of prostituted artistic talent. Painters had planted themselves on the public benches, miming the Paris of Toulouse-Lautrec films with their decorative goatees and speculating successfully on the tourists' bad taste.[78]

Many women from New England let themselves be painted beneath umbrellas and palms in colors of pale green. The carriage horses awaiting guests and food wore hats of fine panama straw, and those wanting to risk a pleasure ride could enjoy the shadow of a roof, one that was colorful as a hood from the Creole time.

One should never forget to visit the cemeteries of foreign countries when traveling. Graves tell a great deal about a city.

The St. Louis Cemetery is New Orleans' oldest bone yard, its basilica is called the "church of death," and I took in and admired the cemetery as a piece of transplanted Mediterranean culture, as an irremovable testimony of Latin life, it was almost a Pompeii, had it not been buried, for its classically styled burial houses looked like excavated villas, and on the old Basin Street, the Negro street, the homeland of jazz, which today was a road of garages, gas stations, warehouses and municipal buildings, the St. Louis Cemetery still represented the old life, the old laughter, the old fear, the colonial epoch, and here they, the French, the Spanish, the upper class and the soldiers of fortune rested as in little pious castles, carried to their graves by black hands and black shoulders, and one felt how unhappy they were, with how much homesickness they had died. "*Medical Doctor of the University of Paris*" was written on one gravestone. Aristocrats' crowns, big names with a historic glow, France's castles and France's landscapes, the dignity of the European conquerors and Napoleonic titles adorned other tombs. They had frequented the "Café des Exiles," they had waited for news in the "Café des Refuges," they had dueled in St. Anthony's Garden for the honor of their king: again and again I came across the lilies of the Bourbons.

And lilies, uniquely fat, running wild, tropical flowers really, flourished in rusted pots and cracked bowls in front of the decaying graves, some of which

---

77. The equestrian statue of Andrew Jackson was erected in 1856, commemorating the Battle of New Orleans in 1814; Koeppen confuses Andrew Jackson and the War of 1812 with "Stonewall" Jackson, the Confederate general, and the Civil War.

78. Koeppen could be referring here to the 1952 film *Moulin Rouge* by John Houston (1906–1987), which focuses on the French artist Henri de Toulouse-Lautrec (1864–1901).

had been broken into by thieves, spreading a heavy sweet smell of greatness gone by and of eternal sadness.

From the air, seen from a plane, New Orleans had its sky scrapers of course, its bold highways, its bridges of concrete and steel, a good harbor with ships, docks, grain elevators, banana storehouses and its factories, its activity and its future. The dead French, the buried Spanish promote foreign business with their bizarre bequest of the Vieux Carré. But the planters, the plantation owners, the families of the Civil War, their progeny and their houses have become the object of literary reproach.

I went through the *Garden District,* the old quarter of the rich. In their massiveness, the buildings were reminiscent of the ungainly beautiful Mississippi boats, with their wooden columns and galleries built all around. Screened windows, screen doors, air ducts, defenses against mosquitoes. In the garden stood ancient trees, upright and fallen down, foliage all around, tropical colors, tropical aromas. The lilies were blooming here as well, here there was also a cemetery peace and quiet, the sweetness could be smelled amid the swelling rottenness.

In these gardens the Negroes were dressed in crude rustic linen. An old man judiciously raked the gravel on a driveway. A girl, a black Venus, sat on the crumbling stoop of a house putting flowers together into a bouquet. A fat cook, as in the book *Gone with the Wind,* sat behind the wheel of her boss's magnificent car and drove to the market. These loyal black servants were not living so badly. They existed, they survived in an intact world from yesterday, they lived and died with it, they belonged to the family property like the big inert dogs, resting in the shadows, they were probably even an inheritance, left to the son, the daughter, like a thing.

These Negroes had very gentle, not at all wrathful faces. A black nanny pushed a baby carriage and bent herself like a mother over the little white prince. It was a glowingly hot afternoon, and I had to think of Tennessee Williams' one-act play "*Garden District,*" which I had seen in New York in an impressive off-Broadway staging, and in which there was a young man from this protected, fairy-tale world of the *Garden District* through which I was going, an heir of these columned houses, slave-holder villas, and hothouse gardens hunted on a beach, beaten, torn apart and eaten by Negro children.[79]

The stars and stripes waved from a white garden palace, which belonged to a sugar planter and had been built according to the rules of the Parisian École des Beaux Arts, as a plaque proudly announced. The flag flew over all American schools, and this white palace here was the *Louise S. McGhee School* in the *Garden District* of New Orleans, and I heard the thudding of tennis

---

79. Tennessee Williams wrote "Garden District," a one-act play, in 1958.

balls, slow, not fast, and I heard irons clank, horseshoes, being thrown slowly, not fast, on a playing field, and on a rug-like lawn under the palms and trees of paradise, hung with green veils, I saw very pretty, very lethargic, very well made up girls, all of the exact same race, resting studiously in deckchairs, the school book light as a fan in a hand undefiled by work. I had never seen such a persuasive image of being well born, and most astounding was that these late heirs of slave mills, of sugar cane plantations and of cotton fields had succeeded at looking snow white in the sun's burning breath and at looking cool in the midday heat.

At the train station, in the streets, I once again found free Negro citizens who were not gentle but who returned hatred with hatred and contempt with pride. I saw the stars and stripes waving over the bare sandbox, over the rough brick wall of a Negro school, I saw black children with text books, holding them fast in their arms, and others crawling invisible in the dust and stores full of energy, and bars for gloomy drinking binges, and the black chauffeurs of the *Sun Cab* taxis, who were not supposed to pick me up, and a black woman in a rocking chair before a car dump, strenuously trying to be a lady, a white lady with a flowerbed hat and a mink stole that looked mangy in the bright sun. I went to the train station buffet and drank a planter's drink, a strong cool rum drink, and then I sat down to linger in New Orleans, *"the Gay City,"* in the Negro waiting room, alienating the whites and the blacks.

The train from New Orleans to Houston, from Louisiana to Texas went through heat, dust, the sun's glare, an oil haze and a cooking jungle. The grass was burnt. The trees looked like decadent moss overcome with elephantitis; their leaves fell like gray, matted hair in a poisonously shimmering, oily pond. I thought I saw snakes and alligators, but it was only bright white birds rising up from the eerie ground.

The sun shone on the shiny train cars, shone on the brilliant twinkling metal dress of the parlor car, where we went to gobble our meals, bathing windows that were not to be opened in light. We were traveling in a rolling oven, we sat as if sunk in flames, getting cooked by the hour. The car's cherished air conditioner failed; it went on strike, it did not want to go on. I had expected it. I saw myself roasted and buried in Baton Rouge.

I had described Baton Rouge in a story. I had liked the name: red rod.

It had been Indian country. Now it was oil country. White aluminum tanks were brilliant as a mirror. Everywhere fire blazed on trash-covered earth; one burned some kind of residue from the refineries, heavy, sluggish smoke crept in thick clouds over the ground. Like sickly, soot-smeared dust-covered weeds, the red chimneys of tankers came up from the water of a canal that was hidden from view.

The Baton Rouge train station was empty of people. The oil-hazed, sun-shimmering air raised the buildings and tracks in a tired empire of dreams. A stack of newspapers yellow in the merciless light, the *Morning Advocate* of Baton Rouge. Next to the papers was a cut-out beer can; whoever wanted to read the Advocate threw five cents in the tin. The paper was a real provincial rag, but it was more substantial than the biggest German paper. The *Morning Advocate* brought news and reports, taking a look at the world, but its love was devoted to local events. Did they take themselves so seriously in Baton Rouge? A resident's birthday, a visit from New York, a school trip were all news, which were described in detail.

A Negro came and threw blocks of ice in a container beneath our wagon as into a pit of fire. Had I described Baton Rouge accurately in my old story? We drove slowly out from the station. The houses stood there, for miles around and set easily in the land, in the dusty green, sun-smoked atmosphere, like an eerie nature morte.[80] I had not gotten it wrong.

Once again mangroves and swamps and the canopy of a glowing sky. We sat sweating in our movable chairs. We spoke about Europe and America. It was easy to get into a conversation. The Americans were very friendly; they even tried to convince me that the terrible heat in the car was bearable. They were gentlemen. They did not take their jackets off and only a little bit did they loosen and adjust their ties. There were women traveling with us.

The women were amazing, they did not sweat, they knew no weaknesses, they had a good appetite and ate chicken casserole spiced with a red pepper like fire. The four women were tall as bean stalks, they wore flowerbed hats and were mostly dressed as if they were using a fashion magazine from a village following the latest collection of 1914. Although they clucked continuously like excited hens, they had horse faces, comically, and they showed their big yellow teeth. I did not believe that these women were the spouses of oil millionaires. But I pictured them as the inheritors of land, oil-producing and petroleum country, and that they defended this land, not giving it away for millions, but extracting gladiolas or radishes from the dollar-rich crumbs, letting ducks graze on the unused capital, and smiling at them in friendship.

The black attendant put a lock on the whiskey cabinet; we were in Texas, the alcohol-hating state of alcohol-loving people. Industrious steel arms were everywhere rising and sinking, pumping the land's richness into tubes stretching across all the fields. The suburbs of Houston were oil tanks, a shiny architecture but one that quickly grew tiring. Oil fires burned. Oil smoke once again sank heavily over the train. A single sky scraper towered over Houston,

---

80. *Nature morte* means "still life."

a hotel for oil dealers; like a modern knights' fortress the powerful building looked defiantly over the city, over the oil tanks, over the burning fires, over the war ships in the harbor and into the red evening.

I was in Houston only to change trains. As if the strain of the heat and the happily survived jungle trip had made us into comrades, the passengers of the old sun journey took me over to the great Santa Fe express train.

As did its name, the *Santa Fe Express* fulfilled all the boyhood dreams of the wild west, of Indian country, of trappers' trips, cowboy pastures, gold diggers' luck, desperado fate, and Gerstäcker, Karl May, Cooper and Sealsfield were traveling with us.[81] Finally I saw their rivers and their mountains, their prairies, their sky and their desert! We went over the Rio Grande, over the red Colorado River, we crossed the devil's canyon and looked at the death rocks. Before our window was the land of the Apaches, the steppe of the Pueblos, the desert of the Navajos, Texas, New Mexico, Arizona, we saw the blue forests, the blue grass, we saw the red earth of the red man, bush land, hardly any meadows, arid terrain of wind and sun, then a mountain range, stones, fields like mythic red mountains, like sky scrapers on *Fifth Avenue,* like the mysterious Inca castles, even like Greek temples, like the columns of Paestum and Selinunte, built through weathering, through the breath of storms, out of the muck of river floods, and I greatly admired those drawn here, coming by foot, by horse, in high-wheeled carriages, those men lured by gold, by the unowned land or simply by adventure, by the lawlessness or the endless distances, the heroes, those who died of thirst, the curious who died on the stake, the unhappy souls, those who had discovered gold streaks and been struck dead by false friends, I had not conquered America, even today, even from the secure train compartment America seemed, in its greatness, in its emptiness, its loneliness, its contrasts and starkness, its inhuman grandeur and natural infinity, to be unconquerable.

There was always a car to be seen on the horizon, struggling bravely and alone through the endlessness. Then a mysterious city of campers suddenly surfaced on the empty expanse. Hundreds of motor vehicles had ordered themselves into proper streets in the most inhuman landscape, it was a true life wonder, life setting itself up quintessentially, radio and television communication with the world and its ideas, smoke rose up from little tin chimneys, laundry had been hung between cars to dry, children had been born and they played among the wheels. Why did this town stay exactly here? How had its people, its car houses found one another, what agreement had they negotiated?

---

81. James Fenimore Cooper (1789–1851) was an American writer; Charles Sealsfield was the pseudonym of Karl Anton Postl (1793–1864), an Austrian-American writer who wrote historical fiction set in America. On Gerstäcker and May, see note 66.

How did they feed themselves? When would they move on? All these questions would remain without answers.

The train had sleeping cars, a salon car, a restaurant car and a car set up like the bar of a big drug store. One sat at a long bar and could watch the black cooks, how they fried eggs, brewed coffee, made toast, mixed milk drinks or one could look past this eating establishment through the window and into wide nature, which again was in and of itself here, not settled and subjugated by people. The restaurant chef was a man from Stettin.[82] He had emigrated to the United States before the war, working as a waiter, he had gone to the train in order to avoid becoming a soldier and having to fight against his old homeland. Already for fifteen years he had traveled back and forth in America. He had not become an American. He was married, he had children, he lived in Chicago. His children were Americans. He wore a Stresemann and looked like a bureaucrat from Bonn.[83]

Where were the original inhabitants of the land, where were the Indians? Along the way, a colorfully painted wooden billboard showed them in feather dress ready to do the snake dance. Get out, the billboard called, visit us. The train went by. After miles there was a town. It rested in a level plane of red stalactites, bizarre fossilization, which found its dusty green mirror image in lonely, strange cactus forms. An extended periphery of campers, car dumps, garbage mountains, oil trucks, tanks surrounded the community. From a little airport, close by the train station, a recreational plane rose up and seemed really to be climbing the empty space. The Arizona sunset transfigured this settlement, which in actuality was miserable. The sandy cactuses, the red rocks, the one-story white houses, even the trucks and the discarded rusted cars seemed to dream of the great manitu, and perhaps this place really was the Indians' heaven.[84]

In the twilight I believed that I occasionally saw high sharp-angled tents, believed I was observing crowds of riders, which the *Santa Fe Express* was following, on unsaddled mustangs, the war hatchet was swinging, but it was surely the silhouettes of the big cactuses that were deceiving me; and the red boulders built ever more mysterious domes.

It was night when the train stopped for two hours at Winslow's train station. A few steps from the train was *Main Street*, its flaring advertisements like a light, very straight dash. The station was built in the Mexican style and

---

82. Stettin, a medium-sized Prussian city not far from where Koeppen grew up, belonged to Germany until World War II. It is now a city in Poland, Szczecin.

83. The Streseman was a formal German suit, introduced in 1925 and named after Gustav Streseman (1878–1929), German Chancellor from 1923 to 1929.

84. Manitu, or Gitche Manitu, means "great spirit" in Anishinaabe, a Native American language.

looked like a backdrop for the film "Viva Zapata."[85] The hotel near the station, called "La Posadana," was also real and, at the same time, imitation Mexico.[86] Even the cactuses and the agaves looked artificial in the lamplight, as if brought by some prop director.

The hotel had dark, empty rooms; a flickering television screen, which no one was watching, ran like distant artificial rain, a tired ventilator hummed, tired rocking chairs were resigned in the equilibrium of still-standing time, a tired elderly bar woman looked without expression at the guest, and the dirty mirror behind the bar doubled the scene's sadness. "Can I have something to eat," I asked the bar woman. "Yes," she said, "in our coffee shop, but it's closed."

I strolled over to *Main Street*. Shady characters out of *High Noon*, extras from a gloomy happening, which could only transpire in a film, leaned against a wall of lime-white stone. They wore wild-west pants, wild-west jackets, daring wild-west hats, and their grimly resolute faces led me to suspect that they were afraid of themselves. I felt for them. What else could one do on an evening in Winslow other than be afraid of oneself?

The main street was before me, a little Broadway with its lit-up advertisements, but behind the colorful, flickering propaganda signs waited only one-story houses, set there like hurried, meaningless decoration.

There were hardly any people on the sidewalk. All the inhabitants of Winslow and its vast, unsettled surroundings seemed to be sitting in their cars, driving up and down the streets in an unbroken chain, like the buckets of excavators. Music sounded from the cars, jazz trembled, songs burst through. Good company, friendship, love, the instructions and social arrangements were experienced in Winslow on rolling wheels.

In Winslow there was the *Grand Café*, the *National Café* and the *White Café*. I chose the *Grand Café* and stepped into light, colorless neon light.

A wheat-blonde Arizona *maid*, in a tight sweater and tight jeans went on slipper socks of some kind, strangely plump like a hippopotamus, to a sparkling chrome jukebox and let Elvis sing. The *maid* wobbled with her breasts, calves, hard backside, dyed-blonde hair, and I wondered whether she was the beauty or the witch of *Main Street*. A family, a man with his wife, with his step parents, with his three little daughters, ate hot dogs with sauerkraut, I too ordered hot dogs with sauerkraut for a dollar fifty, and the man had a chubby, Mexican, very contented face, and one could see in him how delighted he was to invite his family for hot dogs and sauerkraut in Winslow's *Grand Café*. Had

---

85. *Viva Zapata!* was a 1952 film, directed by Elia Kazan (1909–2003), set in Mexico and with a screenplay written by John Steinbeck (1902–1968).
86. This hotel, which still exists, is called La Posada Hotel.

he not come far? I agreed with him. The proud diner paid seven times a dollar fifty, he laid hard earned money on the table, his callused hands betrayed this, that was the reality, and all the rest was deadened boredom.

It had probably occurred to some in Winslow to abduct the wheat-blonde wobbling woman from the café or to fight with the shady *High Noon* characters on her behalf; someone had certainly hit upon the thought, and then the victor would carry away the booty, would have the girl in his car, would drive westward and eastward with her on *Main Street,* letting her enjoy Elvis Presley while rolling along.

In a grocery store, a super market closed but lit with streaming light, a small, perhaps ten-year-old, very charming Japanese girl sat on the stacked grocery baskets and read a book and was in another world. For her parents the American dream had probably been fulfilled, they were Americans, they had become property owners, proprietors of the great grocery store of Winslow. What was the child dreaming about? About Japan? About the cherry blossom? About old demons? About the doctoral cap of an American university?

At this late hour small a pale boy was going through the town delivering newspapers. I followed him for a while. With a skillful swing the boy threw the newspaper to the doorsteps of the lonely houses, letting out a high shout, which I couldn't understand.

In the waiting room of the train station a real Indian observed the bathing beauties of a poster, which encouraged all the world to spend the summer in New England. The Indian wore a creased ready-made suit, which made him look stiff, as if he were cut from wood.

For a while the train passed through a Japanese landscape. Foreign evergreens stood with night-dark tufts of branches on gnarled boughs, extending wide, before the backdrop of a snow-covered mountain, which looked very much like Fujiyama. Then came a fossilized forest. Its red scaly stumps resembled fallen columns, and it could seem that one was going through a city of ruins, which was once of awe-inspiring size, perhaps with political power, destined to rule the globe and then destroyed because of the wrong decisions or because of word from an angry god.

In the morning light a lonely rider really halted on a steep ledge, hesitating before the awakening day, alone in a magic kingdom or alone there with an equal-born enemy, who was now, hidden from the rider's view, lingering in a similar way on another rocky plateau, wanting to look at the field clarified by early light and bereft of people.

America was no land of the masses. It was a land of loneliness, far and wide undeveloped for tour groups. The train passed through the desert while its passengers had breakfast. Twisted cactus trees beckoned like the ghosts of those who had died from thirst. An Indian woman stood by a can of milk, a red calico dress in the land of the dead. All at once an oasis ringed with bricks appeared like a fata morgana: bungalows, umbrellas, lawn chairs, a swimming pool with blue water, girls in bathing suits.[87] How did all this get here? A few steps further there were only stones, thorns, sand, vipers.

At the edge of the desert, forward-going attacking man was on the move: derricks, oil pipes, tanks. Then there were orange groves, a Mediterranean landscape. The San Bernadino train station looked like a Spanish cloister. A green that was polished and shining, lemons, oranges, oleander grew around it. The platform stood in the shadow of high palms. The sky was improbably blue.

A sturdy concrete waterless river bed, awaiting a terrible flood, accompanied us to Los Angeles, to the light creations of Hollywood and to the Pacific Ocean.

The sky was improbable, bluer than the sky over Frederick II's Palermo, it was higher than the Athenian sky in the golden age and more pure than the sky of the shepherds and the three kings from the East, it was the stainless expensive sky of the film operators, its ether was the domed horizon of a massive stage, and the sun made up the lights, which illuminated the decoration, the wonderful city of Los Angeles, the true home of the angels.[88]

The angels live in paradise, as is well known, and Los Angeles is an American paradise, it is the Garden of Eden in its last perfection.

Los Angeles, which is not a city but a monstrously spread out area of settlement with cities, beaches, gardens, valleys, mountains, is the American future, a place of promising. Los Angeles offers room, Los Angeles warms, Los Angeles has palms and fruit at the ready, giving as a gift dreams of Hawaii, of the happy island of Bali and of Metro Goldwyn Mayer. Los Angeles is the place where everyone in the United States, the peoples of Asia and Mexico aspire to be. Los Angeles is the city where the rich are gods, where the poor become rich, where the industrious relax and the old try to buy immortality, it is the happy community, in which the statistically average and model families already own two cars, two televisions, two refrigerators and here all blessings are doubled, if not tripled.

I stood before the administrative building of a well-known oil company, and it was the spitting image of the Ghent altar, made by the Van Eyck brothers, grown here to the height of a skyscraper.[89] Not without emotion I observed the dividend-carrying holy shrine. Golden lines pressed upward with gothic piety, leading up to the roof, which was crowned by a little Eiffel Tower, itself

---

87. *Fata morgana* is a mirage.
88. Frederick II (1194–1260) was Holy Roman Emperor and King of Sicily.
89. Ghent altar was a large and magnificent altar piece painted by Hubert van Eyck (1366–1426) and Jan van Eyck (1395–1441) and finished in 1432.

holding up a globe; below in the display windows, on street level, an exhortation to passersby, a supersonic hunter flew by with the company fuel, faster than the others, into the beyond.

In Los Angeles one loved above all to dress things up. The train station was built like a Spanish church, churches conformed to the style of businesses, a restaurant had been decorated as the historic site of Golgotha, cinemas invited customers in the form of Chinese temples, and one of the area's famous cemeteries was an expanded vocational school for the dead.

My path led me to a bible institute, and the building appealed to me because it was exactly like the Excelsior Hotel that Thomas Mann had described in Venice.[90] The institute was Moorish nineteenth century with minarets and towers for the edification of secret business councils, and above its entrance was written in iron letters: *For ever, o Lord, thy word is settled in heaven.*

I soon noticed a "Church of the Open Door," and its nave was a mussel-shaped room in a giant modern cinema set up by an architect who was both avant-garde and business savvy; where one expected to see the Almighty or the film stage one was staring at a map of the world that took up an entire wall, on which white and red bulbs were set on the globe like strategic points. Only three rather lonely lights were burning in Europe, while dark Africa was lit up by many little red lamps. Before this map, worthy of a general staff, a man stood, spoke, preached, he looked and was dressed like the manager of a big company, an extremely successful general director, a public-relations fox, who presented himself as unaffected, a good guy, although with every natural and studied gesture, with every spontaneous sounding and painstakingly considered word one could see through to the monstrous power, perhaps the power of heaven itself, that he was representing.

Whom was he influencing, whom persuading, whom did he recruit, baptize, confirm, whom did he save from damnation, to whom did he give last rights, whom did he send on into eternal life?

On the beautifully cared for, laboriously polished pews in the back of an otherwise empty room sat a pair of young people, whom I took for business students during a break from school. The students talked softly with each other, though not respectfully, and they ate bananas. It was unknowable whether they had come to the "Church of the Open Door" to listen to the smart preacher or to eat bananas.

Finally a big organ with all of Wurlitzer's sonic jokes boomed praise for the almighty God.[91] The pious efficient man was swallowed before our eyes,

---

90. Koeppen is referring here to the 1912 short story "Death in Venice" by Thomas Mann (1875–1955), in which the protagonist stays in the Excelsior Hotel in Venice; during World War II Mann lived in Southern California, not far from Los Angeles, in Pacific Palisades.

91. Wurlitzer was an American company that made musical instruments.

lowered down as if by the maw of hell. The white and red bulbs on the world map went out, and all the earth lay in the same darkness.

A shiny, elegant, flourishing store in this area of churches and businesses specialized in vitamin concoctions; despite the streaming sun, despite the cloudless blue sky everyone seemed to need the life-giving pills. Customers crowded around as if before a healing well, as if before the shrine of Asclepius, and they got just enough water to wash down their pharmaceutical boosters.[92]

I heard a waterfall pouring down, I heard the Niagara plunging in the middle of downtown Los Angeles, between the stores and the banks, and I saw the real water roaring over moss-green, magically illuminated rocks, over red and blue glowing water lilies, through the weathered fairy-tale fields of an old-fashioned toy landscape, until it divided at the entrance of a restaurant, where, as the advertising script announced, one could eat as much as one wanted and pay what one wanted.

I suspected that the establishment belonged to a Viennese psychiatrist, and went in invoking the holy Freud. Inside an organ boomed, as in the church, and the host's voice spoke from the wall, "Be strong, so that nothing disturbs the freedom of your spirit," and young girls came up to me and called out, "You need food for your soul"; and they led me swiftly, the beautiful houris, the communicants, to meditation and inspiration in the garden of Gethsemane, and the garden, you see, was right out of Hollywood.

In a circle of moved customers I caught sight of the Kidron River, the wondrous city of Jerusalem, the mountain of Golgotha and of three boys sleeping beneath olive branches.[93] A ghostly voice said: this is the night of Christ's crucifixion, and one was asked by the same voice not to smoke or to talk. An invisible boys' choir sang a song of heavenly joy, delicate-voiced church bells sounded, and we were let out into a self-service restaurant, in scenery giving the fake impression that the buffets, the tables, the chairs and the guests were deep beneath the sea floor, corals and seaweed slumbered at our feet, fish and algae watched us during the meal, which the biblical and maritime extravagance did nothing to justify, while over our heads glowing sunrises and sunsets alternated to the constant sound of the organ.

My spirit felt quite confused, my body regrettably unsatisfied, they seemed not to trust me at least with the pay-what-you-want, while a very strict old lady counted as exactly as possible what I had had on my table, and while she raked in my money, the full sum set by the menu, the saying sounded from

---

92. Asclepius is the god of medicine and healing.
93. The Kidron River runs through the Kidron valley to Jerusalem; it figures often in the Bible.

the host or from the archangel's mouth: "You have so much fault to find with yourselves that there is no time to criticize others."

The Broadway of Los Angeles is a street of warehouses. On Sunday afternoon it was occupied by a thick pressing mass, which wanted to spend its money. I stayed standing on a corner for a long time; I lingered in order to be amazed. I was aroused, I got excited; I was astounded by the beautiful, the free, the proud people, whose colorful, joyful show passed me by.

The Broadway of Los Angeles was no shopping street for the rich, it belonged to the people, I had never before seen such a people, whites of all shadings, Negroes light and dark, Asians yellow and brown, Filipinos, Mexicans, Latin Americans, Indians, old peoples, a new people, which looked beautiful, proud, uninhibited, free, stepping straight. The eternal sunshine, the warm air, which wasn't damp, the desire for mixing and perhaps the forefathers' efforts to reach these happy coasts as well, had brought forth a new race, which was only to be recognized still as black, yellow or white in origin, but no longer distinguished from one another in their life's joy; they had all grown bigger, more straight, more self-confident than their ancestors in the distant, forgotten or damned homeland, and what most amazed and delighted me was that they tolerated one another, they looked at each other in friendship.

The Broadway of Los Angeles was no street for prejudices, the crowd made no room for arrogance, the sky made a gift of joy.

Bananas grew in front of my hotel in the middle of the city, and a kind of Hyde Park life arrayed itself on Pershing Square beneath the broad, meaty leaves of the banana trees.

Wild orators spoke to little gatherings, reformers strolled hopefully up to passers-by, preachers of all skin colors stood, overcome by the Holy Ghost, on step ladders carried there laboriously they made rhetorical gestures, whispered urgently, they shouted themselves hoarse, but they all wanted the good, they were striving for holiness, teaching reconciliation, tolerance and friendliness.

In a truly moving manner Negro men and women pressed bibles to themselves like their most precious treasure; they displayed the text in a somewhat surprising way but always in a way one could love, and in their black eagerness, the holy book lifted to their breasts, they often resembled icons from the old Byzantine church.

Vagrants were gathered around these speakers and prophets on Los Angeles' Pershing Square. To me it seemed that they had found their way to the banana trees of the angels' city from all the states of America, even from the whole world. They were peaceful, friendly people, tanned by sun and wind, marked by floods of rain and by the endless country roads. Some of them seemed like old, though not grown-up German Wandervögel; they dressed themselves in the Steglitz style of 1900, going in jungle shirts, in short pants and in sandals, strumming guitars, they did not beg, they only took donations, they hummed songs, fifty years old and older, songs from "Zupfgeigenhansl."[94]

Their faces were amiable, at the same time deeply sad and obstinate after many blows from life. They were themselves white-haired, disappointed children, and there was something touching about them.

These poor and pure, who may have read too much Karl May or Hans Blüher in their youth, had their own bars and shelters among other impoverished folk, less spiritually pure, in the slums of Los Angeles, extensive like the city itself, in a street where those who hadn't found paradise in Los Angeles came to drink in very dark bars barricaded against the sun.[95]

Here one got Mexican food, hot-as-hell chili con carne served with red beans. I ate the dish at a bar, which belonged to an old, deformed Japanese, for whom his young blond waitress had developed such a passion that she had to stare at him intently and in her otherworldly state she confused people's orders. The Japanese man, unpleasantly, in a dollar-hunting way, returned this limitless love with caustic talk, his English words sounding like they had been emitted from an enraged parrot, while a few Negroes in overalls, a Central American with a scarred face and a dead-tired vagrant, who, I gathered, had once been a professor at a German university, indifferently gulped down their red pepper with cheap liquor.

There in a dirty street doorless shops, open day and night, well-proportioned exhibition rooms equipped with viewing walls, a rich assortment of pornographic newspapers and postcards were once again for sale, and these banal erotic dreams of the exposed next-door neighbor found their dreamy viewers and buyers, again it astounded me, even in Los Angeles, this free-living city, as in all of big America.

In the morning, fog and a light humidity pressed down on the city, by afternoon the sun was shining, the air was clear and pure, the evening brought the most pleasant cool, and the night glittered with strong, splendid stars in the ever cloudless sky.

The center of Los Angeles is not Los Angeles, however. Los Angeles is a province, a veritable city province and positioned all across the compass.

In this expansive area anyone who does not have his own car, and who has none to rent, is as good as exiled; even the praiseworthy community bus company cannot save him. The company's transportation map looks like the sewing

---

94. *Wandervögel*, a youth group promoting a return to nature, was founded in 1896, in the Steglitz neighborhood of Berlin; their songbook was called the *Zupfgeigenhansl*.

95. Hans Blüher (1888–1955) was a German writer and philosopher and a participant in the *Wandervögel* movement; Karl May (1842–1912) was a writer of wild-west novels much beloved in Germany.

pattern supplement of a housewife's newspaper, confusing, with lines crossing and running into each other, stretches of hundred-kilometer distances, but between the black dashes lie expansive white fields, unreachable areas for the carless, for those expelled from society.

It so happened to me that after my arrival in Los Angeles, not knowing its topography, I accepted a telephone invitation to dinner and then drove through the landscape in a taxi for over an hour and for twenty dollars. Through a wondrous landscape. With six lanes in every direction the highways swing like giant seesaws through an area of wasted space, human habitation and always more sublime, always more decorative nature. The *Harbor Freeway* seemed to be hung on the snow-covered Sierra Madre mountains. U.S. highway number sixty-six went through a real paradise; orange trees bent over it with their heavy fruit, and the floral magnificence of a tropical garden shimmered in transports of color.

And now seen for the first time! The sky, the waves, the beach, the high coast with its palms, its pepper trees, its carpets of flowers, even the lawns had such a strong coloration that I thought I was seeing light blue, true green, real red and a truly white beach for the first time.

The sea fulfilled all dreams of the Pacific Ocean, and looking directly across to China, to Japan and to India held a strange fascination for me.

On these shores America had already been wedded with Asia, and it occurred to me as I stood on this coast, when I saw the fast airplanes in the air, the great ships on the distant horizon that I was here at a new Mediterranean, before the natural cradle of a new great culture, that I was going along the edges of an immense field of political power, in which the future of humanity might be decided, a future of the finest development or of eternal damnation, and I asked myself whether this future might already have begun.

In the water, on the beach, on the paths, the broad boulevards, the gardens and parks were teeming with people, with people who had carried their heredity from Europe, from Asia, from Africa to these friendly coasts, with people who called themselves Americans though they were different from the Americans of the other United States.

Everywhere they were going around naked, their purpose seemed to be a game and music their continuous accompaniment, which they carried with them in small handy little bags; they had solved a problem, the problem of being in the city and being outdoors, of being workers and of being at leisure. The question of equality and of freedom was solved here in a happy manner. No beach was fenced in or closed off, there was only the entrance cost to be paid, there were no reservations for hotel guests, not a single tour group fell on happiness like a swarm of locusts, here humanity should sun itself, the poorest could come and go as they liked. Little boats thronged near the shore, and in them were not fishermen, sentenced to hard work, but people who had cast their nets for fun, into which the sea's inhabitants willingly leapt, as in some dreamland. Fishermen clustered at the Santa Monica pier beneath a sun that was warming but not burning. I saw Negroes, Europeans, Americans, Asians, I saw men, women, children, elderly, serious and comical and cheerfully tragic faces. They stood peacefully in a friendly proximity to one another, and the ocean was benevolent, it had a reward for everyone, each found his own fish; sea crabs, starfish and Pacific Coast spiders were raised up into a light that must have been horrifying to them, and the most unfortunate were already cooking, the seafood turning a kingly purple in big vats before the pier's food stands and restaurants.

What diligence had been conceived to entertain these people, to amuse them, to stimulate their desire, to take from them the pressing burden of time and loneliness! Everywhere great buildings tempted people, to walk in the shade for a change, to play sports, to go bowling, bowling tournaments had been arranged, a wide concrete space was there for people to go on rollers skates in their bathing suites, there was an ornate carousel, and on its white foamy-maned, smooth wooden horses the prettiest girls imaginable bobbed up and down.

Wrestlers trained their oiled bodies beneath the sun in pure, fine sand; strong men lifted up balls and bars, advertising their muscles in the suggestive manner of gigolos. A red-haired, voluptuous girl practiced acrobatic dance moves on the heroically majestic breast of an equatorial African, and when, because of exertion and exuberance, she gulped the air, she showed her older sister her tongue, like a snake, strawberry red beneath a lather of chewing gum.

Music floated over this earthly paradisiacal world such as no Gulliver had ever seen on his travels. The area that the eye and ear could comprehend was drenched with musical tones. Jazz flashed out from little bags, jazz flew out from the flamingly colorful juke boxes, which stood everywhere and were liberally used. Then, when the sun first sank into the West, into the sea's hazy perimeter, into its waves at sunset, the drumming began.

The drumming spelled out taps for the old Europe, it seemed to me, and nowhere in the New World was Europe further away. Negroes had gathered on the beach in the hundreds, they had brought high drums, and under the black, talkative, magical hands free, wild rhythms were born on the stretched skin, the old powerful voices of voodoo. And dark dancers stood up and listened to the compelling voices and danced barefoot in the sand, and suntanned girls raised themselves up and succumbed to the spell of the drumming and the lithe dancers, and I saw what I had missed in New Orleans, the slave rebellion, almost the Negro heaven.

From that wondrous place, Santa Monica Beach, Ocean Park, a little trolley went on soft rubber wheels, alongside the beach and the sunset, to an even more wondrous place, to Venice, and there Europe and the devil had crept into heaven, in Venice they didn't lie out in the sun, in Venice they were reflective, in Venice they didn't cultivate and strengthen the body, in Venice they neglected the body, they ignored it in the medieval manner. In Venice they weren't friendly, they didn't smile; in Venice they were furious. They also played jazz in Venice, but not because they found it fun or exciting; in Venice the music was something sacred, then it was an expression of revolt and finally it was an occasion to ponder the architecture of the fugue and the mathematics of world destruction. Every trombonist in Venice was Kierkegaard, who had been thrown existentially, Sartre-style into this hell and was crying out from it.

For Venice was a hell, sprung from the brain of a real estate speculator who was probably crazy, who wanted to build an imitation Venice, with palaces and canals, with a St. Mark's place and a Doges Palace and a Campanile, and everything from cloth lath and plaster, postcard true look of the beautiful model. The speculator failed, went bankrupt, left behind ruins of yesterday, half-finished, buildings that had no renters and graves, in which water and garbage festered.[96]

These vaults of impotent romanticism and dead rebirth, which stayed cool and damp even in California's warm climate, now attracted the tired or the defeated generation, *the beat generation,* as they called themselves after their testament, Jack Keruoac's *On the Road,* a bohemia with two dead gods, Charlie Parker, who died of morphine, and James Dean, who died in a car crash.[97] They hadn't grown up in Venice, they didn't dress themselves up, they had renounced the State Department, the Pentagon, the refrigerator, the television and Hollywood once and for all, and so the movie business was just about to discover them. But film and fame were neither here nor there, they too, these tired figures, were America, they proved that also in the New World, as in the Old, usually at exactly their great cultural moments, there were people who could renounce the Madison Avenue ad agent's desk chair or the well-paid positions, which provided for old age and for widows, in television, in the universities, in schools and in the Washington bureaucracies, people who were ready for spiritual rebellion and for the negation of conformist thinking or not-thinking, not dissolute, not satisfied but ascetic and hungry for life. Venice

96. Koeppen is referring here to Abbot Kinney (1850–1920), who studied in Germany and was enamored of European art. His Venice of America, which opened in 1905, was, as described, a failed attempt to build a Venice in California.

97. *On the Road* was, in context, a new novel, published in 1957 by Jack Kerouac (1922–1969).

was soil, nourishment for trees, from which the institutions and, as it goes, the new conformity will eventually pick their fruit. In a room behind broken window panes or with windows boarded up with wood, in ruins as if after an earthquake that had destroyed this imitation of reality in movie-making land, they sat morose, disheveled and dirty with their slender beer bottles and their recorded jazz that sounded like strict old church music, perhaps it would have delighted their ancestors, the Puritans.

When the door to this hell of enraged hermits and nihilistic revolutionaries was opened, one looked, as far as the eye could see, out to a fence, behind which a new speculator, probably no less crazy than the first, had erected a monstrous Luna Park.[98]

And then there was another Venice, less hell-dark but also terrible, inhabiting a square that was really almost Italian, not the splendor of Venice, but with a Southern poverty and Wailing Wall grief, residing in small hot guest houses and cafeterias reeking of fat, on many of the cloudy window panes sickly looking Hebrew letters were written. They were Jews from Europe, who had saved themselves from the raving monster by going as far West as they could, stranding themselves forever on the Pacific Ocean, old people, teary women, beaten-down men, dreaming of Breslau, of the Hausvogteiplatz, of the Prague old town, of their old Vienna neighborhood. They sat timidly, shriveled by fate, reflecting each other's sorrow on little marble tables and on marble benches. The country's friendly sun was shining on them, but I feared that it did not warm these refugees, who also didn't see its light.

Hollywood Boulevard, Sunset Boulevard, Wilshire Boulevard, Beverly Hills, the villas belonging to those shadows on the screen, mile-long, strangely senseless seeming street cars, highways, bravely crossing over each other and coupling on the open fields, cement visions of a future architecture, parkways that reminded me of the Riviera and of Sochi's Black Sea coast, then the walled-in sites of the dream factories, the Hollywood strip with the most expensive restaurants in the world, the bars for the extras smelling of ketchup and powder and the girls who've run away from all parts of the earth to make an American movie, all this big and famous Hollywood is, when you have a car, the most boring place in Los Angeles and, when you go by foot, the most stressful. Again and again I wandered through unbuilt areas and past uninhabited gardens. The land seemed cheap, it seemed to be wasted there, but it cost a great deal. Many buildings were tall, they were small skyscrapers, soaring bravely into the blue sky, but even on the grand boulevards one-story, barrack-

---

98. Hermits could also be translated here as anachorites, or *Anachoreten* in Koeppen's German, who were early Christian ascetics; the first Luna Park, which became a popular name for amusement parks, was in New York's Coney Island and dates back to 1907.

like buildings, looking like their owners had run out of money for the tower of Babel, stood next to the skyscrapers.

Daytime, I observed older women more than anyone in the Hollywood streets, not very well-off representatives of the middle class with correspondingly modest flowerbed hats. With wishful disapproving looks, the women scrutinized the fashion store displays, which offered skillfully cut copies of Parisian tailoring, patterns sewed so one could be naked in them and so no one could be noticed. The women didn't buy the refined dresses, and I have no idea who bought them. In the empty stores, between racks and mirrors, waited women who looked like hunted but still prosperous Russian duchesses or like actresses who had once appeared with Sarah Bernhardt.[99]

The flowerbed women then turned their attention to the display cases of the many photographers, who made their living in Hollywood by producing so-called artists' postcards for people wanting to be in movies and considering themselves lucky to have arrived in these vanity cases. One was opposed to such ambitious stupidity, but the women may not have seen this as stupidity, they seemed strangely to like these compulsively smiling provincial faces, which would never light up the movie-theater night. One clever photographer had specialized in portraying children as little stars, and the mothers brought their children to him with evident desire and hope, and truly the flowerbed women were charmed by the likeness of such youthful affectation.

In almost every building there was an institute offering dancing, acting and singing lessons, and one of the brilliant displays promised an especially successful enterprise, to teach charm, to improve one's natural posture and to bring the underdeveloped aspects of female attraction to full flower. I saw the pictures of the charm students in the entryway, as they had first come to the beauty master, poor and without any of Venus's attributes, wallflowers from some Main Street, and then one got a look at them, hardly transformed to the impartial eye, equipped with all attractions, which make them desirable and irresistible in the institute's estimation, with more studied posture, raised breast and practiced charm, though before and after as deformed as saved, those on display smiling with the same ambitious and striving stupidity. There were a dozen beautiful girls on all the Los Angeles beaches, and on Hollywood Boulevard those who had come up short wanted their revenge and they wanted to sit in the light.

The life of those actually crowned with cinematic fame, the fairy-tale existence of the world-famous shadows seemed to play itself out entirely in automobiles so big that one could sleep in them, live in them, resolve problems and even make love perhaps.

---

99. Sarah Bernhardt (1844–1923) was a French actress.

In the fortresses of their mythic popularity the chosen and the world-famous drove by Grauman's Chinese theater, whose Chinese funhouse rococo
appealingly recalled the early days of movie making, in front of it the idolatry
of flickering figures has been cast and set in concrete and one can admire
the footsteps, the sweet hands, the meaningful script and the bravely curving signatures of the great cinestars preserved for eternity, united with such
earth-shattering expressions, exclamations and dedications as "*Love to you
all*," though I sought out and failed to find among all the beloved concrete
squares, which looked like thespians' grave stones, the characteristic name,
saying, hands and feet of the singular geniuses who had created the medium
of film. Charlie Chaplin had not been memorialized in stone, perhaps he had
not loved everyone and Mr. Grauman enough to be remembered and they
wouldn't have to drive past him, the new dream figures, who no longer make
one laugh, they raced to the valley in their hundred-horsepower cars, to look
after their rights and their bank accounts, driving undeterred and untempted
past those eating, drinking and sinning stations holy to the readers of film
magazines, the Brown Derby, Romanoff, La Rue, Scandia, which from the
outside all looked like the mess halls of some poor postwar era, like barracks,
though inside they were laid out with maximum opulence, traps for the children of Texas oil millionaires and managers' widows, the lights led through
the door of the entryway, greeting its public with glowing porcelain crowns.
Here one could speak with the boss about money and about one's share, estab-
lish the percentage of one's earnings, creaming off the best, sticking it to the
company, and then it was back to the big cars, to the accountant, to the real
estate agent, to the money manager, and always the same conversation, money,
percentages, investments, amortizations, and in the evening they drove home
exhausted, aggrieved at Hollywood and at a world enslaved into worshipping
them, back to their villas, entirely un-American in their whiteness and lying
in sub-tropical flora on their hills, surrounded by high walls, and they weren't
especially fine, not as the fans reading the postbox names had hoped; in West
Germany every mid-level factory owner, every director and statesman had a
bigger house.

Only in the Beverly Hills Hotel did they celebrate the high society Hollywood life so eagerly depicted on the screen. The swimming pool, the terrace of
rocking chairs, the bar, the restaurant were ready for business, ready to begin,
but again it was only the film city's secret kings, the accountants, the real estate
agents, the bankers, a group of managers gathered for a conference, here they
arranged the high society of artists, constituting their reality from the model
afforded by the shadow plays.

Hollywood lived its most exciting hours after midnight. According to local
law alcohol could no longer be served, the orchestras were silent, the dancers

had taken off their makeup, the waiters had made their final calculations, their guests felt unburdened or socially elevated, and then countless little sports cars buzzed and raced through the world's most spread-out village, darting like lit-up insects over the hills and through the valleys, screeching on the boulevards with their overextended brakes, stopping at the big nighttime newsstands with all the major American and European papers, and in a beautiful, well-stocked bookstore, open at night, they met for free literary and arts talk, taking in the newest from Paris, London, Rome and perhaps from Munich as well. It was the Europeans chased over to Hollywood who were here with their nervous enthusiasm, those from Europe who had become restless Americans, the assistants to the directors, the screenwriters, the gag makers, the second cameramen, the film city's inner emigration meeting up near Genet and Beckett, making plans that Hollywood's bankers would never finance.[100]

At the end of my visit to the empire of shadows I stood, a man on foot, a shipwrecked man, alone on a street still lit by advertisements.

The last night bus had failed to come, the automobiles of the restless and the sleepless whistled happily though mercilessly past me. Finally a taxi appeared and was ready after long negotiation to return me to my downtown Los Angeles hotel. We used a highway streaming with light, to its side stood motel after motel, hostels and hospices for car drivers. Dreams were also fulfilled in these buildings, set up like airy summer homes, sporting many lamps, one was in Hollywood, one was breathing in close proximity to the great screen storms, one could drive into bed with the car, but sleep wasn't so desirable, for sleep meant relinquishing one's dear friends, and here an eternal Venetian night beckoned at the film city's edge.

The motels gleamed in the light, the guests sat on terraces and verandas as if on little stages, in courtyards open to the street, beneath garlands of light bulbs, palm fronds and ripe oranges, and I believe I observed happy nomads, wandering actors acting themselves, and again it was Kafka's America that I saw, it was the big world theater of Oklahoma.[101]

After the city of shadows I was drawn to visit the empire of the dead as well, the famous city of graves described so magnificently by Evelyn Waugh in his novel *The Loved One*, presumably with much ironic and grotesque fantasy.[102] But after I had seen the Hollywood cemetery and the green hills of

---

100. Jean Genet (1910–1986) was a French writer, and Samuel Beckett (1906–1989), an Irish-born writer who lived in France.

101. Toward the end of his novel *Amerika*, Kafka refers not to Oklahoma, but to the big world theater of Oklahama. In Koeppen's text the word Oklahoma is used.

102. Koeppen is referring here to the 1948 novel, *The Loved One: An Anglo-American Tragedy*, by the British writer Evelyn Waugh (1903–1966) and available in German translation as *Tod in Hollywood* (*Death in Hollywood*).

Forest Lawn, after I had driven on the beautifully curving Cathedral Drive and Westminster Road, past the mountain of memories, the hill of meditation, the grass of inspiration, the brook of loyalty, the pond of mercy, the flowers of eternal life, the bordering haven of peace and sun sleep, vesper land rondels, dream land, baby land, lullaby land and through the bushes of whispering grove, I was exhausted and overwhelmed and I had to admit that Evelyn Waugh had not discovered anything, not invented anything—it is impossible not to write a satire of Forest Lawn. At first glance, however, Forest Lawn gives off the gently moving, calming, harmonious beauty of American cemeteries: suitably simple white grave stones on well-tended grass standing on green slopes beneath wide crowns of trees.

Forest Lawn has the effect of a dream become reality, a confectioner's dream of a peaceful place in the form of a sugar cake. And in reality, the man who had thought up this cemetery, who had created it like the lord almighty, had called himself a dreamer and was a skilled businessman blessed by God.[103] In front of the big mausoleum in the middle of the park I saw a marble plaque several stories high, almost as big as a skyscraper, behind which only a Cecile de Mille's version of Moses' tablets could be concealed, and it proclaimed the cemetery builder's faith in a happy eternal life, lived out in the subdivisions of his enterprise best recommended for this purpose.[104] "*This is the Builder's Dream, this is the Builder's Creed,*" so went the last sentence of the pompous confession and in front of this Hollywood gospel there stood, day and night, in sunlight and in starlight, all through the year, looking on in amazement, in a posture of high emotion, a little girl and an even littler boy and a little pug-like dog fashioned from plaster.

I couldn't fend off the shameful suspicion that the builder and dreamer had obtained this cute ensemble from a Moscow factory, the one that supplied all the Russian culture parks with plaster figures. But this was the only sign of Bolshevism in Forest Lawn; the graves were intended exclusively for capitalists.

In the Church of the Last Supper liveried servants, resplendent from head to toe, welcomed me and led me to an auditorium resembling a movie theater with comfortable leather chairs. A blueish light went on, the visitors' faces went pale as they encountered the first breath of Forest Lawn's eternal beatitude, and an organ spread its festive sounds through the room.

Behind a big black curtain a tape recorded voice rose up, like the angel of the annunciation, and spoke about the dream and the proclamations of the

---

103. This builder was Hubert Eaton (1881–1966).
104. Cecil B. DeMille (1881–1959) was a film director; his film, *The Ten Commandments*, came out in 1956.

builder. Then the voice, switching over from its angelic tones to those of a business conference, narrated anecdotes from the life of the great man, how he had seen Leonardo's Last Supper in Italy and decided to bring it over to Hollywood's dead. After these words the black curtain spread apart and, as heavenly choirs rejoiced from powerful loudspeakers all around, I saw Leonardo's painting lit up and cinematically magnified, in the form of a movie poster slide.

The dreamer had brought home much of value from his European journey. Not only Leonardo but also Michelangelo had appealed to him, and so he placed David in the harmony department and Moses on the low-cut lawn of loyalty. The builder had gotten the inspiration and the model for a round temple from Rome and from Scotland and England the pattern for old, fully furnished village churches, which in Forest Lawn stood beneath a piece of real highland heaven; this gifted and resourceful man did not hold himself back from serving as a patron of contemporary art. In the crucifixion hall he had given the place and the inspiration for America's biggest religious painting, titled simply "*The Crucifixion,*" "*longer than a twenty-story building is high,*" and "*this dramatic presentation is given from 11 a.m. through 5 p.m. on the hour.*"

The crucifixion was in the best Hollywood style of the "Ben Hur" and "Quo Vadis" directors, and to those interested, to those who wished to lie in peace in Forest Lawn's good society, it offered the pleasant certainty that Christ had died for them and will resurrect their beautifully bejeweled and privileged corpses, unlike the decomposed flesh that Matthias Grünewald had painted.[105]

But more than anything I was struck by the buildings in which the richest of these wealthy dead had prepared for their sleep and their blessedness. The rooms were marble and suggested the safe-deposit vault of a great bank and simultaneously a modern freezer. The dead rested securely in lockers, behind bronze doors decorated with golden laurel wreaths.

From many of the shrines came a soft and romantic music, Mozart, Haydn, La Paloma or even Schoenberg, for it was one of the builder's dreams that the dead, when they were still alive of course, could buy a musical subscription for eternity, for two hundred years, all paid in advance. In the cool passageways, transfigured somewhat horribly by music, there were open bibles of marble, and a "*Lady of Florence,*" also made of marble, sat in a grave-cold armchair, dressed in the turn-of-the-century style, her posture casual.

As I was leaving this cemetery of the comfortable dead, I read the just motto on its door: "*Visitors are reminded that Forest Lawn is a Sacred place.*"

The garden of Gethsemane as a strangely busy, modest restaurant, the dead garden-gnome un-holiness after the visions of the great dreamer, there on the edge of Los Angeles, still belonging to the city and incorporated into

---

105. Matthias Grünewald (1480–1528) was a German painter.

it, two bus stops from Pershing Square, two hours through the oil fields, oil camps, desert and through settlements looking like they were blown together from sand, two hours under the clearest sky, in the purest sunlight, *Knott's Berry Farm*, an artificial ghost town, a beloved destination, a drugstore in Gold Rush style, the costumed wait staff forced to perform a honky-tonk song-and-dance, and then what was probably most beloved of all, Mickey Mouse's expansive, palisade-defended empire, Disneyland, an instructive funhouse display, a morally pure fairground, the friendly or terrible past that was only viewed humorously, a comforting optimistically conceived, purely technical future, as if all problems were to be solved on other stars, the scenery from all the Walt Disney films, approachable, set up like an ice palace and unmoving in its essentially primitive naturalism, entirely alien to fairy tales; didn't all these sites in beautiful Los Angeles, the comfortable dances of death, the kitschy paradises, the false inspirations for sale, the clichéd meditations that were sold, these sites and the love for them, spring from the same desire, an effort to flee from time, from discontent with the passing hours, an oppressive, unbearable fear of death and the despairing desire for bourgeois longevity, for beatitude and eternity in lived-in clothes and familiar furnishings?[106]

In Los Angeles they were ever ready to dissolve reality, although small, shabby, visible ghosts always turned up beneath the blue sky, perhaps because the sky was too high, the sun too warm and the reality more horrifying and much harder to grasp than the dreams, the clothes and the scenery.

Real and eternal and heavy with the future, this was how the ocean's coasts and beaches struck me. I found a piece of reality, of life not yet made into theater, in Little Nippon, Los Angeles' Japanese neighborhood, where small Japanese men, lost in thought, drank green tea in the lacquered fronts of clean homogeneous shops. Reality, averse to scenery, was life in a church on the old square near the train station, where very, very poor Mexicans led their children to communion and the poor little girls in long, dragging, white bridal gowns, wrapped in blowing veils were married off to a poor life in Christ. Reality was the drilling towers for oil around Los Angeles, reality the airplane factories with the mile-wide starting places of the wonder pilots who tried out the planes, reality the lonesome, phallic tower on the Paloma mountain, not far from the film decorations, from which one can look furthest into the big secret, and in fact the desert was immediately behind the city, the infertile dead land, on which the weapons of our destruction had been tested.

The daily train from Los Angeles to San Francisco went along a proud coast, hanging over precipices and splendid views, revealing a fetching Riviera, which in Europe would have made travel agents and hotel owners delirious.

---

106. Disneyland opened in 1955.

How many hotels, resorts, pleasure palaces, shops, kiosks and camping places there were to set up here, how many beaches to fence in for profit, what waves, what surf and what forests these were to administer! How easy it would be to have a full season on this warm sea, in this mild air, and to get thousands of thank-you letters from satisfied customers.

But in America one encountered once again the absence of people, un-settled broad beaches, unused paradisiacal bays, look-out points that had never been climbed up to; a postcard beautiful nature, ready to lift the hearts of every travel company, still resting in the innocence of the first creation.

Sometimes the train went over rocks that plunged down to the sea, and there was the Pacific, visible and beyond measurement like an unsoiled blue carpet.

The company in the parlor car was sleeping, the backs of their chairs put far back, sleeping the sleep of the just, or they were leafing through the surpris-ingly cheap newspapers and journals, thick as an address book and with an amazing amount to offer.

The United States was and remained in all its parts the homeland of the literate.

It was raining when I arrived in San Francisco. The blue sky had stayed in Los Angeles.

San Francisco is the older of the two cities, proudly calling itself the queen of the Pacific Ocean and looking down on its younger sister, which had grown too quickly and had given in to the movie business; Los Angeles, however, had set its stock on the future, while San Francisco is one of the few places in America with history and tradition, a natural, sheltering harbor, discovered by adventurers, criminals and dubious nobles, an old secure refuge and proud polis, connected to the past, to what cannot be repeated, and even the earth-quake, one believed, once one had wandered through the city, will not happen again.

San Francisco was built on steep hills, not like Rome on seven hills, here they could be a hundred. So it had always been, wherever one saw the city, like a painter's beautiful vision.

The taxi climbed up the street, the tall houses climbing along on both sides, it was so steep that I feared the car would fall back and we would tear down the slope, and at the top I saw, behind houses and hills, the sea, the ocean and the bay all around, at this hour, as a full sun broke through the rain clouds, it was lizard green, and then it became steeper still, almost turning us over, and then down, it was a trip through hill and valley, a roller coaster ride, which one enjoyed best when using the old San Francisco cable cars, justly famous, with their airy, amusing cars they clattered up to new heights, new views, new crashes and new charms.

The sun was not victorious. It rained steadily. The hotel had a small garden courtyard. It belonged to the hotel bar. The rain beat down onto the over-stretched awning. Cages full of colorful birds hung on bamboo poles. The birds cried out. A young Chinese woman came, a sweet child's face, her tight skirt slit high up the thigh, and brought whiskey.

This drew me to Chinatown. I studied the city map. I hurried up and down the hills. I feared that the rain would cloud Asia, but to the contrary it made the neighborhood, so foreign to strangers, even more cozy, more Chinese, the lamps more aglow, the houses and shops more like temples, the roofs more like pagodas, the street signs more like the eyes of foxes and lynx, and which made more mysterious all the faces, all the voices, all the playing children, pretty as puppets.

The food was served with grace and with chopsticks. Of course there were also places for Americans and for visiting groups, but others, in side streets, cellars and courtyards were a piece of the real China, they were the foreign and attractive land of the dragon, and it smelled yellow and red, of old fans, it smelled of river god legends, of silk, of tired mandarins, of calligraphy, of wisdom and the spicy, slightly sour aroma of soy sauce.

To the left and the right the Chinese were eating happily, sitting at long tables, they were workers, handworkers, small business folk, they were Americans no doubt, it was not easy for them to earn money, but they paid it out for this meal, and then a sisal carpet on the steps to red light, to smoky candle air, Chinese music and recorded songs stirred thoughts of Kin Ping Meh's symposia, and in reality the morally inclined American club and flowerbed-hat women of the yellow society could have attended these symposia.[107]

They were industrious until late in the night, all the stores were open, all the food stands attended to their customers, the names of Chinese newspapers were called out, people sang and telephoned in Chinese, a cinema played Chinese films, Chinese dancers made an appearance in richly embroidered robes not at all exposed, mahjong stones clattered behind thin venetian blinds, and there was only one thing that seemed entirely un-Chinese here, a Taiwanese general who, with a tight-lipped face, was driven through the cheerful streets in an American military limousine like an evil god.

There was the chance for other encounters at the edge of the Chinese domain. Immigrants from the Mediterranean played bocci on lively streets, throwing the shiny ball, getting excited, getting fired up, singing Italian canzone. Singers in silly long-skirted evening dresses were festive, Spaniards

---

107. Sisal is a plant fiber used in China, and elsewhere, to make carpets; *Kin Ping Meh* or *Jin Ping Mei* is a sixteenth-century Chinese novel of manners.

complained about the melancholy of Madrid bars, sailors from all the harbors of the world looked for girls and consoled themselves with whiskey and gin, as for some reason there were no girls.

The international zone, a small, very shabby Reeperbahn, a preserve of strippers, was unlit this evening, deserted, as if destined for demolition. Next to closed doors, pictures meant to entice you in, naked skin made from paint showed cracks, rents and flaking like some ancient painting of hell long kept in darkness.

The tired, beaten generation had its place in San Francisco and in this area. *The beat generation* was in an even worse mood on the delightful San Francisco Bay than in the dungeons of the Pacific Venice; they were entirely turned away from the world and totally anti-American.

Their hangout was a dirty room, in which three unusually tall Negroes made music that sounded like shooting. The guests dressed in stained sweaters, regardless of their gender, they despised the hairdresser and the comb, the girls did without lipstick or used it clownishly; all stared with a fanatical gaze and with the apocalypse in front of them, it was only a lemon-colored, bitter beer that nourished their drunkenness.

Only one, a loner among the uniformed nonconformists, who had dressed himself strangely like a gentleman from a Rubens painting, he wore high spurred boots, a sword, a velvet skirt with a dirty white lace collar and a turned-up worn-out hat, an ostrich feather waving above it. This bizarre anachronistic knight had an unpleasant shrill voice, he strutted from table to table, coming also over to me, saying he was from Chicago, had fled Chicago, had fled Chicago a hundred times, and then he drank down my beer, and I honored him with a new glass, for I understood this late descendant of Rubens to be a touching, if unattractive, personification of the great American loneliness.

On the streets a bit further on, past philosophical cats, tolerated here as they were in Rome, was another of San Francisco's Bohemian bars. It was called "Poetry" and was a little literary bar, which belonged to a fat Italian, who stood behind his dirty bar like an obese, bloated yet sensitive newt.

His guests were the city's young poets. The young poets had the faces of Caligula with the head of Heliogabalus or the young Nero, and as I entered their hut they were pelting each other with peanuts.[108] The floor was covered with nutshells and sand. A torn-open piano, stripped of its wood, stood there so nakedly that it resembled an abstract representation of itself. On a nightmarish painting a hand clung tightly to a wall, grasping the red stone despair-

---

108. Caligula (12–41 C.E.), Holiogabalus (204–222 C.E.) and Nero (37–68 C.E.) were all Roman emperors, none of them pleasant ones.

ingly, and the painter had captured exactly the moment when the hand was giving up, exhausted, and coming loose from its last handhold, succumbing to an invisible but unspeakably terrible fate.

Newspaper clippings decorated the walls next to this portrait of deeply felt angst; headlines like: Nixon Stoned in Peru, Why Do They Hate Nixon? shrieking their fleeting excitement into permanence in this room, overpowering the artistic proclamations, the poetic manifestoes, the programs for new "isms" written out in green ink and the many invitations and announcements, which suggested connections to the university, where the creations of the disgruntled young were printed, brought out and discussed.

The university in San Francisco was Greece, it was Hellas beneath the Californian sun. The university was in Berkeley on the other side of the Bay, and I drove over the water on a kilometer-long suspension bridge, trembling in the air and swinging in the wind, over the most beautiful natural harbor in the world, through an oft-praised panorama that truly didn't disappoint.

San Francisco and its skyscrapers were behind me, carried by its hills, in the morning sunlight, a golden city in a landscape from antiquity, and water, earth, air and even the works of man appeared so pure, so light, so shining that it was almost difficult to believe in their presence, and they carried one's spirit into a dream of the past or a dream of the future. At this moment I felt as if Sicily's gift to Goethe was being given to me: the clarity of the sky, the breath of the sea, the aromas into which land and sky and sea resolved themselves into *one* element.[109]

An American university is overwhelming. It is more overwhelming than the abundance of the stores, than the highways of the big cities; the university's wealth makes the European feel poor. It's not a showy wealth, it's self-evident, showing itself in the extensiveness of the lay-out and in the overall generosity of the university domain, in which the pathways, the roofs, the trees, the shrubs and even the air participate. In general it's not the state that builds these splendid universities; their riches derive from foundations, donations, which can fund the most obscure kinds of scholarship, a fine example of American idealism.

Berkeley is a little town or Berkeley is a big park, in which the academy buildings stand white and proud, buildings of which Athens could only dream. That is the external image: light, airy lecture rooms, institutes that are little fiefdoms, libraries that, as always in America, awaken my envy, administered with the greatest liberality, their stacks accessible to all, their offerings ready to be used, the reading rooms, work rooms, and always, for European eyes,

---

109. Sicily was the highpoint of Goethe's trip to Italy in 1786–1788, chronicled in Goethe's *Italian Journey*, which he published in 1816.

astonishing amounts of space, and outside the lawns, trees, shaded pathways, benches, steps for leisure, for conversation, for thinking. Perhaps I was deceiving myself, but I saw the students, I saw Alcibiades, but I didn't meet Socrates who had inspired them.[110]

When I was in Berkeley everyone, professors, students, boys and girls, were streaming into the Greek Theater.

The theater was more real and more perfect in its proportions than the old buildings in Greece, in Sicily and in the South of France, only the stone seats and the stage had been so freshly washed that they aroused the suspicion of disinfection, from the unquiet spirit and the knowledge of tragedy. The establishment could be the center for cult worship, and it was glorious; it was a foundation of the newspaper magnate William Hearst.

The students were attractive, they had candid faces, they were casually dressed in white t-shirts and creased pants. I had sat in the topmost row, I could see the gathering and the landscape, from which cypresses emerged, intensifying its Mediterranean feel, over to the Bay, the image would have pleased Apollo. But it was Billy Graham who appeared, the successful itinerant preacher, the public image of morality, the evangelist, as he called himself; they had come to see him, to hear him, sitting in this Greek curvature, though I don't know what Apollo would have had to say to him, Graham and his preaching, his virtue and his gospel seemed to me like a not quite first-class refrigerator.

The preacher wore a blue suit, and in it he seemed to have two personae, sometimes the head of the YMCA, sometimes a very efficient businessman, a market researcher, a propaganda man; this was how he started, but in the course of his address, his holy preaching acquired the hectic gestures and the hysterical, cracking voice of the political agitator, the evil drummer, and for a while I shocked myself by asking whether I was listening to America's future Hitler. His thoughts were banal, par for the course, his intentions and his goal were vague, as they had to be, and he was popular, which was where the danger lay.

Would he be raised up on the shield? Did they accept him as their leader? Not in Berkeley. Here the students swear him no loyalty; after an initial curiosity, quickly satisfied, they talked with each other, laughed rudely, made dates with girls and ate hot dogs, which in a single moment were in all hands, as if by magic word or by sabotage, disrupting the leader's applause points.

I saw Billy Graham once more. I lay in bed, and he visited me. He appeared as a television star. He was brilliant on television; not only his face but also his voice seemed polished. His public relations agent introduced him. What skillful direction! Unassuming, excellent adaptation to a television audience. Noth-

110. Alcibiades was Socrates' student.

ing more of Hitler, hysteria and demagoguery. An insurance professional was trying to persuade a modern company, rationalized from a salesman's point of view, the advantages of gaining assurance from the Bible Incorporated. It was religion hour for cool calculators.

The United Stocking Manufacturers, who had gathered in the hotel for a conference, could be heard for a while in the small courtyard's bar. The small Chinese woman with the split skirt and the child's smile darted from table to table, friendly and in something of a rush. The effort of clothing legs had brought on thirst. The wives of the stocking men sat in the lobby. I was struck by their social discipline. There were some young, very pretty, probably even married women among them, but they were already wearing the flowerbed hat and subordinating themselves to the leadership of their old sisters, positioned higher in the nylon hierarchy. Old or young, the women stayed up til long after midnight, they were at the conference for themselves but also with their spouses, they concerned themselves with relationships, steered along the careers and the popularity of their husbands, doubtless they acted in the firm's interests; and it was explained to me that the big commercial and industrial companies advised and influenced their employees in choosing a wife and in their marriages by using psychological tests.

On soil so prepared, Billy Graham may indeed be called to higher stations, it seemed to me, and I changed the channel, choosing another program and saw people who were determined not to laugh. They were people from the public and had been seated upon a throne of sorts. Then comedians appeared before them, fresh guys willing to pull out all the stops to get these people to laugh. They were brutally seductive, in my opinion they insulted the character of these willing sacrifices, who expected money if they could survive the round with a straight face. The ones I saw all laughed in the end. I couldn't understand why they had lost the competition. I would certainly not have laughed. I would have stared back at the offensive, stupid seducer and would have gotten the money. But the program directors knew their collaborators and their viewers better; to me these directors seemed to be outstanding psychologists.

A professor had been recommended to me. I searched for him everywhere in Berkeley and didn't find him in the pathways or the academic buildings. Finally I asked about him at the information bureau, where an extremely helpful Chinese woman worked at fulfilling visitors' wishes. This Chinese woman did not wear a split skirt or have a child's smile. She was feminine in the American way, efficient in the American way, social in the American way; she was star-spangled proud and believed in the good, which is also the useful. She tried to organize my itinerary; she made a phone call, let the distant response sound on in vain and acquainted me finally with a young Negro, praising him for having won an athletic prize. The young man wearing this laurel wreath led me with

Olympian steps. Had he held a torch, he could have stepped from a Pompei-
ian wall painting. He had the genius' light foot; though sadly we couldn't find
more to say to one another than that the sky would probably stay blue.

This was how I reached my professor's door, he had left a note saying he
would be right back, and he came breathless from a quick run, he had been
in the library, to educate himself on his visitor, and he had actually found
something about me, this time I was the victim of the astounding American
library system, the professor confronted me with my old thoughts. The room
was a small library as well: walls of books and a window to the green campus.
An American scholar's cell: here one could work, one could think, one could
converse. The professor invited me to the cafeteria. With the students we ordered a rice curry, got strong coffee poured into heavy cups, sat down with the
others, sat and ate without embarrassment, jokes were exchanged, teachers and
students behave courteously toward each other, I liked it all very much, and
when the professor mentioned that he would be coming to Munich to learn
about the new German literature, I offered to make introductions for him, but
the scholar had Geibel and Heyse in mind, to whose graves I would not lead
him, and so in the end I understood Berkeley to be a university not unlike the
German universities.[111]

But in the offices of the university press, having attentively gone through
the catalogue, I once again saw what a fine refuge the United States had provided in the years of the latest European blackout. Great names could keep up
their research under the Californian sun, and now this free press was printing
books of notable exclusivity, books that were impossible to sell. They showed
me a two-volume, beautifully made work on Johann Gottfried Herder, which
would hardly have found a publisher in West Germany, and I believed that in
Berkeley they would have hired and published Nietzsche, had he lived in the
madness of our times and had he been homeless.[112]

The part of Berkeley that didn't belong to the alma mater was a sandy dusty
street, in which nothing was happening and on which one had to endure a
long wait for the bus back to San Francisco, nearing despair at the thought
that it would never come.

An evening before the bay. The cable car carried me, lifted me up the hills,
taking me down into the friendly valleys. A robust camaraderie prevailed
among the passengers. The trip was a Southern Oktoberfest.

---

111. Franz Geibel (1815–1884) was a German poet; Paul Heyse (1830–1914), a German
writer. Koeppen is frustrated by this professorial interest in less-than-major figures from the
past.

112. Johann Gottfried von Herder (1744–1803) was a German philosopher; Friedrich
Nietzsche (1844–1900) was another German philosopher, who spent much of his life outside
of Germany.

I went to Fishermen's Wharf. Street musicians were playing. Young people. A big choir. Their straw hats recalled the business in Rüdesheim's Drossel-gasse.[113] But it wasn't so bad: the musicians were far and wide the only ones making noise. Only the seals were crying out more powerfully. Their hoarse roaring barks touched the heart. The poor animals lay in a narrow container, surrounded by the sun's last rays as if by an oven's embers. They were hungry. Their owner had put them next to a vending machine, which, when you inserted a dime, gave out tiny little bags with dead, stinking fish. You were supposed to feed the seals with these fish. Their noses pressed greedy and damp against the bars that closed off their container.

Fire was burning everywhere in redbrick stoves. Fish soup was cooking in shiny gold copper vats. Huge crabs, sea stars, sea urchins and sea spiders lay in purple-colored broth, ready for the connoisseurs. Families refreshed themselves; they camped on the curb of the street. At a little stone marina they were swimming before white sails. Out in the bay was the friendliest of islands. At the fishermen's wharf they had pay telescopes, with which one could bring this sweet island closer and observe it.

Seen through strong lenses, Alcatraz was not at all alluring. It looked like a factory, whose walls had a sinister aura; one could have concluded that dangerous explosives were being produced out there, for security reasons in the middle of the water. Alcatraz was the most feared prison in all the United States, the dungeon of those sentenced for life, the last station for those on death row, and as we stood in freedom, the taste of fresh shellfish still on our tongues, looking over to the barred windows, we saw a prisoner whose execution had already been called off six times at the last minute and who had yet to be pardoned.

If you took the looking glass from your eye, the island and the bay were once again brilliant and beautiful. This was how distant paradises could deceive.

A kind American, a young lawyer, unbeholden to me except for wishing to be friendly to a foreigner, drove me to the other side of San Francisco, to the open sea.

We saw the houses of the rich, villas, row houses, flat-roofed, suited to the landscape, covered in Mediterranean green, airy, modern, reflecting a feel for building.

We entered the Golden Gate Park on a far-Eastern moon bridge, we saw real Japanese temples, and Japanese girls in Japanese gowns beneath Japanese trees offered us Japanese green tea.

Nobody was swimming in the sea, which was warmer than the North Sea in August; they were swimming in a heated pool behind the beach, and the

---

113. The Drosselgasse is a touristy street in Rüdesheim, a German city on the Rhine.

water was so clear that you could see all the divers, like dancers, hanging in some strange element.

On this coast one's glance swept less freely over to China than it did in Los Angeles. Battleships stood gray on the horizon. A submarine burst from the deep like a water-spouting whale, exciting a little zeppelin so much that it exercised a terribly complicated maneuver over the waves. The round aircraft drew close to the submarine, and one couldn't tell if it wanted to kiss the black steel fish or to gobble it up.

Alone again, I went to where the poor lived, long gray streets, freezing despite the sunshine.

Sailors who had not seen a ship for a long time, men who had dressed themselves as gold diggers or trappers, victims of the Gold Rush who had come a hundred years too late, they were all begging. A one-armed vagabond with Verlaine's touching physiognomy but with an empty face moved in on me with a drinker's self-assured instinct.[114] We went into a bar; like all real hells it was long and narrow as a tube. San Francisco's failures stood shoulder to shoulder. The liquor burned as if it had been peppered. The Salvation Army was across the street; it was in a poison-yellow house. Before the house, a man with a peg leg was going back and forth. He was dressed like a pirate. I thought about Stevenson's *Treasure Island.* The peg leg was both real and unreal. It was unclothed. With his arms he begged with intimidating gestures.

In the Hotel Netherlands wretched Asians sat in a store window. They looked as if they were for sale there, but no one seemed to want them. There was something rare by the garage: black prostitution. She had lost all her black beauty. *"Entertainment for the Esoteric"* was written on the dirty glass door of a red brick building. I rang the bell. I was all too glad to acquaint myself with this entertainment for the esoteric. But the entrance remained barricaded.

Beneath an overhang Negro boys were getting their heads shaved by an old, embittered, white-skinned barber, whose cradle may once have stood in friendly Copenhagen. Their laughter was garish and menacing, as if they were only getting their hair cut to annoy their elders and to gain revenge on all the whites.

I sought out San Francisco-style jazz. It was there. It was ascetic, it was gloomy, it was meditative. It was better suited to New Orleans than to the California freedom.

In a jazz workshop, in a black coffin illuminated by a single candle, a bass and a piano conducted a judicious dialogue, and their masters, two dark men, reminded me of the Imperial Crypt in Vienna, for they made music in the

---

114. Paul Verlaine (1844–1896) was a French poet whose experience of poverty and whose alcoholism were a part of his literary legend.

manner of two long embalmed Habsburg emperors, placing demands on the world, despising the world and subject to the rules of strict ceremony.[115] Two tall daughters turned out to be waitresses and looked, in their striped chemise dresses, like two worried moths who had mistakenly flown into a hell. The listeners were Negro and white; they sat in equality on hard stools and, black or white, they looked seriously and sadly into the flickering flame of the lone candle.

Another cult locale for San Francisco jazz was *The Black Hawk,* the black hawk, the black trickster. *The Black Hawk* had a *jam session* on Sunday afternoons. Whether hawk or trickster—its nest was black and it stood exactly like a coffin in the dazzling sun.

A quartet was playing. The black men had priestly, Assyrian beards and were dressed as if they had done their shopping on London's Savile Row. The men's hands were graceful, exceptionally delicate, and the sounds they created seemed to express an ultimate, excessive sensitivity. They too were not playing to entertain but to edify their cloister of skeptical intellectual Trappists.

This style was in open contrast with *The Black Hawk*'s commercial practices. Here there were no tall daughters, no stray moths, but waitresses concerned with turnover. This led to conflicts with the audience, which did not concede anything to the simple ideas of business Americans.

A woman was there in a fur hat despite the summer heat. Her baby-doll dress flowed over her swollen body. She couldn't pay for her drink; she had forgotten her money or she didn't have any. She was punished, removed from her table to a chair by the cash register, where the fat owner of *The Black Hawk* dallied with her, first angrily and then with animation. A young lady expressed in her beautiful unornamented face the bitterness of amaryllis, as Rückert had described it in his famous poem.[116] She was clearly rich and cultured and she regarded life without joy, traveling alone. She reminded me of the bitter girls in Carson McCullers.[117] Then I saw a Jewish face. It was a woman's face. It was disfigured by terrible scars, as if squeezed out of its form by vicious force. The Jewish quality in this wounded countenance was its pure spirit; it led one to think of crucifixion and resurrection. The beautifully made-up mouth of a very dainty Negro woman was a red bloom above a plant-green shirtwaist

---

115. The Imperial Crypt, in the Church of the Capuchins in Vienna, is the Habsburg dynasty's burial place.

116. Friedrich Rückert (1788–1866), a German poet, wrote "Amaryllis" in 1812; amaryllis is a flower native to South Africa, and the poem concerns a man in love with a cruel woman, his love likened in stanza XLI of the poem to "sweet poison" (*Mir ist vor deinem süßen Gift nicht bange!*).

117. Carson McCullers (1917–1967) was an American writer who specialized in down-and-out characters; Koeppen may have her 1940 novel, *The Heart Is a Lonely Hunter,* in mind here.

dress. A very serious Negro couple who, man and wife, looked like pessimistic philosophers, had come and sat near me without saying a word.

Meanwhile, in their *jam session* the quartet's black men had found themselves with white colleagues. The whites kept rhythm with their feet and wanted to fly into an entirely unimpeded joviality, but the blacks remained motionless, dark pillars of holiness, far superior to the others, subjecting their notes to the strictest ritual.

I didn't want to leave San Francisco; it was a place to stay.

One could easily linger at the *Top of the Mark,* the tower bar of the highest hotel on the highest hill in San Francisco, something sensational for nightlife and for tourists.[118]

One swayed as in a balloon gondola over the beautiful public. Amused, well-dressed guests. The food was French. They laughed and talked and looked with cries of joy into the shining night, to the noisy, whirling city, running over hill and valley, they looked out to the bay, the lights around its shore like glowing strings of pearl, one recognized the ocean on the rocket emblems of the battleships and the military jets, one drank a cocktail and forgot that, notwithstanding all its lights, the earth was a dark and unexplored star.

The city beckoned friendliness at the moment of farewell, as the next morning I took the ferry across the bay to the Oakland train station. The hills beckoned, the houses beckoned, the cable cars rang in a continuous party, the sky was shining. All the Chinese and Japanese were smiling, all the beggars, the pirates, gold diggers, the peg-legged, all the bars' Verlaine-faced regulars, all the rich ladies and gentlemen at the *Top of the Mark* called out *good bye,* even the most serious high priests of jazz looked young as the morning, and the young poets in *Poetry* did their best to do the same.

The *California Zephyr,* the San Francisco-Chicago Express, with a to-the-minute connection to New York, was among the greatest of train trips, hurrying from the Pacific to Lake Michigan in forty-eight hours, and I was in my little compartment, in the thick air of the cleaned shiny silver can-like wagon, which passed through a continent, through America, and despite the artificial atmosphere arranged for on-board conditions, designed for maximum comfort, despite the glassed-over look-out area, named the dome, on the top of our car, despite the bar, café, restaurant and club room, I felt like Jack London's railway adventurer, as we went through the land of the Indian wars, through the hunting grounds of the Sioux, the land of heroes, of scouts, of leatherstockings, of conquerors, of the last of the Mohicans, past the scattered traces of wagons, of the historic trek, of the postal carriages protected by riders but

---

118. *The Top of the Mark* is still in business.

attacked nevertheless, over the Sierra Nevada, through the salt desert, over the Rocky Mountains, past the memories, the ghosts of those who had starved to death, who had died of thirst, those who had been killed, this was rattlesnake country, bow-and-arrow country, spear country, this was the paradise of buffaloes, wild horses, grey bears, here arched the great Manitu's sky, here the sun heated the purgatory of lost sons, we reached Sacramento, the gold-digger city, the American River of the first prospectors, here rice was grown, Japanese worked overflowing fields and exported the corn to Kobe, to Yokohama, to Hong Kong, to the homeland, the old, hungering rice lands, and there were peach trees and canning factories and once again there were oil speculators' shacks, ghost towns, desperado villages, reminders of Bret Harte stories came into view.[119] Feather River Canyon, blue mountain ponds, in which the colorful stones and the somber pine trees were reflected, we stopped in Portola, the sky was clear, smelling of yesterday, of freedom, courage, independence, the adventure of the snow-covered Sierra and the giant forests, this was the America of discovery, the continent without borders, the ravines of danger, the valleys of lawlessness, the mountains of traps and furs, rivers of gold and of death, for dinner there was oyster soup and roast Brazilian chicken, an extra-dry martini, whiskey, juices, ice-cold fruits, the night came, the bed rocked on its springy steel, the battle of Red Mountain, the attack on the Virginia range, dreams, children's stories, films in a suburban cinema; I got up early, went to the look-out wagon, the crew was still sleeping, the head waiter slumbered in an easy chair up in the dome, a wide, cheerful African face, a father's face, a citizen's face from the black neighborhoods of Chicago, we were shrouded in morning light, aurora, a sun that came up fire-red against the train, we were in Utah, the Mormons' state, barren land, God's kingdom, the great Salt Lake was shining, its shores covered with brine as with brittle ice, a gong was struck, waking the sleeping man, he was distraught to see me, the black professional face, the dark smile, the readiness to serve gathered together slowly at first (and who knows from what dreams), a copper mine appeared, a crater, a pair of houses, a work road as if on the moon, we had reached Salt Lake City, city of Zion.

The Mormons, the saints of the last days, says the American Encyclopedia, are a religious sect founded in 1823 by Joe Smith, after having tried several professions in New York State, Smith saw an angel on the Cumorah hill in Palmyra and dug up holy brass plates, covered with a script that he could not read; among his discoveries were miraculous glasses, named Urim and Thummim, with see-through stones rather than lenses, which enabled the unknow-

---

119. Bret Harte (1836–1902) was an American writer who set many of his stories in California.

ing Smith to understand the mysterious signs, revealing the future to him. In 1830 Smith went among the literate and released the English translation of the plates titled *The Book of Mormon.* The book is astounding, a mixture of Jewish and Indian sayings, falsified, copied from obscure novels, tainting the late-to-literacy man who had assembled them with the charge of plagiarism, but in real life the Mormons' story was one of grandiose drama, oppressive tragedy and astonishing success.

In the early morning, having stepped out of the *California Zephyr,* I could believe the tragedy. The very success of Salt Lake City seemed a tragedy to me. After I left the train station and went with a taxi through comfortless dusty streets, in which the desert heat was rising, even though the sun was hardly up, I no longer believed in the existence of the joyful beautiful train, whistling its departure, the dear *California Zephyr,* it seemed a hallucination, and I had the feeling that only Kafka has described of being forced to stay in Salt Lake City.

The heat of all earlier days boiled in the Temple Square Hotel; the hotel was narrow, built for a small town, one couldn't get away from the sun. In the Coffee Shop the waitress looked peroxide blonde rather than pious, she was in a bad mood and so was anyone, apparently, who had to get up early in Salt Lake City and to eat breakfast in the Temple Square Hotel. The food and the drinks had an insipid aroma-less taste.

The Mormon temple across from the hotel resembled a supernatural vision; with its six towers set into the façade of a three-story apartment building the temple could have been the dream of mid-level bureaucrat working for some heavenly post office. I didn't know which letters God would answer. He seemed to bless the tribulations of serious business folk.

I went to *Zion's First National Bank* to cash a check, but Zion's first bank, which looked like all other financial institutions in America, namely granite-hard, was closed.

The sun was burning. On a one-tone commercial street, provincial to European eyes, there were no trees and no shadows. The cars and the employees going to their offices looked morning-tired as they did everywhere else and not particularly otherworldly. The girls were pale but, as usual, they were made up, ready to be charming and to spread joy with their appearance. Were the Danites still going around, the angels of destruction, the secret thought police of the Mormon priests?[120] In a warehouse window was a shadow man of black paper, whose outline reminded me of Kohlenklau, our old comrade-at-arms, and beneath him was a book, *The Naked Communist.*[121]

---

120. Danites, at first a fraternal organization, later became a term for militant Mormon groups in the first half of the nineteenth century, whose survival was a matter of legend.

121. Kohlenklau, the coal thief, was a propaganda figure from World War II-era Germany, intended to teach Germans to use less energy; Willard Cleon Skousen (1913–2006), an Ameri-

I wanted to tour God's city and went to the travel agency. A laconic man said to me, "in the summer?" I asked: "and what season is it now?" "Winter," the man said. The sun was burning. The thermometer neared a hundred degrees Fahrenheit.

I went back to the temple. A few visitors, looking like vocational school teachers on holiday, strolled through a dusty meager park. The windows of the temple looked dead. Only the managers of angelic service have the keys to holiness. They were not in. Perhaps they were in Zion's first bank, tending to God's mercy.

In this area of temples the great tabernacle was indeed accessible, a circus-like building with a big and beautiful organ, on which an organist, diminutive among a choir of organ pipes, played Robert Schumann's "The Prophet's Birth." Had Schumann thought about Joe Smith? Had he known about him? Would he have praised this temple and this city in the desert?

I visited the Mormon Museum, where among the touching, modest, entirely quotidian objects of memory, only there because they were from the great Mormon pilgrimage, I realized that Salt Lake City, a city that I didn't like, was a place with tall buildings, businesses, schools, a university, all kinds of industry, a city of wide-ranging if provincial character, only a hundred years old, for they had first come to the Salt Lake in 1848, after their deportation, their expulsion from Illinois *"the beautiful,"* as a picture in the museum put it, and then they were in the wilderness, in the desert, a great journey, men, women, children, their carriages laden with household goods, and they had gone hungry and thirsty, and many died under the strict discipline of this new Moses, yet they did not abandon the belief, the mocked, perhaps stupid belief in Joe Smith and his angel's message on brass plates, and then the miracle happened, one had to recognize it, here, in a dry desert of salt and stone, on ground that nobody wanted, Brigham Young, their leader, as Smith had already died, said "this is the place," and it was the place, a desert place, a presumptuous challenge from God, and they stayed, and Young announced: "this desert shall bloom like a rose," and it bloomed, if not like a rose, then with gardens and crops, and a city of one hundred and twenty thousand arose.

In the museum I saw Brigham Young's marriage bed protected and displayed there, a petit-bourgeois rack only good for the necessity of sleep and for God's own progeny, Young, who looked like a small-town banker, had had nineteen wives, his settlers he had called them, and on an 1897 photograph, as the city was already growing, the work already blessed, I saw the surviving

---

can writer and conservative, taught at Brigham Young University in the 1950s and was the author of *The Naked Communist,* a collection of communist writing (intended for anti-communist instruction) first published in 1958; he also wrote a book titled *The Naked Capitalist.*

Mormon pioneers, those saved from persecution, veterans of the great pilgrimage, hard, tanned godly white faces devoid of smiles.

The sun was burning. Salt Lake City was a city in an oven. So much holiness, so much strictness and so much heat depressed me, I had to drink something, but they told me that in law-abiding Salt Lake City strong drink was only available in government-run alcohol stores. I went down the shadowless street to the government-run alcohol store, and intimidated figures, granted no respect in Salt Lake City, were shuffling around a counter in an office. The man behind the counter subjected me to an inquisition, asking about my eye color, counting my hairs, weighing me on a scale, and then he gave me a license that allowed me, once a week for up to a year, to obtain a bottle of liquor in the new Zion.

The bottle protected in my arm, I walked the shadowless way past sleepy little shops to the train station.

At this time the train station was also lost in deep sun dreams. It looked as if no train had visited it in years. At the counter I knocked on the glass, an official came as if from a deep sleep, and I asked him about the *California Zephyr*. I was worried about the train coming on the next morning and taking me away from Salt Lake City. The official said, "There's no *California Zephyr* here. I've never heard of it." I responded: "I got off the *California Zephyr* in this station a few hours ago." The official shook his head earnestly, "You couldn't have gotten off the *California Zephyr*. I'm telling you it doesn't exist." I had a presentiment that I was K. from Kafka's *The Trial*, I was the surveyor from *The Castle*, I was the country doctor following the wrong people, and there was no way to set things right. I turned pale, and the official was human and had compassion for me and revealed a great secret to me: only a few steps down the shadowless road there was another train station in the Mormon city, and perhaps, perhaps there they knew about the *California Zephyr*.

The second train station resembled the first as one egg resembles another. It too seemed to be sleeping in the sun, but it slept at the expense of another railway company. They knew my train here, and the official assured me that everything was alright. By noon the morning's taxis had disappeared. I staggered from one house's miniscule shadow to the next on my way back to the Temple Hotel. Those who met up with me looked like dwellers in the underworld.

In the hotel lobby, heated by the desert air, the guests were watching a distant baseball game; they were in the prophet's hot breath or already in purgatory.

I secured some ice and some publications from the Temple and went to my oven-like room with my whiskey. I looked out the window to the bare salt mountains, which were like sparkling sun mirrors. Salt Lake City was roasting like an egg in a pan. I pulled the drapes shut, but they were hardly any protection against the glaring rays of merciless light. I lay down on the bed, mixed the whiskey with ice and rejoiced that I was on the holy city's list of drunkards. I read the treatises of the Mormon printing press. I fell asleep reading them and was in Brigham Young's marriage bed with nineteen Mormon wives, who had settled down next to me, and Joe Smith appeared to me with a glowing sword.

In the evening a General called me. The General had heard about my stay in Salt Lake City, and he was an American and a very kind General, who wanted to show me the city.

We drove to the monument, to the historical site, "This is the place," where Brigham Young stood on a base in a patriarch's godly robe with his traveling companions before a still bare mountain reddening in the evening light.

Salt Lake City lay at our feet, a hundred years old, it filled the great salt valley, it was green and blooming, roofs were laughing, chimneys were smoking, the faithful had extracted a homeland from the stony earth, they had harvested and shown themselves to be charitable, they had been the first to send care packages to hungering Europe, to a destroyed and ostracized Germany, and the General said that Salt Lake City was a fine city, a community without slums and with only seven hundred and fifty Negroes.

We went slowly through residential neighborhoods, driving in the General's beautiful big car and we saw American peace, American happiness, an American ideal realized, nice, one-story houses on green hills or on even lawns, trees giving freely of their shadows, nothing fenced in, a great neighborliness, a single normal family, nice, pretty children who resembled one another, dogs and cats similarly taken care of, grass that was everywhere trimmed, cars that were everywhere washed, the building style, the plans for building, the furnishings, the music that was played, the abundant food on the table, *grand dad's* comfortable rocking chair, everything fit together like two shoes from a pair, and I asked myself whether there are people drifting through this well established, friendly neighborhood, doubtless always ready to help, who prefer not to fit in and who let their lawns grow wild.

The kind General drove me back to *Main Street.* Its advertisements flashed as in Sodom and Gomorrah. Zion's fist bank also could be seen, flaming and promising interest in the night. The General and I shook hands, and I went down *Main Street,* going back and forth.

The sidewalks were empty; only two cinema sales counters enlivened the street, two glass boxes, simply placed before the theater on the street and in which the sales girls were locked up like Snow White in her coffin. One Snow White smiled as I went past, but the other Snow White, fully aware of Zion, gave me a black look.

In a drugstore university students, nocturnal and unrighteous, sat at a long counter, Salt Lake City's young intellectuals, spooning up a pale ice cream they had dipped in a foamy red, aroma-less sauce.

My whiskey drew me to the Temple Square Hotel, which gave me the gift of restless sleep.

The *California Zephyr* had me back, holding me in its artificial environment on the next day's early morning, I had escaped Salt Lake City's furnace-like heat, and the sun had a friendly shine.

The *Zephyr* was fleeing to the East, rolling toward Chicago, we crossed the River Jordan, the great salt valley, in which despair had overcome the angel's pilgrims. Cracks went through the gray earth like trenches, and the beautiful train, the railroad tracks, the train's messaging system gave the impression of being unreal and unbelievable in this landscape; things and people were specters, and the salty earth and thirst and death seemed to be the only reality.

Rocks formed the *skyline* of a ghostly skyscraper city, a Manhattan without life, then came the Green River, and the powerful Colorado Valley was around us, towering over us, building itself up over us, as we climbed up its reefs, seeming to sway in the air over the river, whose water was forever timeless, pre-historic, a friend only to the adventurer, the red stones rose up like totem poles, building themselves into monstrous castles, powerful forts, fantastic palaces, and nowhere was there a human being in sight, it was entirely beyond belief that the train tracks had ever been laid down, in the club wagon a flowerbed-hat lady read "The Miracle of Lourdes," though not the one by Luise Rinser, the train's stewardess went coolly through the car, blonde-haired, dressed in zephyr-blue, manicured, made up and painted, what was she actually doing?[122] An older man spoke about Hawaii, where his travel agency had sent him, "I'm telling you, it's heaven on earth," here was Death Valley, a ford for dead horses, serpents, a tunnel, wounds exploded into the rock, the heights of the Rocky Mountains, anchored in nothing, bridges swaying over chasms, we were climbing, corkscrewing into a valley, and we reached the city of Denver, which was lying in mist.

It was humid in Denver. It was darkening into night. Air as in a kitchen heated with coal soot. On the platform stood a young woman. She looked frail, though without moving she held on her arm a fat boy dressed in a wild-

---

122. 1958 marked the one-hundred-year anniversary of sighting of the Virgin Mary in Lourdes; the book Koeppen saw on the train is Ruth Cranston's *The Miracle of Lourdes* (New York: McGraw-Hill, 1955). Luise Rinser (1911–2002) was a German writer who published *Die Wahrheit von Konnersreuth: ein Bericht* (*The Truth of Konnersreuth: A Report*) (Frankfurt am Main: Fischer, 1954). Rinser's book is about the Catholic mystic Therese Neumann (1898–1962), whose Bavarian village of Konnersreuth was, like Lourdes, a site of pilgrimage.

west outfit, wildly shooting with a water gun, as she bade farewell to her husband, leaving for Chicago and already thinking about his business. The heavy boy hung on his mother like a vampire.

The city, as far as one could see from the train station, looked like the setting for a horrific detective novel. The houses were ugly and seemed to be enemies of one another. In the sky a thunderstorm gathered, reddish, sulphurous yellow and leaden.

The *California Zephyr* pushed itself slowly into a mechanism for washing, past rotating brushes, cascades of soapy foam and rubbing towels, emerging shiny, hermetically sealed, a little earth satellite, indifferent to everything but its travel plan, ready to travel on into the night.

With the new sun came another landscape. We went through farmland, wheat land, through corn-yellow grain factories, and past properties that looked like the big German farms, the house cowering before the wind, as in East Frisia, the stables under the trees as in Holstein.[123]

Chicago had eaten far into the land around it, in hundreds of satellite cities and thousands of satellite suburbs. Streets of elevated or depressed anarchy, at once monochromatic and wild, ran past us, rejoicing when they could join up with highways, jumping up over the present like visions of the future, but Chicago had projected itself furthest into the countryside in its used-up cars, we were welcomed by mile-long cemeteries of distended sheet metal.

I stood high above Lake Michigan, it had a silvery surface, a playground for wind, as big as an ocean, the other shore was invisible, massive cargo ships completed the horizon, and behind them had to be Canada, the continent's great Northern empire, which had not known the ancient world or the middle ages; white sail boats were rocking in the foreground, and from their decks Chicago or Manhattan could be seen, a line of the most powerful skyscrapers, competitive with New York's *skyline,* though on this shore and on this territory luxurious greenery had sprung up left and right, trees grew, flowers bloomed, parks enticed, which did not correspond to the popular images of Chicago.

In a fourteenth-floor office, its windows affording me an expansive view, a community plan was covered with extended green dots. "We are a city of parks," said a man who was showing me around. "And the green districts?" I asked. "Slums," he replied. "We're eliminating them, we have the biggest *slum clearance program.*"

The man was a Chicagoan and an idealist. Only in Russia have I met as many idealists as I did in America; I say this without mockery, and it seems to me the biggest, perhaps the only hope for our world's state of confusion.

---

123. East Frisia is a region of Germany on the North Sea and Holstein a region in the north of Germany.

Chicago is a white and a black city, it has the biggest Negro population in all America. The blacks have migrated from the South to the North, fleeing the cotton fields for the factories, from discrimination to equal rights, and one day this migration will be comprehended as the South's loss; once again the South will lose the Civil War.

In this Chicago idealist's office Negroes and whites work together. They worked in the same room, sitting across the desk from one another, they ate in the same cafeteria, everything smooth, taken for granted, a good working environment, as they say.

Yet it was a Negro who explained to me: "Wonderful. But would my colleague Smith introduce me to his sister?" I answered: "But you're working with Smith's sister? Perhaps she's your secretary." The Negro conceded the point. "But," he added, "after work she gets into a different bus." He wanted to say that she left for another world, she lived in houses, which in Chicago would not be rented to me either.

The idealist said: "Look at the big picture, we're not Al Capone's city, we are not a zone of speculation, we don't just have slaughter houses." He wanted to say that we're making efforts, we have achieved a great deal, and in our city the future will be beautiful.

For me Chicago was a backdrop for Theodore Dreiser's novels, author of *An American Tragedy*.[124]

I went to the Loop, the business center, enclosed by the old elevated train tracks as by a lasso. I walked among the skyscrapers.

What distinguished a street in Chicago from one in New York? Unlike New York Chicago was not cozy. Chicago was hard. Chicago was not cheerful, it was serious. The wind that came over Lake Michigan was not the sea's lively breeze. Its gusts contained the threat of tornado in summer and of blizzard in winter. The wind spoke of harvests that were either too rich or too poor, from years that were too fat or too thin, it came from the grain provinces, but it also knew about soil erosion, was acquainted with despair and with hope and was therefore sober and capable of remaining calm.

Everything one could desire was in the store windows. The department stores stood tall.

But everywhere alleyways extended out from the streets of commerce and exchange, strangely neglected emergency exits from the business life. Here the facades were black, the fire escapes stretching grave-black or fear-red to the ground, and on the pavement was garbage that interested cats and old people, men and women, poor in a peculiarly American way, and each with some-

---

124. *An American Tragedy* is a 1925 novel by Theodore Dreiser (1871–1945), the beginning of which is set in Chicago; Dreiser is a writer very much associated with Chicago.

thing grotesque about his clothing, men with women's hats, women with men's boots, with something dictated not by need but by eccentricity or perhaps by perversity, the grotesque element was there to clarify the isolation, their status as outcasts, as step children, to compel this clarification of their status, as I had already observed among the Negroes.

The nexus, the high temple of business, the fabled land of speculation and of an eerie, anonymous dominance, bringing poverty and war and making life more expensive, was the Board of Trade, Chicago's grain market, the world's greatest bread company.

It was an imposing building! One first encountered it as the base of a deep canyon of streets. One had to look high up to it. In its pathways one walked as if through a mountain range.

As I came to the stock exchange, I thought that they were beating each other, or they were simply communicating with each other.

It was a market. Despite all the perfection, all the communications technology and global interconnectedness, despite the invisibility of things and of money, things and money replaced by little scraps of paper, it was an old market, and buyers and sellers stood in their pits, on eight-cornered risers, the corn pit, the wheat pit, the soy bean pit and the pit for cotton and oats, as der Billiger Jacob had once stood at his market stand.[125]

They worked, they created, they earned, esteemed citizens, big businessmen, fathers, brothers and sons from the best families, shrieking like madmen. Telephones were ringing right and left, the telegraph and ticker sounded front and back, it was a spider web, spanning the earth, and I watched them as they received, observed, registered and interpreted the network's messages, the vibrations of its threads, as they did in London and in Frankfurt, in South America and Australia, in New Delhi and even in Moscow and Peking.

For laymen looking at the spider web not much was happening. The actual event was not to be seen, the power anonymous. It was as if those operating on the floor could not understand their own words, acting as if they were deaf and dumb. They implored one another with signs. A broker's raised finger meant five thousand bushels of corn, the corn may not have existed yet, but it was bought and sold on deadline. Some hoped that wheat would be cheaper in six months, and others that it would become more expensive. A speculator, called the bear, tore down prices with his claws, and his colleague, the bull, drove them higher with his horns. Both were simultaneously interested in making money, and one had to dole out the difference. But perhaps it was the entire world that paid for this party, and high above the roof of the tall, mighty *Board*

---

125. Der Billiger Jacob is a phrase used to designate a merchant who sells cheap goods at low prices.

of Trade stood a figure, I couldn't tell if it was the god of trade or a broker, keeping watch on the world's harvest and on its level of hunger.[126]

Safes were built into the cellar, in the *Board*'s foundations, probably holding money and the secret of speculation, the plan for power, but perhaps there was only a corn cob behind the armored door, a sole corn cob beaten from the harvest, and a salesman came now and again to look at it contemplatively and thought proudly that he was the one who fed all the poor, and among the safes there was a bar, where one could drink to life's vicissitudes and to its fertility.

A prince of the church had died in Chicago, America's first Cardinal, his funeral mass was celebrated on television, and holy Latin melodies filled the stock market's cellar bar, and the cook, slicing up a roast, and the bar tender, mixing drinks that restored confidence, and the men, in need of drinks and of confidence, and a young woman looking like a *pin-up-girl* out of *Esquire,* in need of confident men, looked on entranced at the blessings and the arrangements for heaven being administered to this crimson figure.[127]

Chicago did not lack in piety in other respects as well. In the Loop there was ringing at midday. It was ringing as if from every roof. One heard church bells that one couldn't see, perhaps they were hidden in the skyscrapers, the skyscrapers' true voices, sounding powerfully and brightly, as if in a valley, and employees, hurrying through the streets to the drugstores, to the automated restaurants, to the open grills for cheap tough steaks, were included in this ringing and lifted up above the earth for a while.

And the ringing bells were not all. From the street a door opened into a simple room, in which people who had been writing business letters, adding numbers or reflecting on profit and loss gathered and listened to a man who looked like an announcer from the stock market but was singing a spiritual song in a clear beautiful voice, in order to edify the other clerks.

The next day was a holiday, Memorial Day, devoted to veterans of all the wars, from which the New World had not managed to escape.

I walked to a park on the lake. The park was directly in front of red factories and black warehouses. Stones were stacked up by the shore. A sign stated: "*Danger. No swimming!*" People in bathing suits sat on the stones. Occasionally one jumped into the murky depths. A policeman came and genially asked if the water was cold. The bathers called out that it was cold, and the policeman seemed to shiver. Girls did some kind of dance with each other. They were ugly faeries, not at all American, stooped, having grown up unfree, friendless and without love. There was no music, no little bag with a stereo, and they followed

---

126. A aluminum statue of Ceres, the Roman goddess of grain, stands atop the Chicago Board of Trade building.

127. The "prince of the church" was Samuel Alphonsius Stritch (1887–1958), Cardinal and Archbishop of Chicago, who died on May 26, 1958; he was not America's first Cardinal.

the rhythm of numbers called out like figures from a sad balance sheet. The flag was at half-mast on a well-known cheese factory. Everywhere people were sleeping in the grass; their faces looked dreamless and exhausted.

I came to a wide bridge for cars, which passed over a pool in the harbor. The bridge had been raised to let a steamboat through, and almost endless rows of cars accumulated before it. When the car drivers saw the ship, its chimney and masts rising up above the shore, they got out of their cars, went to the area at the edge of the pool, watched the ship's passage, a colorfully dressed herd of Sunday day-trippers, a loud, curious nomadic people, Negro and white, people from Germany, from Poland and all the countries of Europe, who now, thanks to the automobile, which the New World had given them, wanted to gobble up many miles of American land, now, saved for a moment from the madness for speed, they waved to the sailors, while their cars, in their usual marching order, but without drivers and passengers, had a ghostly look, as if they had finally made themselves independent and had been the ones planning this trip without people.

On this day of commemorating the dead, the poor, the carless and the provincials had occupied the business district. Among the skyscrapers, the famous stores and the much esteemed banks they slept and yawned and were amazed. There were many policemen out, and the watchmen carried long, brown-colored truncheons.

The American Legion, the club of front-line fighters, gathered for a march. Colorful hats and decorations let the veterans believe that they were the heroes of the day. Perhaps the veterans had no illusions and were not dreaming of glory and heroism. In general they looked shabby. Perhaps a few of them believed in the flag being carried ahead of them. Perhaps they were fleeing the day's monochromatic schedule, fleeing their home, their wives, their children, perhaps they were thinking back longingly to the chaos of war, to the manly camaraderie, to a street in Paris, to life in Augsburg, to a girl in Tokyo, to the exhilarating feeling of being a crusader. Perhaps they had forgotten death in the Ardennes and the dying on Okinawa Beach. Perhaps in Chicago death no longer frightened them.

A hat lay on the asphalt in the middle of an intersection, a civilian's old hat, and a troop of legionnaires passed over it with their firm steps.

As was often my experience in American cities, I found myself suddenly in a small, quiet, entirely empty street.

It was an alley in the garment district, I read the business signs, German, Czech, Jewish, American names, through opaque windows I saw the pieceworkers' tables scrubbed blank, the immovable rows of sewing machines and steam presses, clothes that had yet to be worn in the iron racks under coarse protective sheets, like shrouds for the dead, it was a gray still life, and then in the street there was a store for remembering Europe and Asia, where one could buy tiny, breakable Dutch windmills and little, splintered Japanese rakes designed for scratching your back in the bath.

An excited police siren sounded far away from me, then it was everywhere, I was surrounded by them, and planes invisible from my standpoint howled and buzzed overhead; the great air parade had begun, and on this street, belonging to dead things that til now had been quiet, I was in the middle of the coming war. I gathered that no fire escape, no firewall, no police car would save me; I saw that the industrious garment workers' clothes would never be worn; I knew I was powerless, I could do nothing to prevent this destiny. No man could have. Man had been condemned from the beginning, and the little, holiday-quiet street in Chicago shouted out this truth to me.

A bit later I observed a hundred thousand who had come together at *Soldier Field*, a horseshoe-shaped stadium on the lake; the crowd's compact mass rolled past a background of Doric columns, and among these Doric columns, in the reality of having reached them and in the arena's people-encircled playing field, regardless of what was happening there, was the continuity and the curse of race, from Delphi to Chicago.

Near *Soldier Field* a big bar had four televisions on, each showing a baseball game, and on all four screens one kept on seeing a fat man in white sports clothes, who evidently couldn't decide whether or not to hit a little ball with his big bat. In the bar, drinkers, legionnaires, men and youths looked up to this four-fold white-dressed fat figure as if he were a god.

The underground went above ground, bridging a part of the Negro city, going through the old and bad neighborhoods, showing the gray areas on the idealist's city map. Dilapidation, loss, cheating, things left unfinished. Houses of unspeakable sadness. Little abandoned workshops. Dirty barracks with optimistic advertisements on their roofs. Splintered wooden porches. The faces of black children behind broken windows. Occasionally a shining automobile in a run-down yard. Two expensive, groomed Saint Bernards slept on a sloping, makeshift veranda. Piles of rubbish, piles of junk, smoke, rubble, demolition, each one taking what he wants. Burnt-out shells, suddenly empty places, hope for some real-estate speculation, here and there a little alley with trees, everywhere gray-colored clothing standing and sitting about, as if to take advantage of this sad everyday life.

The elevated train stations were wooden, mere ladders for entering and exiting. No money had been allotted for these passengers. On the train they had unreadable faces. They did not look at me in a friendly way. I climbed down the exit with them.

I asked the way to the *Maxwell Street Market,* joining a stream of black people, among children who were like dirty smoke.

The *Maxwell Street Market* is not a flea market like in London or Paris, it is not at all picturesque, it is a place for the poor to shop, serving necessity not opportunity.

One could also live as a beggar in Chicago, one could feed oneself on pennies, and even at the *Maxwell Street Market* there was incentive and envy and competition, and everything was as flashy as possible, each item was supposed to outdo the others. Everywhere people were lying down, the sick, the drunk, the old, the weak, lying on the bare ground, rolling in filth, and one stepped over them without concern. I was overcome with angst, though it was not the fear that I could be beaten up or robbed here, where they stood around like the dead from all the world, like black or sometimes like white ghosts, I was only afraid of tripping, of feeling weak, of falling, for one would never again rise up out of this abyss, for all eternity misery would step on the fallen with its thousands upon thousands of ancient legs.

In a store window on this street I saw white, veiled bridal dresses waiting for a wedding day. I saw a church in which candles burned before an image of Maria and in which sermons were held in Polish and Lithuanian. I saw a priest in a brown habit, playing handball with delinquent children who knew every kind of crime. I saw an old blind man, eating from a garbage can like a dog without a master.

From a pile of garbage, from a collapsed building, from a break in the street one could see the skyscrapers in the Loop. They were much further than the clouded sky.

And I went further through the streets, which in the middle of Chicago were like country paths, went over train tracks, past storehouses, camp grounds, past cracked scales, beaten-up shacks and inhabited huts to the *stock yards,* to the terrible slaughter houses.

Here there was much that looked Southern, like Virginia, like Georgia. Shacks rose up on open fields, but it was a field of dust and garbage, thrown-out packaging, emptied cans, exploded tires; as in Alabama they sat on the porches, the colorless verandas, the rotten steps and looked, as if they were blind, at the great city's garbage fields.

It looked as if it were about to snow, frost covered the wounds, but it was very small feathers carried here by the wind, depositing some white on me as well.

Here and there you could see a tree; a tree struggling for its life.

Fifty years ago Upton Sinclair had described the *stock yards'* stench of blood in his novel, "The Jungle"; they still stank of blood, smelling of manure and need, of fear and the desire for survival.[128]

---

128. *The Jungle* was published in 1906.

I had expected perfection, a thoroughly rationalized, technological landscape of death, but the *stock yards* were boorish and primitive, they were back-
wards, similar perhaps to how they were in Sinclair's time, monstrous to be
sure, but no conveyor belt from the pasture to the can. The animals stood
cramped together in slatted pens, and the sight of them was so fantastically
terrible and infernal because countless numbers of these pens had been hap-
hazardly, asymmetrically built up on top of one another, wooden bridges and
planks combining them into a labyrinth, and in its entirety the scene had the
effect of a hellish cage, like a prison that is both horrifying and shoddy. Behind
these death cells, through which dead-faced drivers stepped with their whips,
technology triumphed after all, a factory with silos and chimneys stood and
a tower, which looked exactly like a fairy-tale mosque's minaret, raising the
question of who here was calling to the one and only God.

Western Union's telegraph machines ticked out the latest meat prices. The
stench of blood descended on the office, pressed upon the lungs, the hair, the
clothes of the scribes, laying itself like a mask, cosmetic and disgusting, on
their skin.

A Negro woman slept in the slaughter house workers' bus, her head cradled
in her hand, like the Medusa in Rome.

Chicago was a strategic field; there were gradations of power to observe.

The university had built itself an Oxford, gothic circa 1892 and given generous support in 1913, well endowed, a respected school, incubator for the
descendants of industrial and commercial money, it was at the foot of a grassy
lawn, villas, and private kindergartens sheltered the heirs, though when one
went through the university gate, over its old-fashioned courtyard and out the
back, then one was once again in an underground urban street, with people
who seemed to have given up, who no longer took care of their homes and
who, whether sitting or standing, carried the heavy burden of existence.

I found a big hotel here, closed down in front, a real palace hotel, if falling
apart, I thought it was a rooming house for colored people, it interested me
and I went in, and I was in a home for very poor whites, wheel chairs, and
stashed baby carriages were standing there, and the floorboards were broken,
but the hotel business carried on in some strange ghostly way. A grave pale girl
stood behind the reception counter, sorting unreal looking letters, while guests
sat stranded in the worn-out, burst-open chairs, like wounded in these once
luxurious seats, which were far too big for them; and it all resembled a chapter
from Kafka's Amerika.

The street went under an elevated train track. It was again a black street,
a store of little shops and countless people who gave the impression of being
urban, moving gracefully, though they all seemed to be standing on the same
spot.

The oppressive shadow beneath the train track came to a sudden end, and the narrowness of unkempt homes, of junk shops and bars broadened out and directed one's gaze to a field illuminated by streaming sunlight, at the edge of a lovely little forest.

The field lay like a carpet before a Negro high school, giving it its playground, and its students, who were well dressed in the usual collegiate style, conducted themselves in the English public-school manner, their lawn sports included. Only a minute's distance from the old black slum, and this could be Harrow. These young Negroes were a new, different generation, no longer stuck in fate's dead-end but extremely active and trusting in the future.

They filled a bus, and I went with them along Park Street, *Hyde Park Avenue, South Park Way* and *Drexel Boulevard.* They talked the school talk, assignments, grades, mathematics, languages, science, a pretty Negro policewoman stepped on the bus, white gloves, a white hat slanted on her head, an official pride, social pride, citizen's pride, and there were the *slum-clearing-action* buildings mentioned by the idealist, tall buildings standing in greenery, dreams made out of glass reflecting the air and the clouds, they were friendly, they were bathed in light, they had been designed by Frank Lloyd Wright's disciples, they were modern, they were well thought out, they had garbage disposal systems and were *air conditioned,* they stood in the prettiest nature, in one of the best neighborhoods on the lake, and in the side streets there were hotels like the new expensive ones on the corners of the Kurfürstendamm or the Champs-Elysées.

The black students got out and were at home. Was this a new era for them? The residents of *Drexel Boulevard* were walking their dogs, black ladies and black gentlemen. They carried briefcases, serious lawyers, accountants, attorneys, in their offices, and there was no shortage of shiny cars. But the elderly were still sitting as they were accustomed to do, contented or apathetic, on steps and curbs, observing life, which was not just cause for their resentment.

After a while the pretty neighborhood came to an end and transformed itself back into a street of barrack-like buildings and shacks with a mixed white and black population. They looked, the blacks and the whites, with the same bitterness and sense of defeat at the passer-by, at me.

I took the underground to the business center. All the Negroes and all the poor were striving in this direction. I got out of the car with them, an escalator went directly from the subway station to a department store, into a paradise of special offers and abundance, of seduction and of money changing hands; this was *Sgott & Co.,* but an error in the lighting above the escalator led me to read the company name as God & Co.[129]

---

129. The department store was, in fact, Scott & Co., but Koeppen's misreading allows him to see the word God, *Gott,* in the company name.

Who was the influence here? Who was skimming the cream from this operation? *Sgott & Co.* advertised in the Negro papers. Marshall Field, the department store king, stepped from his airy aromatic floors, from the paradise of flowerbed-hat-wearing women, over to God's black children and preached to them the gospel of fur and of underwear. Black men stood nobly on advertisements, casual members of the club, drinking *Lord Calvert* whiskey, and thanks to Elizabeth Arden their wives remained forever young. The Negro was a salesman. He was a customer. He was courted.

Ebony was displayed on the newspaper stands, the black sister of *Life,* the dark image of the great American illustrated magazines, and just like *Life, Ebony* was excellently edited, richly put out and printed on high-quality paper. A black *cover girl* was laughing on the title page, black high society let itself be photographed. Negroes who were rich or famous, Negroes doing very well or who had desirable jobs, looked out at the reader. Their faces did look a bit exhausted to me, as if they contained great exertions within them.

Ebony was disseminating optimism. Its heroes gave parties and married their daughters in the ballrooms of flower-laden hotels. I learned about black millionaires. That delighted me. One of these black millionaires was the publisher of *Ebony.* This gave me pause. To me it seemed that the Negro illustrated magazine had fashioned too comfortable a peace with the world and the condition it was in. In the magazine the black man's ascent took place in an isolation that elsewhere was fought for, in a black world which mostly coincided with the white world, coming into contact with it through luxury but remaining separate from it. Was *Ebony* a mouthpiece for black apartheid? *Ebony* educated the Negro: you have civil rights, you should exercise them, become rich, drive good cars, watch TV shows, buy yourself fur, drink the best whiskey, let your sons study, Little Rock is a disgrace, but in New York and Chicago please retain your independence and your racial pride while living in a black ghetto.

I visited *Ebony.* The publishing house was on a street with small auto body shops, cheerless bars and many commercial and technical schools in garage-like buildings, as well as government-run night schools, providing everyman with steps for elevating his place in life and society. In this environment the press was a palace and a fortress of belief in personal advancement.

Ebony was a black Ullstein press; it had the position among black people that *Life* had among whites.[130] A black beggar approached me and was

130. The Ullstein press, founded in Berlin in 1877, specialized in popular magazines and newspapers.

handled as a white sponger would have been handled by the white competition—he was thrown out. The receptionist was efficient and unapproachable. She spoke on several telephones at once and asked me to wait in a soft leather old-English-style chair. They were not about to lose face at *Ebony*. Oil paintings by a black artist, who had learned his art in Paris and was now continuing on in Chicago as if on the Left Bank, hung on the hallway walls. The paintings showed the melancholy of Montparnasse; they did not show America's sadness; compared with black jazz the paintings were without originality and without engagement.

The press's manager came and kindly greeted me; she could have been the director of Marshall Field; Marshall Field would have been delighted to have such a skillful colleague. She led me through her well-organized office. *Ebony* apportioned honor to each work place. Clean rooms, tidy desks, smooth machines. The people were clean as well, smooth, tidy. I met the managers and the employees. They were managers and employees. In the mail room a girl reminded me for an instant of the choir from "Carmen Jones."[131] But she wasn't singing, wasn't dancing, wasn't fighting. Of course not. This girl would never fight again; she had assimilated white mores, she was domesticated and had lost her temperament. What had I expected? The manager showed me the studio for photo shoots; I saw the black photographers, I saw a beautiful, black model, the frizzy hair smoothed into a fashionable international style, and the clothes copied from Dior. The manager showed me the trial kitchen. The pots and pans were flashing and shining. I remarked on the elegant cheerfully colored cafeteria. My guide gave me a challenging look. My amazement surprised her, had I expected a den of thieves, she thought? Yes, what had I hoped to find? A better world? Better people?

The editor-in-chief was a great man. He had the head of Napoleon and he spoke like a businessman, like an important director. He didn't seem to be either a dreamer or a fighter, not someone who hoped to make things better or different, he took the world and he took America as they were; he only wished that the most capable of the blacks could get their piece of the pie. Europe didn't interest him. He was an American and only saw America; but of the Americans I had met the best were those who saw the world. *Ebony*'s editor-in-chief accepted the reigning morality, the general taste, the widespread illusions, he adhered to ideas that had long ago become suspicious to the best Americans. The man was a conformist; in his black modesty he wanted to belong to the ruling class. Probably he was a Napoleon committed to elections.

---

131. *Carmen Jones* was a 1943 Broadway musical, made into a film in 1954; it was based loosely on the 1875 opera *Carmen*, by Georges Bizet (1838–1875) and set in an African-American milieu.

He was a contented rebel. He made me sad; and perhaps I was the foolish one, and he was right.

The airport bus stopped in front of the elegantly busy, sinfully expensive Hilton Hotel. A man got out, he took his bag, he went past the entrance to the Hilton, past the doormen, the sound of an organ, flowerbed-hat matrons, *call girls,* today's stock market reports, the morning's election slogans, he entered garage land, backdoor land, little honkey-tonks, little cinemas, little shops enticed with their gaudy advertisements, the man went decisively over to a gray cement block, to the YMCA. The man was no longer so young, but he was signed in, he was taken in, his name or the name he had chosen, he went through registration, his affairs put in order, the man got a key from a board with a thousand keys, he got in the elevator, carried his bag, went up to the eleventh floor, went through honeycomb doors, found his way, found his cell among a thousand cells. He looked out the window. He saw garage roofs and the heights of the Loop in the evening. He saw lights, those he knew and those that had nothing to do with him. He had not come to conquer Chicago. He had business in the city. Small business that for him was important business. The man undressed, got in the shower, refreshed himself, changed his shirt. He gave the key to the man at the desk, he left the building, he made his way to the warehouse street. The man inspected the goods, and since he came from Minneapolis, he criticized them. The night's business yielded a crowd that pushed out onto the street. All the store's goods were being auctioned. The man looked on, he calculated the auctioneer's profit, he made a bid and won a plate with a dog's head. He went into a restaurant, took a tray, grabbed silverware, went to the buffet, selected a salad, a piece of meat, carrots in a brown sauce, and a sweet potato baked in its skin. A glass of milk and a cup of hot, strong coffee were sufficient. He went to the cashier, paid, went into the guest room, and sat himself at a table. A Negro came, cleaned away the dishes from the previous diner and poured the new one a glass of ice water. The Negro did this as if he were mute. The man ate his meal. The food had no taste, but the man didn't notice. He had drunk the ice water and the milk, and then he drank the coffee. He strolled to the airline company street. Their offices were lit up; under the supervision of the uniformed air goddesses passengers waited to be transported to the runway and were ready to entrust themselves to the stars. The man confirmed his return flight to Minneapolis for the next night. He put twenty-five cents in an automat and once again insured his life with his wife the beneficiary. If his plane crashed tomorrow, his wife would get ten thousand dollars. With the money she could keep up the business. For a moment it seemed to be the solution to all problems. He went back to the YMCA. He lingered before a display window, in which a Chinese man was tattooing two flags and the head of a television star onto a sailor's chest. The man observed the sailor's face, how he pressed his lips together and bit down on the pain. The man envied the sailor, and it pleased him that the tattooing needle was inflicting pain on him. The doorman at a cinema offered the man shadows of nude girls. The doorman of a cabaret offered him the girls live. After brief hesitation the man went to a bar with a long counter. He sat among the men and ordered a bourbon. He took a dollar from his wallet, and the bartender gave him a bourbon with fifty cents change. Then the man watched television, like the other guests. He saw a man who looked like him, and a prosecutor was questioning this man as a courtroom witness. The man on the screen was turning back and forth. In a close-up his eye was seeking an exit. The prosecutor was honing in on the man on the screen, and this pleased the man at the bar. He laid his recently acquired fifty cents on the bar and ordered another bourbon. This time the bartender shook more whiskey onto the ice. He was a good boy. The man went home, took his key, went to his cell. Chicago lay before his eyes, a monstrous spectacle. It didn't interest him. He pulled the curtain across the window and went to bed. On the night table a bible lay beneath the lamp. The man opened it randomly, but it made him tired. He thought that tomorrow he had to go to Brown first; perhaps Brown would give him a good price.

I went North up Michigan Avenue, I crossed the bridge over the Chicago River, in front of me was the *Wrigley Building*, the chewing-gum fortress, white and strange like one of King Ludwig's castles.[132] From this part of the avenue I could look down upon streets, rails for the transportation of goods to the harbor warehouses crossing under the avenue. The streets lay there like dark dried-out canals. Here and there a person was strolling, walking in the shadows of buildings. Above on the avenue journalists went to bars from their editorial offices and publishing houses. The journalists knew Paris, Bonn and Pankow, they knew Moscow and Peking and Tokyo, and several even knew Lhasa and Weimar.[133] They didn't know how the world would end. In a very complicated way they would bet for drinks, betting on war or peace, and then they would go up the stairs to the avenue and to their papers, as if returning from Hades. The avenue was a neighborhood of specialized stores, elegant young people, expensive cars, very rich flowerbed-hat women, snobbish hotels, exclusive restaurants. Policemen stood before the hotels with wooden clubs. The elegant young people were out on the town, greeting one another with the warbling horns of their sports cars, dining in a courtyard decorated in Florentine style. A society photographer was exhibiting his targets. Many had rat

---

132. King Ludwig refers to Ludwig II (1845–1886), a Bavarian King known for building extravagant castles.

133. Pankow is a neighborhood in former East Berlin with many government buildings.

mouths, each was intent on showing his worth. A Negro, who was very young, very decadent and very, very rich, was out with a luminously beautiful, delicate black girl and he was very, very alone. An old water tower stood like a Saracen palace, though the Palmolive building towered over it in a small park. For its part the Palmolive building shone like the Castle of the Grail. I thought it was a shame that Richard Wagner had never seen the Palmolive building![134] A real lighthouse watched over the high roof, throwing its light over Lake Michigan, over its green or stony shores, over the skyscrapers and garages, over the legendary Loop, over the battlefields of commerce and crime, over the business and pleasure districts and the seductive magazines, over all the nations, who had come together here to work and to acquire, and also to die and to inherit, over all their priests, over all the Negroes, over the *Board of Trade* and perhaps over the homeless sleeping on Maxwell Street as well. But I didn't believe it. Maxwell Street did not get the grail's slightest shimmer.

In the elegant bustling lobby of the Hilton Hotel an organ player sat in the reception area's gallery and let Händel and Protestant chorals and a Stabat Mater float over the illustrious guests. The Hilton was the place for political conventions, the big meetings, here the new president would be put to the vote. One saw priests and preachers, one lived piety. Flowerbed women grew on all the carpets, they bloomed in all the chairs. Michigan Avenue went through these conference rooms and ran through to Wall Street in Manhattan and to the White House in Washington.

Here one saw the avenue of beautiful and expensive things, mink even in summer, girlfriends for politicians and corporate executives with their discrete elegance, many driven by in royal English cars, and in the art galleries wonderful color prints of the French impressionists, up to Braque and Picasso, were hanging. All of Michigan Avenue was overflowing with French colors. They were reflected in the boutique displays, in the jewelers' stones, in the bottles of expensive perfume, a little girl went by holding her governess' hand and was dressed from a Renoir painting, but the light over the lake was not smiling, and the wind was not gentle.

Chicago in the early morning, the streets were grave, quiet canyons, water ways, brush rolls and rotating scrubbers did their work, the asphalt was being cleaned, an old man was looking through the garbage heaps, he fed himself from Chicago's refuse, the newspapers predicted a tornado, it was raging on the lake's north shore, destroying the wheat fields, helping the *Board*'s optimistic bulls, the sky sailed down into grayness, in Monroe Street the wind

---

134. The Castle of the Grail, *Gralsburg*, figures in the 1882 opera *Parsifal*, by Richard Wagner (1813–1883); the juxtaposition of Chicago's commercial architecture with imagery of the Wagnerian quest is an irony practiced here at Wagner's expense.

stung with a sword of ice, it didn't cut into the passengers, and in the bus to the airport I realized that in the United States planes are the favored transport of the petit bourgeois.

There's space in all the continent's train cars, it's never crowded; but to fly up in the air they stand, they wait patiently before the gates, the departures in all directions were announced, jumps to the desert, jumps to peaceful places, to the storming ocean, to the warm Caribbean, they waited with bag and baggage, they flew with their own and with foreign companies, they rose up for births and for deaths, they made their way excitedly to honeymoons, the tornado came closer to Chicago, and soon I was hovering in the azure, I flew with little cowboys and their water guns, with cinema star puppets of youthful flowerbed-hat women, I flew with briefcases and bridal bouquets, I hung over cloud beds and probably over Lake Michigan, then the sky opened up, Detroit lay in the sunshine, cars growing like plants under glass, Edsel Ford appeared to me beneath my feet and among his empire, he watched the engines being fit together, saw wheel after wheel added, he donated a million to the university in Berlin and five hundred thousand for the preservation of the old cloisters in Cluny, and there was Lake Eerie, a track of ice blue, Canada's dark-green endlessness, we sank down to Buffalo, the bridal flowers got out and hurried to Niagara Falls, solemn beginning to their married life, the wind was already coming from the Atlantic, blowing here from Europe, tasting of English fireplaces, we stretched our wings over Pennsylvania and Massachusetts, whose green fields were like counties in the old kingdom.[135]

Massachusetts is New England, it's the land of the pilgrim fathers, the Mayflower's coast, the forest of Salem's strict belief and Cambridge's liberal lawns, and Boston is the city of tradition and of the great American revolution.

I could feel both tradition and revolution. Here they drank tea instead of coffee, the streets were cozily crooked instead of straight, they had honorable names and no numbers. In my view, Boston could still have belonged to the British monarchy, even the wind had an English tang, cool and northern, but it was Boston's pride to have been the first to break with the English crown, to have prepared the defection, to have stirred up the rebellion, though the buildings, the locales, the churches, the squares of the revolution had remained so ur-English that one wanted to visit them with a rolled-up umbrella and a stiff round hat.

Boston's heroes were two handworkers, they were a printer and a goldsmith, Benjamin Franklin and Paul Revere. One could go by their houses, one could contemplate their work places: very slender houses, very small workshops. But

---

135. Edsel Ford (1893–1943) was the son of Henry Ford (1863–1947) and president of the Ford Motor Company from 1919 until 1943.

the spirit of these men had triumphed over a king and over all his advisors and officers.

They had not been wild revolutionaries. Before they had attempted their revolution and proclaimed their new-world freedom, they had consulted with their God, a strict, unornamented, Protestant God. They had sat in the Old North Church as in little living rooms, in separated berths with their families, with the Almighty, with their faith, with their temptations, with their conscience and with their rebellion, each family in its place, situated exactly according to their standing and their church donations in the strict ordering of the berths.

The ordering has been kept to this day. The wood, the chairs were swept, brushed, rubbed clean. Their meticulous cleanliness was not in the best taste. And yet the wild will to freedom, the firm belief in unconditioned human rights had lived in the hearts of these decorous citizens. Only a red curtain decorated this house of God, and otherwise its sobriety conveyed a strong alert sense for the separation of powers and for proper representation.

A monument showed Paul Revere as a daring rococo rider.

The monument stood in *Little Italy,* Boston's Italian quarter, and in the square, men sat on stone benches in the evening and played cards. They sat and played as if they were in a square in Bologna. A house was burning. The fire department came. But the fire wasn't dangerous; the people were saved and the property was probably insured. And so people watched the welcome spectacle, and the participants enjoyed the good fortune of being actors in a fate insured against misfortune. An entirely Italian, black-haired teenager took me for a reporter, and she found it interesting that a foreign reporter had come to see her house burn, and she said proudly that she was an American, even if she had been born in Modena.

Everyone on this square with the Revere monument to the little handworker and rococo rider for freedom and human rights was a proud American, an even more proud owner of the chrome-plated car, yet Italy lived on in the vegetable and wine stores, in the flickering light of the much-visited chapels and in the people's hearts.

In little shop windows there were pictures of the Madonna, of the saints, of Lincoln, Washington and Eisenhower framed in little American flags. Two old men with drooping white mustaches and bulbous rolled umbrellas came out of Cino Cinotti's *Funeral Home.* Their businessmen's faces showed that they were pleased with the day. In their real American hotel for the dead they gave up to the peaceful night Alberto Pagnanelli, whom they had laid in his open coffin as in a bridal bed, whose cheeks they had painted red, his beard and hair beautifully colored, and into whose folded hands they had put a crucifix; and Pagnanelli smiled thankfully, a man from a hovel in Naples, but still successful in death, a sir, a mister, who had honestly earned his respectable and not entirely cheap American grave.

Abraham Lincoln winked at the Cinotti men, but they didn't notice him; they were lost in a conversation about bad times; in *Little Italy* one lived well and didn't die gladly.

Strangely there were more newsboys in Boston than in any other American city. Even at night they were prowling about, hurrying as if they were just about to become millionaires. They hawked their papers before the train station, before the bars and the little middle-class furniture stores on Washington Street and before the old warship "*Constitution*," which had triumphed over many Englishmen in 1812 and was anchored at a pier, honored like the battleship "Aurora" in Leningrad.[136]

I had seen the "Aurora" and the "*Discovery*" in London and now I was visiting the "*Constitution*," and I stood on the military boards together with school children, who were being taught history, the greats from the past, the greats who had conquered, the greats of the revolution, greatness, heroism, national pride, and at each point they forgot to tell the credulous children that elsewhere there were ships loaded with heroism, sacrificial courage, national pride and with blood dried into their wood.

Boston's newsboys didn't bother with the old fame of the "*Constitution*"; they profited from contemporary history, they lived, as did others, from new blood.

I walked through the first park to have been laid out by white immigrants in America, through the continent's first artificial nature, and in the middle of Boston everything was laid out in exact concordance with London's St. James Park, and all the world lay on the lawns beneath the trees.

Kingly civic freedoms predominated. In this English city girls met amiably with boys. In Boston there was not much American loneliness, much less sadness and even less of this strange fear, which one felt in other American cities: something was about to happen, someone was about to start shooting, shouting, screaming, running amok. The girls did a wild, celebratory dance. They danced as they were supposed to dance. These girls were English in their kindness as well, and the first time at the front door they probably said "no."

In the evening Washington Street was the sailors' joy and the playground of the shoeshine boys.

Horseshoe shaped counters in the bars. Booming music. Male or female hips shaking with or without singing. Young and old prostitutes. Children's

136. The battleship Aurora is said to have fired the opening shots of the Russian Revolution, the comparison yet another subversive suggestion by Koeppen of similarity between the United States and the U.S.S.R.

eyes and hyena's faces. *Blue jeans* over small rear ends and black tops on withered breasts. A midget pushed himself through the subterranean air of sweat, perfume, stink and aroused libido. He was selling chocolate and was on good terms with all the girls. They stroked him like a cat. An absurd drunk climbed up on the bar's brass railing. He demanded a drink, brought the glass to his mouth, then he cried out and poured the alcohol down on his head, ordered another drink, paid, cried out, poured it out, continued on, and the bar tender took his money and, his demeanor unshaken, served him full glasses. The doorman-bouncer directed an evening dress to an Uncle Sam. Uncle Sam was cooked. The navy held together. Drinking as the neo-Teutonia once had drunk.[137] A united front against the maritime police. The absurd drunk had finally poured out his last half dollar. The bar tender said "that's it." The doorman-bouncer grabbed him by the collar; only then did one see how small and seedy he was; he dangled from the hands of the professional tough guy like a rabbit caught by the nape of its neck.

He flew out onto the street and lay in the dust. A little shoeshine boy set aside his box and tried to help the man, but the man continued falling down and he cursed the little shoeshine boy. The little shoeshine boy, who did not know this helpless man, began to cry. Perhaps he cried because he grasped the futility of goodness.

The furniture dealers lived at the end of the street. They sat in their dreadful lacquered, petit-bourgeois shops and spoke into microphones, which eerily broadcast their voices via loudspeakers on the street. Little Chinese children were rocking on a seesaw set up for them by a gray-clad nun, in a parking lot for furniture vans. A small bordello stood across from the fire department as in Hamburg's closed-off streets. The bloated whores sat in red lamplight, stuffing their swollen mouths with fruits and sweets; they knocked invitingly on the windowpanes, and the firemen who were enjoying the evening at their lookout station laughed amiably.

In front of the opera house women promenaded in long evening gowns that touched the ground. An unusually fat woman was covered from head to toe in lace and looked like a blue tower. The men were in black tie and had club faces. In order to manage high society's exodus from the opera house, the policemen had put on white sashes, reminiscent of guardsmen on the Kaiser's birthday.

At a nearby oyster restaurant guests waited patiently in long rows, and when there was a free place a policeman without a sash called out to the next

---

137. Neo-Teutonia was a student fraternity; the protagonist of the 1918 novel *Der Untertan,* which has been translated as "The Loyal Subject" by the German writer Heinrich Mann (1871–1950), is a member of this fraternity.

gourmet. The oysters were fresh as waves, delicious and cheap. The men eating at the bar all looked as if they should be addressed as colonel.

A cozy turn-of-the-century subway, bumpy, so high-wheeled that one could imagine it being pulled by horses, went from Boston to Cambridge, to Harvard University and three hundred years back into the past.

Cambridge, Massachusetts is Harvard, and Harvard is Oxford or Cambridge in Cambridgeshire. Heidelberg, Göttingen and Jena are cities with a university, but Cambridge, Massachusetts is a university, to which a small town belongs. The campus, buildings and courtyards are cloister-like, and Harvard had preserved fully the character of a medieval scholarly center, though it does not give the impression of being narrow or narrow-hearted but wide and on-going with ever more new, free green squares laid out, occasionally showing its worth with columns of Greek origin.

Everywhere I saw the most cultivated lawns, and from one end to the other Harvard smelt of freshly cut grass, a stimulating smell that included the people, the female students made one think of meadow white linen, the male students of mowers' sweat and the professors of dried hay in a stable's manger.

They camped out on the lawns, on the lawns their diplomas were handed over, the mortar board set on hopeful head, I saw them as they lay in the grass, reading, studying or playing with an enviable abundance of time, sporty young people, who did not look as if they had had to earn their place at the university, and all around the churches, the libraries, the lecture halls, the dormitories, and especially the all-female *Radcliffe College* had the scent of wealth and good nurseries, and the *Harry Elkins Widener Memorial Library,* founded and richly endowed as a memorial to a young millionaire and Harvard graduate who went down with the Titanic, with its Athenian-academic portico of columns, its collection of Renaissance manuscripts and Shakespeare first editions, was an appealing symbol of the transformation, always possible in America, of money into spirit.

In a big hotel in Boston old boys sat at the bar, which unaccompanied women could not enter, who had come to their alma mater's yearly graduation party, checks in their pockets, with clownish red *Alpha Pi Beta* hats on their heads. Secretaries, wait staff, chauffeurs were continuously running by and reminding the academic young-at-heart tipplers of their business, and it was apparent that with a successful Harvard diploma and brilliant career, spirit had been transformed back into money. Perhaps the cycle was healthy.

Students from Boston University frequented the *coffee shop* in my hotel. They were very different from their fellow students at Harvard, they seemed to be smaller figures, more middle-class, more conventionally dressed, as if following a good recommendation, they seemed to be working for their place at the university, to be financing it themselves with hard work, they were not

Greek at all, they did not embody academic freedom, even with the pursuit of knowledge, if it's to be conducted independently, they didn't have the leisure, they were apprentices to practical trades, enlisting the next generation, house doctors, lawyers and technicians, they were disadvantaged, their wing for high flying had already been clipped, but because they were young, they laughed, and because they were hungry they ate a great deal of sticky toast drenched in melted butter.

Many old women lived in the hotel, the elevator groaned beneath the burden of the years, its own and its passengers' days, and the women ran and limped down the corridors, disappearing into their rooms like mice into their holes.

The mouse holes were enormous. This was a third-class hotel, but even here, as everywhere in America, the rooms were three times as big as those in the best European hotels.

I looked out from my window onto a dead train station; they had ripped the tracks from the gravel, they had scrapped them, but the grooves from the tracks were still striving forward, as if sending ghost trains from fallen platforms forward and out into a wild endlessness. It was a melancholy picture, and in its background rose up the powerful dome from the mother church of *Christian Science.*

From a distance the church, around which the sky was particularly blue, truly looked like Saint Peter's in Rome; only Saint Peter's had been placed in a dead world.

I visited the church on a Sunday afternoon and found a building that was governmental and bewildering at once, a circle of doors standing open like entrances to the circus. Through its doors came an aroma as if from the opened wardrobe of a woman who had just died, lavender, silk starting to crumble and suppressed desires.

There were box offices behind each of the entrances, and the alphabetically ordered counters framed the hat-wearing women in such a way that they looked like their own passport photos. Above these women and these box offices sayings had been painted, writings derived partially from Jesus and partially from Mrs. Mary Baker Eddy, the saint of Christian Science.[138]

In marble halls festively dressed men and women had formed receiving committees and greeted guests as in a very elegant clothing boutique. Sociable groups had gathered in the other rooms, while with exceptional energy flowerbed-hat women pulled the stops of a small organ.

The faithful streamed into church from all corners of heaven. What distinguished them was affluence, sobriety, solidity. Nobody looked stupid and no-

---

138. Mary Baker Eddy (1821–1910) was the founder of Christian Science.

body looked fanatical. The streets filled with parked cars, and by some of them contented, well-fed chauffeurs waited. An elderly Negro couple also came to the service and looked affluent, solid and sober like all the others.

The nearby houses seemed to belong to the church. They had been built in the manner of the Renaissance and the great banks. A *Church Reality Trust* rented apartments and stores.[139] The *Christian Science Monitor,* a respectable paper, whose lead articles were paid attention to in Washington, was housed in an extremely solid, granite building.

In the display window of shop where you could buy paper and aphorisms there hung the portrait of the woman who had created all of this, the church, the aphorisms, the reality trust, the world-famous paper and the reading rooms across the globe. Mrs. Mary Baker Eddy, president of the Metaphysical college, pastor emeritus of *The First Church of Christ Scientist,* looked out at me, with her white curly hair, a friendly old aunt in her good rooms. The wardrobe smell was accurate. That a worldwide church and powerful operation could emerge from this demonstrated America's limitless possibilities once again and strengthened the conviction that the efficient ones could find a pleasurable existence in God's country.

Now they, the efficient and rewarded ones, had gathered in the enormous, sparkling auditorium, beneath the Saint Peter's dome, and they thanked God with assured voices, in which there was no hint of doubt, rising up over the granite building, over the secure financial investment houses and the *publicity* offices and over an old woman's smile.

I came back to New York at night. Seen from the countryside, Manhattan was a big light house promising happiness. The skyscrapers shone above the stony forest of the suburbs like red and white stars.

The train went through tunnels, it hurried beneath rivers, and wherever it stopped there was some drama. New York did not sleep. Lovers embraced each other before the backdrop of the commuter rail. Betrayal, separation, farewell, return and already the certainty: never again! People were walking, running, driving, feeding themselves, leaning against hotdog stands, emptying vending machines, transporting goods, hauling garbage, working hard, working gladly, giving up on work, they had had enough, they gave in, when they were sociable they lived with abandon. The morning bloomed like a rose. Water wagons, garbage machines, mountains of newspapers, a truck full of flowers, pigeons washed themselves in a fountain on Fifth Avenue, early mass in *St. Patrick's Cathedral,* looking like the Cologne Cathedral on Fifth Avenue, the protected heart of mystery glowed in the glass window over the portal, night hawks, cleaning women, homeless catching an hour of sleep filled the nave, I arrived

---

139. Koeppen must be referring here to a Church Realty Trust.

in the hotel with the airplane passengers, they had flown across the Atlantic, without flair, according to contract, they had come from the older parts of the earth, light-colored fluttering hair beneath caps from Stockholm, an audacious moustache from Israel, others from Mexico, Brazil, the world was small, it upheld camaraderie, pulling camaraderie down from the sky perhaps; no breakfast could be cozier than the one at the corner drugstore, into which the city was streaming, the New Yorkers, friendly, tolerant, open to the world and related to Berliners.

New York was a place of eternal seduction, a place of smiling offers, above all Manhattan ensnared women, the enormous city was always ready to decorate them, while the men fixed the streets, the display windows, the colors, the lights, the forms, the aromas and the newspaper advertisements designed by cunning psychologists, the men who were in turn bewitched by women to buy something for the beautiful and un-beautiful.

Going through the streets and avenues, you needed a woman, in New York or anywhere else in the world, to give her something of Manhattan's riches. The confirmed bachelor had to feel rejected.

I too wanted to bring a dress to Europe, one of those adroit New York creations imitating Paris, though it was impossible to imitate, I went to the department stores, daring to enter the women's empires, and I met up with queens. Here they were still at the customer's feet. Entrance halls for every age, floors for every size and color, the latest Parisian idea, hardly drawn up on the Avenue Montaigne, was here a cheap pleasure in a hundred variations. Every piece hung in the freely accessible racks, within reach of the desiring hand. No salesman to burden or hem in the greed. The women reached for their dreams, put them on, looked at their reflection in the crystal mirror, passed on the first, second, third choice, new models were pulled down from the shelf, tried on, they hardly went behind the curtain, they were without shame, what they didn't like they threw on a table, on the ground, friendly employees came to clean up, with a smile hanging the spurned fashions back on the rack, and no one paid any attention to me, no one asked about my wishes and desires, they probably took me for a fabric inspector, for a eunuch in service to the women.

The normal American man did not dare enter this seraglio. But they had also taken him into account, he who wanted to bring his wife or girlfriend something from this ready-made garden of Eden, and so in each of the best stores there was a department for men who wanted to buy women's items. I visited one, in order to make myself clear. I described what I wanted. The director gave me a motherly smile. She asked about the size. I didn't know the American measurements. The director led me to the mannequins. They were very beautiful girls, they looked like groomed horses, they too were smiling but not in a motherly way. Among the girls I chose the one who fit the dress I wanted to buy. Then I chose the dress. The mannequin put it on and showed it off. The mannequin's step once again reminded me of the steps of a beautifully dressed horse in a riding school. One didn't know whether to buy the dress or the horse. I thought of Prince Pückler, the lover of parks and writer of beautiful letters, who had brought his wife a beautiful female slave from Abyssinia.[140]

The mannequin was no slave, she was a New Yorker, she thought I didn't like the dress, taking it off unwillingly, changing, showing off another, and this time with the smile of a princess.

Wind on the corner of *Central Park South* and *Fifth Avenue.* The women held down the hems of their skirts. Then the flowerbed hats flew from the Atlantic to the prairie. They let their skirts sail. Tops and nylons, little crinolines, loose parachutes; the high-heeled women rose up to the sky. Expensive five-o-clock tea, expensive ladies' tea, expensive gigolos' tea, the material emphasized men's shoulders and hips and muscles, fresh complexion, red make-up covering the rich widows' blue furrowed brows, hair rippling in purple waves. A little girl besieging the exclusive shops on roller skates, pulling behind her a terrified white rabbit hopping along on its leash, and she was entirely confident in her rich family and in her feminine worth.

The little shops of fifty-dollar-bills opened their doors like sacred shrines, porters wore tailor-made suits and disowned France, striped awning protected the guest from the car to the soft carpet. Workers on strike paced in front of the famous Stork Club. They carried placards, asking people not to patronize the club, and their faces inspired thoughts of sour soup. The club ignored them, a policeman watched over them, the guests came and went. A homosexuals' bar was in the basement, their bright vibrating voices rose up to the street, the men and boys crouched below like parrots on a pole, and the loudest juke-box music fought in vain against their fear and their loneliness.

One could view a Chagall in the *Museum of Modern Art,* an angel and magical horse wanted to ornament the skyscraper home, one could look at the Indian valley of the Hudson and at the old synagogue in Vitebsk; in the museum's cinema "The Cabinet of Dr. Caligari" did its frightening work.[141]

On 23rd Street they ran from the sewing ateliers, from the assembly line, from piece work and banded into colorful bouquets, white, yellow, brown, black, Jewish, Chinese, Puerto Rican girls, proud Negresses and pale Swedes. How beautiful New York was!

---

140. Prince Hermann von Pückler-Muskau (1785–1871) was a German writer who excelled at travel writing.

141. *The Cabinet of Dr. Caligari* was a 1920 German horror film.

An attic theater had attempted an experiment, putting on "*Ulysses in Night-town*," a night and dialogue piece based on James Joyce's work.[142]

The theater was far from Broadway, it had installed itself and its black décor under the roof of a tall, dilapidated commercial building on the Bowery, and it was as if the streets of bars, the dim and fascinating boulevard of Manhattan's poorest drinkers belonged to the worldly writer, while the theater offered the stage setting. Here the Joycean inferno arose directly from the visions of the unhappy, the poor, the downtrodden, the addicts, who shouted their drunkenness out into the evening or lay dazed on the pavement, the horrible birds of delirium above them. They begged. They all were begging. They begged in a businesslike way, abruptly, rudely. They did not debase themselves. This was how people often begged in America, and it seemed to be always the same man, who went begging throughout the entire country, with a gray face, dressed in gray, his lips gray and thin and the hand he put forward was hard and gray.

The city had put a playground for children near the Bowery, however, a fenced-in piece of cultivated earth with plants that looked as if they had been cut from old paper, and the drunks were lying here on a green that wasn't green, sleeping off their drunkenness or sleeping in exhaustion and agony, whispering their internal monologues, shouting out their curses, while children of all races clambered over their humiliated bodies, the children hunting each other without inhibition, playing cops and robbers and swinging happily on rusted metal see-saws.

A food market, well stocked stands of Italian, Spanish, Greek, Levantine merchants, led in its colorfulness, its shouting and smells to the Jewish quarter. It was a Sabbath night. The Jewish stores were closed. Their owners walked with festive steps to the houses of prayer; they went to their God, as they had gone in Eastern Europe, black, bearded, serious, they were black, serious shadows in a colorful, care-free, unbelieving world. Kids sat and played on the steps of a synagogue built at the turn of the century from rough bricks, in the style of a fire department, and a pious old man drove them out exactly like an outraged Moses. An ice cream salesman went by on an old-fashioned tricycle, and the bell, which he rang with his hand, sounded like the bell of death.

The theater performance began, and the viewers who had climbed up to the attic were the best and most alert audience, they had come from all over New York to see Joyce's wild eerie journey through the night and to see Zero Mostel, a comedian well known in the neighborhood, who had appeared in Yiddish-language productions and now was playing Leopold Bloom, the Dublin insur-

---

142. "Ulysses in Nighttown," a play created by the playwright Marjorie Blakentin (1891–1974) and based on the 1922 novel *Ulysses* by James Joyce (1882–1941), previewed in 1958.

ance agent, the role of his life.[143] He reminded me of the very great, enchanting moments of Max Pallenberg, and his performance is one I will never forget.[144] What I had doubted, what I had thought impossible, he did; the unimpeded eruptions of the unconscious were made visible, the play of thoughts, the inner monologue, the spirit hunting for adventures, deals, illusions had been put on stage, given over to the audience, and I was struck by how similar this ghostly excerpt from "Ulysses" was to the second part of "Faust," with Joyce as classical as Goethe was modern.[145] The New York night was magical.

Through old streets, through the place of the first immigrants, through New Amsterdam, right through the downtown, dead buildings, died out, a population sinking into the grave, without sparkle, without light, boarded up windows, cracked walls, cats, rats, dogs, everything unreal and ghostly, an old man with his bag on his back, a world empty except for an inexplicable crowd, young people, bent backs, glimmering cigarettes, an image from the cover of an old Nat Pinkerton magazine, pulp fiction, the people were taken away from me, they disappeared forever, surfaced again, were lively, deserted streets, warehouses, garbage dumps, new buildings, glass palaces, a new shine, new light, new people, I had reached Greenwich Village, New York's village, the Montparnasse of Manhattan.[146]

It was a pretty, mild night. In Washington Square under lanterns and trees they played chess on the city's tables and benches. The Sunday evening crowds pushed their way through the crooked streets. Artists painting in all styles set their work out on fences. A bookstore lit up the sky; they had everything in every language, and people pressed up to the tables as they did when buying shirts and shoes elsewhere. Young people filled the hundreds of bars, it was impossible to get a place, they drank standing, a white girl and a black girl kissed each other, and another, a skinny one, still a child, from New York, snuggled up to a boy, in whose face defiance and light delighted as in a Rimbaud portrait of a boy.[147]

I went further to Italy. At the corner of Mott and Hester Street the neighborhood was celebrating the feast of Saint Anthony of Padua. They carried the Madonna and the Saint in a celebratory procession through the New York

---

143. Zero Mostel (1915–1977) was an American actor; Leopold Bloom is the (Jewish) protagonist of Joyce's *Ulysses*.

144. Max Pallenberg (1877–1934) was an Austrian actor.

145. The second part of Goethe's *Faust*, which was written as a play, is almost unperformable in its complexity; its wild imagined journeys prefigure, for Koeppen, the modernity of Joyce's *Ulysses*, which has turned the experimental in Goethe into something classical.

146. Nat Pinkerton was the name of a prewar detective series, which appeared in magazine form.

147. Jean Rimbaud (1854–1891) was French poet and archetype of the bohemian life.

night. Light bulbs decorated the church and were put up over the street in colorful links. Barrel organs rejoiced, as if one were on Naples' latitude here. They danced on the street. A swing boat had been backed onto a truck.[148] The grandchildren of Sicily, Calabria and Tuscany floated up to foreign stars.

And it went directly on to China, one could still hear the barrel organ, but here there were already the Chinese sounds, Chinese lanterns replaced the colorful light bulbs, fireworks burned, rockets rose up in the air, and Chinese girls in blue studded jeans and with taut black braids clapped their hands excitedly.

The nearby Wall Street district was dead; only at the *Police Night Court* was a light burning, and whoever came here in the night, whoever was brought here, was entangled in a drama or less often in a farce. The policemen and the detectives led their prey up before the judge in groups. Everything went very quickly. A conspicuous camaraderie predominated among the detectives and those they had captured, and often the captives and their capturers resembled one another. Many of the delinquents were Negroes, coming out of the night into the court's garish light, letting accusations and punishments pass over them like a burst of rain, which couldn't be avoided. Never did a judgment elicit a complaint from them. Despised lawyers sat on a long bench with nothing to do, like servants to be rented, doing crossword puzzles from the paper. The judge looked rushed and stressed out. He proclaimed the last word each time with a hammer blow. The judge was not malicious, but sometimes impatience overwhelmed him.

On Sunday everything was pushing toward *Coney Island,* the people's beach in New York.

I went with the subway, traveling for over an hour, the train rising often out of the tunnel night, becoming an elevated train, roaring over bridges, offering up views.

The large borough of Brooklyn! They tried to realize the American dream of a single-family house over the subway tracks. In deck chairs they lay in the shadows of the rattling trains, playing ball on cement roofs, going to church through canyons of stone, which were built like English village churches, having their weekend. *Coney Island* occupies a kilometer of the Atlantic, its waves coming up on a white beach colorful with people, and the sight of ships showed that there was still the old connection among continents, a proper Luna Park in Utopia. They jumped from high towers in parachutes, they rode a train of life-sized artificial horses, going over streets and houses in steps that had never been seen before. An Indian choir played the national anthem, and

---

148. The swing boat is an amusement park ride, still popular today. It was invented in the United States in the 1890s.

policemen placed their hands welcomingly on the visors of their caps. Roller coasters took up entire city blocks, the car races offered an almost real death, people lay on the beach, in shooting galleries behind booming mechanical rifles, flew through the air, fell into precipices, families had prolonged picnics, pants-wearing men fraternized at card games, young couples built their weddings out of sand, but dominating everything was movement and shouting. Humanity was hunting in a fever of unleashed puberty. Negroes showed the joy of children, they had dressed up as if for a masked ball, black dancing shirts, white socks, red accordion-pleated skirts, one ran in skin-tight, embroidered bull fighter's pants, with a naked chest, an amulet on his muscled chest and a green Tyrolean hat with a colorful peacock's feather in his wooly hair. I went with them onto the ghost train, and they, bona fide big-city folk, were truly terrified by the simulated death, the childish devil, the white castle ghost, the monster's paws, shrieking and at the same time unspeakably charmed they clung to me, whom they presumed to be equally afraid and overjoyed.

And then I saw blood, smeared on the wall and the ground, splattered on the ceiling, in the grisliest room of wax figures; everything shocking was displayed in the most natural way, the strangled, beaten, stabbed women, family tragedies that had actually happened in the city, the body of a thirteen-year-old lay in a bathtub chopped into pieces, a father shut up his murdered son in the refrigerator, a woman mounted the electric chair, her mouth in a shriek, and then you could see seven Negro martyrs, innocently sent to their death in the South, forming a truly moving group of seven apostles in their cell, and of a murdered gangster it was said in a rebellious language, almost honoring anarchy, that "he fought against the police and for freedom," Hitler stood next to John Dillinger, Einstein was presented as the "father of the atom bomb," and children and teenagers crowded into the booth and observed with knowing faces, with the intelligence of the aged, life's dramas, rapes and heroic acts.[149]

The subway took us all back to Manhattan, we stood packed together beneath the big humming ventilator, bathed in sweat, the day's nakedness pressed through people's clothes, giving off steam, of sun, sea, salt, of the ball, all the excitements and movements and now the exhaustion and desires still unfulfilled, the light flickered in the car, the train stood still in the tunnel's darkness, pressed together we trembled—hell's brood.

In the evening I saw *West Side Story*, a big Broadway hit, a musical, that retold the story of Romeo and Juliet in the milieu of young gang battles.[150] It

---

149. The "seven Negro martyrs" are the "Martinsville seven," seven black men who pled guilty to sexually assaulting a white woman in 1949; they were all executed in 1951; John Dillinger (1903–1934) was an American bank robber.

150. *West Side Story* opened on Broadway in 1957.

was a fantastic production, close to the present day, critical of the present day, affirmative of the present day, moving in an unsentimental way, and the young actors were able to do a great deal, they were excellent and always equally good, they were accomplished as actors, as dancers and as singers.

New York was present on the Broadway stage, and later as I went along the streets west of Central Park, I saw groups of Negroes, Puerto Ricans, immigrants from Spain and Mexico, as they eyed each other and crept around and tested each other in the night, we would have called them hooligans, but they were murderously caught up in the danger and stupidity of racial hatred, even when they called themselves with great pride Americans and New Yorkers.

I went down 42nd Street for the last time. I left Times Square behind with its news, its practical-joke stores, its nudities, its tough steaks grilled over an open fire and its people-mixing democracy. Once more I saw the people-friendly, wondrous, marvelous American *Public Library,* the display window brilliance of Fifth Avenue. I waved to the ad agents on Madison Avenue, I didn't take them seriously, at Grand Central Station I went into the prayer room of the Biltmore Hotel, I prayed like all the business people to the great, dollar-spending god of Manhattan, drank my last drink in the manly fraternal men's bar, neared the East River, the sea's arm encircling the half-island, walked through Tudor City, the new hotel city, entered international, entered diplomatic territory, rejoicing at the sight of unadorned, cool, beautiful facades, Paris and Rome had sent restaurants, street cafés, they played as they did on the Place de l'Opéra and on the Piazza Navona, and in front of me the glittering hope of the world raised itself up.

The United Nations building stood like a tall, shiny mirror before uncalm water. The flags blew merrily in the wind; they blew above a fountain, which New York's schoolchildren had dedicated to brotherly humanity.

An Indian woman led me through the building, and others were led by Chinese and Negro women, and all the guides wore blue uniforms, which directed one's thoughts to distant optimistic horizons, only my Indian guide wore her native dress, like a pious veil.

A pendulum swung above a golden ball. Was the ball the earth? And where was the pendulum swinging? And what did its swinging prophesy? A naked Zeus fit his surroundings well. The stairs, the corridors, the rooms, the halls were light and big and devoted to a better future. A black door led the delegates to a meditation room. The black door was like the black entryway in a fairy tale, and if one didn't look back one would probably be lucky. The bird of freedom or of peace was being held or let free by an angel. One couldn't say exactly; perhaps the angel thought that the time had not yet come. Bold swirls of color, painted by the Frenchman Fernand Léger, waved through the main auditorium, and through the wide window at the head of the room the East River looked like the Rhine at Bonn, and beneath its shining surface one could make out dangerous reefs.

Everywhere in this beautiful building it was apparent that the colored people, the long oppressed, had the greater confidence in their world. In all shades of skin color and dressed often in the picturesque clothing of their native lands, men and women gave the impression of having equal rights, as friendly guides, as writers and secretaries, they behaved as suppliants or as helpers of peace, as judges in a conflict, and they were always at home in the perfect architecture, which gave the gift of good thoughts, a creation of our times, the strength of our times, the faith of our times and without stain like an artful fugue.[151]

For a while the visitors also had faces expressing joy in the future. They admired the naked large Zeus, a gift from Greece, and they were honestly seeking peace; it was unclear who would give this gift. A young white priest showed the president's empty chair, empty at the moment, to a group of black adolescents. In the building's bookstore, a fat but free man from Ghana, wearing a bohemian velvet jacket, was offering splendid souvenir maps. In the gift shop, which was not absent of course, you could buy cigarettes from every country, strangely the "Edelweiss" brand was *"made in Italy"* here, and the ashtrays stated "good luck" and *"I love you."*

I went under the river, went under the hope of the nations reflected in the water, went under its reefs, which could wreck every hope, to solid ground, to the borough of Queens, to the airfield back to Europe.

In Queens there were small and tall new houses, freshly mowed lawns and old cemeteries. From the field of the dead I looked over to Manhattan once again; by chance it was a Jewish cemetery in which I was lingering, and its grave stones stood so tightly together and so high on the hill that they seemed, in my eyes, to be a faithful mirror image of the beautiful and beloved, the great and mighty, the sublime and friendly, the people-mixing and most cozy city of skyscrapers.

---

151. With the word suppliants, *Schutzflehende*, Koeppen is referencing the title of the Aeschylus drama, *The Suppliants*, circa 470 B.C., a play about rights, including women's rights, and about justice generally.

Bibliography

Critical Studies of Koeppen

Arnold, Heinz Ludwig, ed. *Wolfgang Koeppen.* Munich: Boorberg, 1972.

Basker, David. *Chaos, Control and Consistency: The Narrative Vision of Wolfgang Koeppen.* New York: P. Lang, 1993.

von Briel, Dagmar. *Wolfgang Koeppen als Essayist: Selbstverständnis und essayistische Praxis.* Mainz: Gardez!, 1996.

Brink-Friderici, Christl. *Wolfgang Koeppen: Die Stadt als Pandämonium.* Frankfurt am Main: P. Lang, 1990.

Buchholz, Hartmut. *Eine eigene Wahrheit: Über Wolfgang Koeppens Romantrilogie Tauben im Gras, das Treibhaus, und der Tod in Rom.* Frankfurt am Main: P. Lang, 1982.

Craven, Stanley. *Wolfgang Koeppen: A Study in Modernist Alienation.* Stuttgart: H. D. Heinz, 1982.

Denneler, Iris. *Verschwiegene Verlautbarungen: Textkritische Überlegungen zur Poetik Wolfgang Koeppens.* Munich: M Press, 2008.

Döring, Jörg. *"Ich stellte mich unter, ich machte mich klein": Wolfgang Koeppen, 1933-1946.* Frankfurt am Main: Suhrkamp, 2003.

Eberl, Dominick Andreas. *"Es geht um Kopf und Kragen": die Auseinandersetzung mit der jungen Bundesrepublik zu Beginn der fünfziger Jahre in Wolfgang Koeppens Tauben im Gras und Das Treibhaus.* Augsburg: MarloVerlag, 2010.

Eggert, Stefan. *"Abfahrbereit": Wolfgang Koeppens Orte: Topographie seines Lebens und Schreibens.* Berlin: Das Arsenal, 2006.

———. *Wolfgang Koeppen.* Berlin: Edition Colloquium in Wissenschaftsverlag v. Spiess, 1998.

Egyptien, Jürgen, ed. *Wolfgang Koeppen.* Darmstadt: Wissenschaftliche Buchgesellschaft, 2009.

Erlach, Dietrich. *Wolfgang Koeppen als Zeitkritischer Erzähler.* Stockholm: Almqvist and Wiksell, 1973.

Fetz, Bernhard. *Vertauschte Köpfe: Studien zu Wolfgang Koeppens Erzählender Prosa.* Vienna: Braumüller, 1994.

Geiter, Michael. *"Der Humorist geht gleich dem Raubtier stets allein": Wolfgang Koeppen im Lichte Sören Kierkegaards.* Freibug im Breisgau: Rombach, 2010.

Greiner, Hartmut, ed. *Über Wolfgang Koeppen.* Frankfurt am Main: Suhrkamp, 1976.

Gunn, Richard. *Art and Politics in Wolfgang Koeppen's Postwar Trilogy.* New York: P. Lang, 1983.

Hanbridge, Carole. *The Transformation of Failure: A Critical Analysis of Character Presentation in the Novels of Wolfgang Koeppen.* New York: P. Lang, 1983.

Häntzschel, Hiltrud, and Günther Häntzschel. *Wolfgang Koeppen.* Frankfurt am Main: Suhrkamp, 2006.

Hielscher, Martin. *Wolfgang Koeppen.* Munich: Beck, 1988.

————. *Zitierte Moderne: Poetische Erfahrung und Reflexion in Wolfgang Koeppens Nachkriegsromanen und in "Jugend."* Heidelberg: Winter, 1988.

Jens, Walter. "Melancholie und Moral: Eine Laudatio auf Wolfgang Koeppen." *Die Zeit* (26 October 1962).

Kimmage, Michael. "Munich/Manhattan Transfer: The Proximity of America in Wolfgang Koeppen's Tauben im Gras." *Internationales Archiv für Sozialgeschichte der deutschen Literatur* 35 no. 2 (December 2010): 122–35.

Koch, Manfred. *Wolfgang Koeppen: Literatur zwischen Nonkonformismus und Resignation.* Stuttgart: Kohlhammer, 1973.

Kurth, Bianca. *Spiegelung des Ich im Anderen: Juden und Schwarze in Werk von Wolfgang Koeppen.* Heidelberg: Manutius, 1998.

Manola, Anastasia. *Der Dichter-Seher als Dichter-Warner: Wandel eines Mythischen Modells bei Koeppen, Wolf und Grass.* Würzburg: Königshausen & Neumann, 2010.

Mauranges, Jean-Paul. *Wolfgang Koeppen: littérature sans frontière.* Berne: P. Lang, 1978.

Ochs, Tilmann. *Kulturkritik im Werk Wolfgang Koeppens.* Münster: Lit, 2004.

Oehlenschläger, Eckhart, ed. *Wolfgang Koeppen.* Frankfurt am Main: Suhrkamp, 1987.

Quack, Josef. *Wolfgang Koeppen: Erzähler der Zeit.* Würzburg: Königshausen & Neumann, 1997.

Reich-Ranicki, Marcel, ed. *Wolfgang Koeppen: Aufsätze und Reden.* Frankfurt am Main: Fischer, 1998.

Triechel, Hans-Ulrich. *Fragment ohne Ende: Eine Studie über Wolfgang Koeppen.* Heidelberg: Winter, 1984.

Uske, Bernhard. *Geschichte und ästhetisches Verhalten: das Werk Wolfgang Koeppens.* Frankfurt am Main: Peter Lang, 1994.

Veit, Lothar. *Einsam in der Menge: der Schriftsteller in Wolfgang Koeppens Nachkriegsromanen.* Marburg: Tectum, 2002.

Ward, Simon. *Negotiating Positions: Literary Identity and Social Critique in the Works of Wolfgang Koeppen.* New York: Rodopi, 2001.

Critical Studies of *Journey through America*

Basker, David. "Ein Bundesbürger geht auf Reisen: Wolfgang Koeppens Reiseliteratur." In *Reisen im Diskurs: Modelle der literarischen Fremderfahrung von den Pilgerberichten bis zur Postmoderne,* ed. Anne Fuchs and Theo Harden. Heidelberg: Winter, 1995.

Erhart, Walter. "Fremdsein, ganz und krass" – Reisen, Alterität und Geschlecht in Wolfgang Koeppens Romanen und Reiseessays." *Jahrbuch der Internationalen Wolfgang Koeppen-Gesellschaft* 2 (2003): 151–67.

Koch, Manfred. "Wolfgang Koeppens ‚Amerikafahrt.'" In *Deutschlands literarisches Amerikabild: Neuere Forschung zur Amerika-Rezeption der deutschen Literatur,* ed. Alexander Ritter. New York: Olms, 1977.

Sabhi, Thabet. *Das Reisemotiv im neuren deutschsprachigen Roman: Untersuchungen zu Wolfgang Koeppen, Alfred Andersch und Max Frisch.* Marburg: Tectum, 2002.

Schuchalter, Jerry. "'… Und Gerstäcker, Karl May, Cooper und Sealsfield reisen mit uns.'" In *Wolfgang Koeppen - Mein Ziel war die Ziellosigkeit,* ed. Gunnar Müller-Waldeck and Michael Gratz. Hamburg: Europäische Verlaganstalt, 1998.

Schlösser, Hermann. *Reiseformen des Geschriebenen: Selbsterfahrung und Weltdarstellung in Reisebüchern Wolfgang Koeppens, Rolf Dieter Brinkmanns und Hubert Fichtes.* Vienna: Böhlau, 1997.

Todorow, Almut. "Publizistische Reiseprosa als Kunstform." *Deutsche Vierteljahrschrift für Literatur und Geistesgeschichte* 60 (1986): 136–65.

1. German Images of America

Barclay, David, and Elisabeth Glaser-Schmidt. *Transatlantic Images and Perceptions: Germany and America since 1776.* New York: Cambridge University Press, 1997.

Blome, Astrid, and Volker Depkat, eds. *Von der 'Civilisirung' Russlands und dem 'Aufblühen' Nordamerikas im 18. Jahrhundert: Leitmotive der Aufklärung am Beispiel deutscher Russland- und Amerikabilder.* Bremen: Ed. Lumière, 1997.

Depkat, Volker. *Amerikabilder in politischen Diskursen: Deutsche Zeitschriften von 1789 bis 1830.* Stuttgart: Klett-Cotta, 1998.

Diner, Dan. *Verkehrte Welten: Antiamerikanismus in Deutschland: ein Historischer Essay.* Frankfurt am Main: Eichborn, 1993.

Durzak, Manfred. *Das Amerika-Bild der deutschen Gegenwartsliteratur: Historische Voraussetzungen und aktuelle Beispiele.* Stuttgart: Kohlhammer, 1979.

Emons, Thomas. *Das Amerika-Bild der Deutschen, 1948–1992: eine mediengeschichtliche Analyse.* Aachen: Shaker, 2004.

de Grazia, Victoria. *Irresistible Empire: America's Advance through Twentieth-Century Europe.* Cambridge, MA: Harvard University Press, 2005.

Mauch, Christof, and Kiran Patel, eds. *Wettlauf um die Moderne: Die USA und Deutschland 1890 bis heute.* Munich: Pantheon, 2008.

Müller, Christoph Henrdrik. *West Germans against the West: Anti-Americanism in Media and Public Opinion in the Federal Republic of Germany, 1949–1968.* New York: Palgrave Macmillan, 2010.

Ostendorf, Berndt. "Deutsch-amerikanische Kulturbeziehungen." In *Deutschland, Europa und die Welt,* ed. Gert Richter and Dieter Lang. Gütersloh: Bertelsmann Lexikothek Verlag, 1986.

———. "The Final Banal Idiocy of the Reversed Baseball Cap: Transatlantische Widersprüche in der Amerikanisierungsdebatte." *Amerikastudien/American Studies* 44, no. 1 (1999): 25–49.

Osterle, Heinz, ed. *Bilder von Amerika: Gespräche mit deutschen Schriftstellern.* Münster: Englisch Amerikanische Studien, 1987.

Pells, Richard. *Modernist America: Art, Music, Movies, and the Globalization of American Culture.* New Haven, CT: Yale University Press, 2011.

———. *Not Like Us: How Europeans Have Loved, Hated and Transformed American Culture since World War II.* New York: Basic Books, 1997.

Rodgers, Daniel. *Atlantic Crossings: Social Politics in a Progressive Age.* Cambridge, MA: Harvard University Press, 1998.

Schmidt, Alexander. *Reisen in die Moderne: der Amerika-Diskurs des deutschen Bürgertums vor dem Ersten Weltkrieg.* Berlin: Akademie Verlag, 1997.

Stephan, Alexander, ed. *Americanization and Anti-Americanism: The German Encounter with American Culture after 1945.* New York: Berghahn Books, 2005.

Wagnleitner, Reinhold. *American Cultural Diplomacy, the Cinema, and the Cold War in Central Europe.* Minneapolis: University of Minnesota Press, 1992.

———. *Coco-Colonization and the Cold War: The Cultural Mission of the United States in Austria after the Second World War.* Chapel Hill: University of North Carolina Press, 1994.

Index

Romberg, Sigmund, 27n2
Rome, 6, 19, 26n21, 32, 44, 65n56, 67, 103, 105, 107, 109, 131, 143, 151
Roosevelt, Franklin, 71
Rousseau, Jean-Jacques, 67
Rückert, Friedrich,
the Russian Revolution, 19, 36n10, 140n136

Sartre, Jean-Paul, 29
Salt Lake City, 2, 8, 118–123
San Francisco, 8, 25n17, 106–117
Scheffel, Joseph Victor von, 53n40
Schumann, Robert, 120
segregation, 9, 16–18, 58, 76, 79
Selassi, Haile, 52n39
Sinclair, Upton, 130, 131
Simenon, Georges, 29, 29n6
Skousen, Willard Cleon, 119n121
Smith, Joe, 118–119, 120, 122
the Soviet Union, 1, 7, 18, 24n10, 25n18, 104, 124, 140n146
Stein, Gertrude, 1, 2
Steinbeck, John, 7, 24n10, 90n85
Steinberg, Saul, 76, 77n64
Stevenson, Robert Louis, 115
Strauss, Franz Joseph, 61, 61n54

Tocqueville, Alexis de, 2, 11, 15–16, 23n3. See also *Democracy in America*
Treasure Island (by Robert Louis Stevenson), 115

The Trial (by Franz Kafka), 121
Twain, Mark, 11, 32, 77

the University of Chicago, 131
the United Nations, 151–152

Vechten, Carl Van, 50n33
Venice, 6, 99
Verlaine, Paul, 115, 115n11, 117
Vidor, King, 82
Vienna, 9, 15, 37, 37n16, 61, 100, 115, 116n115
Viva Zapata! (film), 90, 90n85

Wagner, Richard, 137, 137n134
Washington, George, 47
Washington, DC, 16, 31, 59–74
The Washington Post, 70
Waugh, Evelyn, 103, 103n102, 104
West Side Story (musical), 17, 150–151, 150n150
Whitman, Walt, 11, 17, 32, 36, 36n14
White, E.B., 19
Wilhelm II, 51, 51n35, 53
Williams, Tennessee, 28, 78, 85, 85n79
Wilson, Edmund, 7, 24n10
Wolfe, Thomas, 58, 58n50

Young, Brigham, 120, 122
Youth (by Wolfgang Koeppen), 22

Zola, Emile, 29, 29n5